A LIFE OF
OBSTRUCTIONS

A LIFE OF OBSTRUCTIONS

THE 1973 CONNECTICUT FIELD HOCKEY
SEASON AND FIRST-EVER TOURNAMENT

ROB PENFIELD

atmosphere press

Published by Atmosphere Press

978-1-63988-058-4 (Hardcover)
978-1-63988-059-1 (Paperback)
978-1-63988-057-7 (ePub eBook)

Library of Congress Control Number: 2021916663

Cover design by Robert Penfield

All of the events in this memoir are true to the best of the author's memory and recent interviews with coaches and players. Any views expressed in this memoir are solely those of this author.

atmospherepress.com

Dedicated
to the
Valley Five

Bonnie Tyler
Avon High School

Dot Johnson
Granby High School

Joan Sullivan
Simsbury High School

Jean Hunt
Farmington High School

Linda Hamm
Lewis Mills High School

Dedication

I called them, *"The Valley Five."* In the fall of 1973 and throughout the Farmington Valley, they were the *"Merchants of Change."* This story would not have happened without the commitment and dedication to their roles, responsibilities and their beliefs.

This book is dedicated to *"The Valley Five"* because of the paths they created and the doors they opened. Those many obstructions each hurtled over during their lifetime.

Joan Sullivan was the standard bearer to the assurance of that change with her 40 years of service in the Simsbury schools' system. Change came slowly, but Joan's fingerprints are on every path and gate along the way. Farmington's Jean Hunt was her sidekick in life. Old school to be sure, but flexible and with a heart of gold. Like Butch and Sundance, you didn't mess with either one of them. Together, you couldn't beat em. You liked them or you didn't like them...either way, you were in awe of their legacy, accomplishments and everything they stood for.

Avon's Bonnie Tyler was kind, patient and cared passionately for her work. No matter the situation, she always had words of support for your efforts. She managed her responsibilities in a caring and understanding way, earning the considerations and respect from all those who ever had the good fortune to know and interact with her.

Linda Hamm of Lewis Mills was quiet and reserved, until the bugle played the charge, and it was time to take the high ground. Then, like in a heated battle or a cool game of chess, she seemingly was three steps ahead of everyone and pulling away. She had that rare and wonderful gift of transferring knowledge to folks just by leading.

Dottie Johnson truly loved everything she did during her many years at Granby High School. And her players loved her back. Her words were her actions and results. Her preparation and guidance, both in athletics and life, were uncanny. Her legacy...she just kept setting the bar higher every day, just by the way she lived her life.

My editor, Lou Ball, once pointed out to me, *"A Wise Man Once Said...Nothing! Results Were Achieved Because the Appointed Leaders Led by Example!"*

In fall 1973, the Farmington Valley had good high school sports: football, soccer, cross-country teams and individuals. But, oh my, they had field hockey coaches who didn't just coach. They led by example, created a spot on the map and embedded their huge thumbprints on what would become the very legacy of field hockey in the state of Connecticut. Then they passed on their legacy to the new breed who, ironically, had been taught their lessons in field hockey and in life by, *"The Valley Five."*

PROLOGUE

On November 17th in the year 1973 the world changed.

It was a late fall in Southern New England. A Saturday. The type of day when the grayness of the season is the dominant color. When sunrises came peeking over the horizon with a chill in the air. Leaves on the ground. Early mornings came beckoning with a saddening loss of time. This Saturday, however, would prove to be one of renown. Because on this day a legacy would be born unlike others that had come before...or since.

For on this day a group of young women from tiny Granby Connecticut High School were en route to a rendezvous with destiny. They will win the state of Connecticut's first-ever, girls' high school post-season field hockey tournament. Played on the campus of Yale University. In a tournament long overdue, they outscore and defeat the girls from Guilford Connecticut High School, 2-1, scoring the winning goal with

28 seconds remaining in the second, sudden-death overtime period. The tension-filled action playing out on Practice Field B, nestled in the cozy shadows of the historic Yale Bowl.

I was there. The lone writer covering the game for my paper. A small and well-respected weekly, *The Farmington Valley Herald,* located in Simsbury. A paper that has been publishing for 92 years as a continuation of the original, *New Hartford Tribune.*

The first edition of that paper published on this very day, November 17, 1881.

The Granby girls became legends, stamping their names into the granite history that is the iconic staple of time... eternity. And, whether they, or the girls from Guilford even remotely understand the social and economic magnitude of the moment, the complexities of their accomplishments, or even care about the future long-term impact that goes far beyond winning just another field hockey game...their worlds and their lives had changed.

Granby is a tiny high school by enrollment standards. The underdogs. They played a regular season schedule and qualified for the tournament. And, like 37 other qualifiers, were all thrown into one class. One boiling cauldron with but one simple goal: Survive and advance. Be the last ones standing. The State Champions.

They were not the best or most skilled team in the state. Nor were they the fastest afoot. Or the most aggressive. They were not the highest scoring team. They had been outscored in total team goals by almost half of their regular season opponents. And their regular season conference provided the weakest league competition of any in the state. Yet, when it came time to play, no team was more prepared to play the game than Granby. It's said that in sports, championships are won in practice. And Granby practiced every day as if they were preparing to play in a state championship game.

On the pitch they were led by their co-captains. Two

seniors who served as the on-the-field coaches and team leaders. Disciplinarians when needed. Four-year starters who, during their high school careers, never experienced losing a game and were now riding a five year, 50-game unbeaten streak.

They played a shifting and innovative formation that, at times, was indefensible and often impenetrable. Luring opponents into their zone, letting them come right up to the front door of their goal. Then, with deftness and teamwork of a quiet machine, would run their opponents into the ground with a swift flurry of decisive moves, sending foes to defeat with the coldness of an assassin. Opponents were left standing in the lurch, stunned. Trying to figure out what just happened and now tasting defeat.

The girls liked each other...and they hated each other. They were friends...they were enemies. They were teammates... they were individuals. They did not beat themselves. They certainly didn't let anyone else beat them, either. They had attitude, and it was unbreakable.

They were coached by a lady who did not play field hockey during her formative high school and college years. Yet, her knowledge of the game, strategy and innovativeness would come to rival the greatest names in field hockey history. Inside that lady burned a fire that cultivated a gifted skill for the passionate transfer of knowledge to her players.

She was, singly, the most prepared coach when it came time to play. And that, too, was the signature of her teams.

They won the tournament because, well, they were, by the standards of the day, a damn good field hockey team.

Yeah, November 17th, just another Saturday in the late fall of the year 1973. Granby High School rode their skills and disciplines to the pinnacle of success, winning the first-ever girls' high school field hockey tournament. The *Farmington Valley Herald* would be the lone paper recording the events. And, if the frenetic post-game celebrations of the as-yet undocumented accomplishments of this game continue to go unnoticed, then time and its relationship to the events of this day, is truly of the essence.

For on this very day, November 17th in the year 1797, the tool of time itself, like the Granby girls, will make history. The man is Eli Perry in the town of Plymouth, Connecticut, just 31 miles north from where the post-game celebrations are now underway. Perry, a clockmaker, had applied for, and is granted the first-ever clock-making patent in these new United States by the recently opened patent office.

Perry will build the common tool to measure time.

Now, another clock had begun ticking. Already recording time and growing older. A pendulum for life. Because, no longer were they just a bunch of girls from tiny Granby High School who played and won a game of field hockey. They had become and would forever be, legends in time. It was Saturday, November 17, 1973. Just a late fall Saturday in New England.

And the world really had changed.

Part 1

"The Beginnings"

1

Fighting for an identity. A lifetime battle of overcoming obstructions.

On the day Granby won the first-ever state of Connecticut field hockey championship in 1973, there were 87 public and catholic high schools playing field hockey in the state. Another dozen or so private schools for girls. An estimated 2800 high school girls were involved, both on a JV and varsity level. A dramatic increase compared to just 10 years prior when the number of active participants was about 15 public high schools and about 350 girls.

There were seven conferences operating on a round-robin basis and two more in the early developmental stages. There were 15 new applications to the Connecticut Interscholastic Athletic Conference (CIAC) from boards of education for the establishment of new field hockey programs. There was a backlog of applications for new officials. A growing list of referee wannabes requiring a demanding certification process.

Yet, the game of field hockey, one of fall's only team sports for girls at public high schools, was fighting for its survival. Fighting against the ever-evolving world of change. Of the old guard and its mindset that boys' fall sports—football, soccer, track, cross-country—owned and ruled the resources.

In the 1890's the game made its initial appearance in the USA as "Lawn Hockey" played by men. In 1899 a Springfield College team engaged in a regular season schedule using rules written by James Huff McCurdy. A few of McCurdy's rules made it to England where they were infused into the English rules.

British student, Constance Applebee, first introduced the game to women in 1901 as part of activities classes at Harvard University. The 28-year-old Applebee had engaged in the game before coming to the states. She demonstrated to her female classmates the skills used in what she referred to as, *"A wonderful engaging exercise."*

Applebee promoted her game as a spirited, yet gentle competition, played in long dresses, a formal blouse, stylish neckwear and a long-colored tie. Playing behind the Harvard gymnasium the game quickly caught on with friends and colleagues.

Applebee was invited to take her game on the road, introducing it to eastern colleges. Visits were made to Vassar, Ursinus, Bryn Mawr, Radcliffe, Mount Holyoke and to Smith College in Northampton, MA. She demonstrated the basic skills of engaging, using a club-like stick and a hardened white granite ball. The game was played on a designated flat field with disciplined dimensions at the basic level of competition, one team verses another team.

The rules were few and easy to learn. You won if your team's designated players scored more goals than your opponent. In 1901 that meant knocking the ball between two sticks in the ground about eight feet apart. There were rules of compliance and penalties for over-playing or trying to stop an opponent from scoring. The game official was the on-field moderator designated to callout penalties. Those obstructions in the game of life.

The game grew slowly through the 1920's and 1930's at the women's colleges and private girls' schools from northern New England to as far south as North Carolina and selected locations throughout the mid-west. Applebee, or *"The Apple,"* established field hockey summer camps in Pennsylvania and New Jersey and published a field hockey and lacrosse magazine. She became the quiet trailblazer. Though many were learning about her sport, few played the game.

By the late 1950's about a dozen high schools in Connecticut maintained a field hockey team. Scheduling was a challenge. The late Joan Sullivan began Simsbury's program in 1954. She had to schedule the same opponents two and three times during one season. She played private schools like Ethel Walker School in Simsbury, Miss Porter's School in Farmington and occasional games vs the MacDuffie and Chaffee Schools.

Simsbury played on a lonely expanse atop Plank Hill Road known as Memorial Field, bounded by thick woods and a graveyard thought to be haunted. It was referred to as that place where, *"Visiting teams went to die."* The field was on an incline. Simsbury always played downhill in the second half. And, usually won because of that tilted advantage. Game day crowds included the teams, managers, coaches, officials and what can be described as lovers and other strangers.

An official in 1956 was a local lady known as Mrs. Selby. Since Simsbury always played downhill in the second half, Selby positioned herself near midfield. She explained that it was too tiring to run up that hill and decided to stay in the lower end of the field. Opponents, having to play uphill, rarely got the ball beyond midfield. She sipped on a bottle of coke during play that was known to contain a few shots of rum. She smoked her favorite cigarette. Pall Mall longs in the distinctive red package. In one game, Mrs. Selby, needing a light, hollered out if anyone had a match. A girl on the Bloomfield team, coached by the late Alice Yokabaskas, stopped and gave her a pack of matches to light her cigarette. As she again passed by, Mrs. Selby handed the matches back to her.

I was 10 years old and recall watching Simsbury take on the highly touted Miss Porter's School. The Trojans scored a late goal to pull off a huge upset against Porter's Green and White, whose center-halfback was one of the best players in the state. She was the best and most-skilled player on the field that day. A one-lady wrecking crew who swore at her teammates like a sailor on shore leave.

Leaving the field at game's end, she was congratulated by the Simsbury captain who offered her hand. She stood face-to-face with the Simsbury player and slapped her hand away. She lifted her middle finger, put it in the face of her opponent and said in a frustrated voice, *"Screw You Bitch!"*

Ladylike behavior and good sportsmanship...well, perhaps not. But it was pure passion within every sense of perception. The stress of the battle and mounting frustrations of unmet expectations. A by-product of the battle lost, yet the war still raged on within.

This was the way of the game in the early years. There were pioneers of field hockey in Connecticut. The early torchbearers who stoked the fires and kept the game alive, all becoming Connecticut Hall of Fame inductees. Along with Sullivan and Alice Yokabaskas was Lorraine Splain from Old Saybrook who would become the standard bearer of coaches for what would evolve into the vaunted Shoreline Conference. Roger Ludlowe's Pat Small began producing winning seasons in the early 1960's.

Joan Gauthey's presence in Washington, CT would build tiny Washington High School and Shepaug Valley's field hockey program into a winner during the early years of the Berkshire League. June Olah at Weston produced a series of conference winning teams.

Bea Walko established two programs within a few years, first at Norwalk followed by years of quality teams for Greenwich High School. Jean Hunt would start a program at Litchfield High School, then begin a strong program at Farmington High including a 46-game unbeaten string.

Sally Nelson created a standard of quality and performance at E.O. Smith High School that continues to this day. Virginia Parker's Staples teams were winners from the onset. Angela "Chickie" Poisson, whose exploits as a player, coach and legendary official in the tri-state area would become synonymous with the game in Connecticut. I would come to call her the Babe Ruth of field hockey.

Yet, after 65 years of field hockey in our country, Connecticut had a sparse smattering of high school programs. Few girls were playing the game. Fewer, even, had any understanding of field hockey. For most, exposure came during gym classes. I recall many girls during my high school years admitting they wanted no part of engaging in competition with a group of Bohemian type girls with athletic skills, who liked to run free on open fields, engaging in physical competition verses opponents on a battlefield with wooden war clubs.

This was an observation that was a little over-the-top to be sure, yet due to the nature of the field hockey player of that day, not completely outside the realm of trueness. The real game of the day was not as gentle as Connie Applebee's game in 1901. It was more like the Springfield College men's game of 1899. Most girls opted for badminton or volleyball in gym classes.

These were pre-Title IX times of no conferences and no post-season play. No state sponsored sanctioning organizations for managing compliance to policies and procedures. There were loosely organized rules committees within the officiating ranks. The sport lacked a critical mass presence and a clearly defined path to its future.

When it came to the question of funding, well, you had a better chance of winning a longshot in the Kentucky Derby than you did at successfully engineering a municipality into taking money from a football or basketball program for the purpose of establishing a field hockey program for girls.

Identity and survival. Yes, girls' field hockey was expanding in the state's secondary schools, but, at an alarmingly slow rate. As in any epic story what the game needed was a miracle. Like when the calvary, with the bugle blaring, comes charging over the hill with reinforcements to rescue the doomed souls and save the day.

Little did folks know but that calvary of reinforcements, that cadre of souls, were on their way. Just one or two college graduation classes away. Local and homegrown heroes. From right in Connecticut's backyard and western Massachusetts. From UConn, Southern Connecticut State and Central Connecticut State. From Bridgeport's Arnold College and Springfield College.

That arrival of fresh and hungry graduates beginning in the mid-1960's would, over the next few years, change the face of high school field hockey in the state of Connecticut.

2

The reinforcements came rolling in like a tidal wave between 1967 and 1971, arriving in every shape and size imaginable.

A cadre of female coaches hired for physical education and coaching positions throughout the state. They arrived with knowledge and a freshness to the uncertain but changing times. To a huge throng of young girls who had energy and abilities in sports, but no infrastructure, paths, or leadership. No playing fields and few opportunities to unleash their pent-up skills and show off their abilities.

This new breed worked for paltry salaries. Amounts that would not come close to paying for today's annual gasoline costs. They found equipment closets that were empty or filled with damaged goods. Athletic fields that were not available even for some of the gym classes they were responsible for mentoring. Athletic budgets that did not exist for girls' sports. A continuation in a lifetime of obstructions. What they did find was that veritable army of young girls just waiting for an opportunity to show off their skills.

In the Farmington Valley, things got interesting in a hurry. In Avon, Athletic Director Bob Summers hired a young coach from Maine's Aroostook Valley State College via Springfield College. His requests to her were functional and direct. Take over the regimen of girls phys-ed classes, intramural programs and build a field hockey program. And a young Bonnie Tyler did just that.

She had started a program at Winthrop, Maine High School. Now, she was hired to do the same for Avon. To say the resources bin at Avon was empty would be a huge understatement. Tyler started with nothing...not even a few broken hockey sticks. The school board, through Summers, saw her passion for the job, and within five years through their continued support, she had developed a competitive field hockey team and her Avon Falcons would qualify and play in that first-ever 1973 CIAC tournament.

Atop the mountain in Burlington, Dave McConnell greeted Lewis Mills' newest coach, Linda Hamm, an All-American basketball player from Southern Connecticut State College. Hamm came from close by in Terryville and would come to be known as one of those coaches who, *"Had the gift."* That ability to transfer knowledge and expectations into the performance of others. Whether it was in gym class, the hockey pitch, or her specialty, the hardwood with her basketball teams. Her moves were that of a chess maven. Three steps ahead of everyone else and pulling away.

She too was given a list of assignments including the building a field hockey program with a caveat from McConnell. *"Make it competitive within five years."* In 1974 Lewis Mills' field hockey team would appear in the first, Class M state championship game. Ironically, in that game, they would lose to Granby.

Janet Beck began the field hockey program at Canton with no experience in field hockey, no equipment, no guarantee of a daily practice field and little support from the school board or Athletic Director. What she did have was a group of talented athletes, though not skilled or experienced in field hockey.

Some of Canton's early equipment was provided by their competitors, Farmington and Simsbury High Schools. Still, those early Warrior teams were competitive, first on a JV level before moving up to a varsity schedule. A rumor persisted that those in control of the town's educational budgets and finances felt fewer games might be scheduled to keep the cost of losing seasons lower.

Granby High School scored the coup of the quarter century. Dottie Johnson came out of Westfield, MA High School playing three sports for the Bombers before moving on to Springfield College. Ironically, she never played field hockey in college for their legendary coach, Dot Zenaty.

She played softball, volleyball, basketball and competed in synchronized swimming. After student teaching at Enfield High School, she was hired by the Granby school system. Athletic Director, Ken King, remembers her as being ready and prepared for her first meeting with him. King remembers, *"That's the way she was. Organized and prepared, for every meeting, every practice and every game she coached."*

Granby's field hockey had started in the mid-1950's but fizzled out. It was resurrected in the mid-1960's. Johnson would take over the Granby program in 1969. In her first four games she produced a 2-2 record. Her teams would not lose another game until 1975, an unbeaten run of 67 games.

Under her guidance Granby, a Class S school, would win the first-ever state championship in 1973, defeating schools three to six times larger than Granby's enrollment size. They would repeat in 1974, again setting a mark winning the first-ever Class M title over larger schools and the first-ever Class

S title in 1978. She would win seven state titles and play in 11 championship games in her 34 years at Granby. A standard bearer to the game of field hockey who kept setting the achievement bar a little higher as the years passed.

As the 1973 season dawned, many field hockey programs throughout the state were in their third and fourth years of competition. Feeder programs and summer camps were beginning to create an impact. Rivalries were being developed. Conferences being formed. The early seeds of success being planted.

Pat Mascia was building a consistent winner at Amity Regional in Woodbridge. Pat Harrison and Jan DeLucca oversaw the building of a strong program at Guilford with assistance from physical education instructor, Linda Gavin, and new coach, Becky Clomp. Sue Schwerdtle started the program at New Canaan and in five years had amassed a record of 46-3-5, winning the unofficial WFCIAC title in 1972.

Cyndy Wilson took a losing Windsor Locks program, turning it into a winning team. In Enfield, both schools were on the rise. Carol Albert had the new Enrico Fermi High School quickly on a winning path and across town at Enfield High, Kathleen "Cookie" Bromage started with an equipment closet of broken sticks and cracked balls and led her girls into the '73 tournament.

In Cheshire, Arlene Salvati fought with every available tool. She wrote letters to the school board that fell on deaf ears. Begged athletic directors for new equipment and better fields. Received the support of sympathetic friends and families known as Concerned Parents for Girls Sports and Opportunities. A dedicated group buoyed by the efforts in Washington from retired Lieutenant General, Robert Pursley, a decorated Korean War vet. Their efforts eventually engineered the school board to make some rather dramatic changes in the sports agendas. But, it was Salvati's grit and dedication that took her team into a top 10 ranking in the initial tournament.

In football-driven Stamford, Pat Bradbury started their program rolling, and in its third year, captured the city championship.

Becky Strominger put Darien's team together, and it became one of the most dominant and consistent teams in the downstate area that become known as "Preppy Corridor." Her players were skilled, aggressive and many in her program during those early years went on to successful playing careers at eastern colleges and Ivy League programs.

Wherever you looked, a new coach was in the early stages of developing a program. Maloney of Meriden was becoming a force behind Sandy Piantek. Sandy White had a successful program at East Lyme. Deb Haggerty's efforts had produced a winning field hockey team at Coginchaug and Fran Zaloski was doing the same at New Milford.

In Wallingford, Sheehan's Judy Samaha and her girls were producing winning seasons in the new and competitive Housatonic League. In the Berkshires at Litchfield, Cindy Ferrarotti's teams were now winning games. Newtown had a winning program with coach Betty Bouclier and Brookfield was now a winner under Cindy Adamski.

Westbrook had a young team playing in the demanding Shoreline Conference under the guidance of Gail Perzanoski. Joan Bulmer was molding Nonnewaug into a winning program. Karen Erlandson had a gang of seniors with experience, turning a losing program into a winner at Newington. Hall High of West Hartford was looking to have a winning season for coach Sally Ann Warren and Mary Wallenberg was leading an experienced team at Watertown.

Babby Nunh was in the early years of building her program in North Branford. Bev Thompson's Suffield team was pretty good in the NCCC, playing in the shadows of Granby. At Shepaug, Sandy Bruegger had taken over the reins for Joan Gauthey who was on sabbatical. Good and exciting field hockey coaches were building programs in every corner of the state.

This new breed inspired their teams with the same values that drove them in their lives. That passion that also drove their mentors and predecessors. The drive to take on a challenging project and make it work. A believed audacity to be successful beyond their coaching peers. Not just to achieve a successful program, but to reach higher. To venture further than ever before. With ambition to reach beyond the norm and not be afraid of what might be there. To take their programs to the next level of competition. Like taking a virgin field hockey program and landing it on the moon.

Oh yeah, baby. The calvary had arrived.

3

For all its quirkiness and oddball events, 1973 was a year of unique happenings in Connecticut and throughout the world. Happenings that cut a swath through history creating their own legacies.

In the Nutmeg State, gasoline prices would reach .43 cents a gallon after OPEC raised its costs for a barrel of oil over 200%. Two weeks later the oil embargo would begin along the East Coast as the energy crises exploded onto the world scene. Long lines of cars at gasoline pumps. Lines in grocery stores as folks cued up for the big three of household staples: bread, milk, and toilet paper.

Just a few days after Granby wins the '73 field hockey championship, the Granby Town Council meets to make a critical decision. To vote on whether to shut-down the winter sports programs due to dramatically elevated costs during the energy crises. By one vote, the council decides to play winter schedules. Specifics from the vote were to be withheld from the public. Word leaks out that the decision not to cut the winter programs carried by just one vote. Townsfolk are not happy with the *"surreptitious manner in which the decision was carried out,"* notes the *Farmington Valley Herald* in one of Lou Ball's editorial comments.

Two nights later, senior co-captain, Bob Corneroli pours in 38 points setting Granby's all-time individual one-game boys scoring record in the Bears' 63-55 win over Cheney Tech. Most of the Town Council, many of whom had given negative votes just days before to cancel schedules, sit in the bleachers rooting for Corneroli as he sets the record.

The New England Whalers capture the first-ever World Hockey Association Championship. Then announce their wish to move their team and league operations to Hartford. In Boston they are overshadowed by the NHL's Bruins. Connecticut's Sports Authority quickly engineers approvals for bond issues through a series of accelerated social and political moves within the general assembly, with plans for a downtown multi-purpose arena seating 11,000. An arena that has been on the drawing table since 1965. It will be built and open in 1975 as part of the Hartford Civic Center Complex and will officially be called, The Veterans Memorial Coliseum.

Despite the presence of professional sports and major NCAA games, The Capitol City will never fully recover from this investment into the Hartford Civic Center. The situation is exacerbated by the suspicious collapse of the Coliseum's space-framed roof in January of 1978. A building that I will walk out from just five hours before the collapse. A case that even today, 44 years later, still has open investigations.

NASA, using existing parts and 2.2 billion in funds, launches Skylab. The unit is used for 84 days and then abandoned. It will crash to the earth in 1979. Elvis Presley will perform *"Live from Hawaii"* on a national network. Presley's

TV audience will be larger than that of the Apollo Moon landing. The Watergate Hearings will begin with doubt and mistrust of the committee by a large part of the population, and the suddenly irascible fourth estate, already being referred to as, *"The fake press."*

A fire will occur in St Louis at the National Military Archives. The reported cause will be faulty wiring. It will later be disclosed by whistleblowers that the fire, most likely arson, is the government's continuing attempts at destroying records of Vietnam vets in an attempt to avoid the growing number of Agent Orange disability claims. By 1973 estimated to be over 100,000 claims.

A footnote to the story generates a cloud of controversy.

Investigations find that sprinkler systems and fire-fighting tools heavily re-douse the area with water applications...for no apparent reason other than the hopes by the government, that what the fires did not destroy, the water will. The government is quick to reply, *"We categorically deny such allegations and illusions as bunk."*

In early January the Supreme Court of the United States, by a 7-2 vote, passes its landmark decision, Roe v Wade. The vote will uphold and enhance the fourteenth amendment. It will give women the right to privacy and the fundamental right of decision should they choose to have an abortion. Despite religious and ethical restrictions, procedural limitations in-and-by some states and on-going challenges to wording and content, the public will overwhelmingly support the amendment's legal and lifestyle decisions offered for the ensuing 50 years.

In September, Billie Jean King defeats Bobby Riggs in the *"Great Battle of the Sexes"* at the Astrodome. In the movies, *"The Exorcist"* will be released to long lines of moviegoers. The movie becomes known as the *"Ego Challenge."* A battle of the movie's directors to see how many moviegoers they can get to vomit in the theatres.

In a move that is never fully explained to satisfaction by any member of congress, The American Psychiatric Association removes homosexuality from its DSM-II List, citing that *"the affliction"* will no longer be categorized and documented as a mental illness, either for men or women!

On the final day of the year congress passes the Endangered Species Act designed to protect imperiled species. The US Supreme Court will call the act the most comprehensive legislation for the protection of endangered species enacted by any nation.

Politicos and radio pundits vocally wonder just exactly what species the legislation is targeting. The timing is paired with the APA's removal of homosexuality from the DSM's lists of mental illness. The actions, viewed as compatible, are not lost in the dialogue of the early talk shows and in radical editorials.

In the early spring of 1973 the Connecticut Interscholastic Athlete Conference, known as the CIAC, will announce plans for the possibility of holding a post-season field hockey tournament that fall. No details will accompany the announcement as the CIAC has yet to develop any cost to revenue protocols needed to financially support a tournament.

Tournament rumors begin circulating in late 1972 after Texas Senator John Tower pulls his amendment to Title IX off the docket. It's reported that the action is a result of a budding conspiracy against the Tower groups that goes unreported and is quietly swept away by the Senator's own spin doctors.

Previous attempts for a field hockey tournament had not gone well. A series of surreptitious assessments identified that most Connecticut municipalities were not complying to the partially completed and very confusing Federal Amendment to the Civil Rights Bill known as Title IX. What some in the press refer to as, *"The Bill of Female Education Opportunities."*

Nothing looms on the horizon to give any indication that the uncompleted federal law will be re-written for a clearer understanding of what the act means, or more specifically, what it doesn't mean. The words, target goals and directions for Title IX in 1973, will remain just as ambiguous and confusing to the world as they remain today, 50 years later.

The manner and clarity to which the initial Title IX act was written did not offer much support to the CIAC's investment of resources, especially with Tower's troubling amendment sitting in the wings. If not defeated and removed from the docket, as it was in the 1972 conspiracy, Tower's supplemental amendment will slingshot women's sports opportunities 20 years into the past.

In February of 1973 I am hired as Sports Editor by Lou Ball, Editor and Publisher Emeritus, for the *Farmington Valley Herald*, a weekly newspaper located in Simsbury, CT. One evening I share a conversation with him over the pending decision whether it was time for the CIAC to stage a post-season field hockey tournament. Lou, always the curmudgeonly pundit, who knew of and had written about the pros and cons of Title IX in his editorials, listened to my rationale.

He then offered his editorial summation which typically was delivered like a pub dart whistling past your head, *"Time for the CIAC to shit or get off the pot."*

Lou's thoughts stayed with me for days and resurrected a memory from years past. Pondering his words, I recalled a lesson I had learned from one of my aunts when I was 10 years old. She was, in the terms of those days, an old maid. A spinster. She had once been an athlete who played baseball and basketball with men's teams. From the stories I had heard from my Dad, she could bring it, often outplaying her male counterparts and performing beyond expectations. She was a child of the 1880's, a long-ago time and different era. Her rationales and guidance were old school, sometimes right out of leftfield, but her logic was curt and usually dead center on target. When she wanted to make a point, you listened.

Wanting to teach me a lesson, she showed me how to put

a bobby pin in an electrical wall socket. She instructed me to remove it. I knew that I would get a hard shock if I tried to pull the pin out. She smiled, held up one finger as if to make her point. Her words were electricity, itself.

"Sometimes you have to grab the goddamn thing and see what the hell it feels like. So you will know what to expect...the joy and pain. Know what you're dealing with. "

Leave it to my Aunt Fay from the 1880's to blaze a trail. At some point the CIAC just had to swan dive into that great abyss with their eyes open and see what the hell they had to deal with. The joy of success...and the pain of learning. Time to dive into the deep end of the pool and see if they could swim.

So, despite all its shortcomings, perhaps 1973 would be the year to ride that serpent down that path through the social, the cultural and financial gauntlets to see what they were dealing with.

After all, a post-season field hockey tournament for girls, like getting the hell out of Vietnam, was way over-due.

4

This is a fact. During the early days of covering girls' sports in the newspapers the learning curve was, surprisingly, a very steep hill to climb.

Here's another fact. It was even a steeper hill to climb for the girls to learn about the ways of newspaper reporting. All the good stuff and especially, all the bad.

As dramatic a change 1973 was for girls' sports, especially field hockey in Connecticut, the paths to reporting those changes in the media were equally as stark and surprisingly limited. To be sure there were newspapers. A few were, pro-actively, covering girls' games. But, despite these new wide-open vistas for sports reporting, those newspaper paths were not well-marked, nor were they easy to understand or deal with as one might think. The newspapers were still a business fueled by, *"An Old Boys Network."* Not ready to give up and go the ways of the Dodo.

It was not a gentle path for the coaches, players or school administrators. Nor for the emerging audiences of moms and dads, fans, and friends. Or, for the daily and weekly newspapers and its editors. And for me, too. Because as much as the world would soon change for the athletes on the field and their associates, my life, too, was changing along with theirs.

It was winter, 1973. I was living in Windsor. I received a note in the mail from Lou Ball, Editor and Publisher Emeritus for the *Farmington Valley Herald*, a paper I had known all my life. It was the first newspaper I learned to read in 1951 during kindergarten classes. I was a *Herald* delivery boy from 1955 to 1959. Lou wanted to talk and asked me to reply. I called and we set a date for me to stop by the offices, then located in Simsbury on Hopmeadow Street on the backside and lower level of the Simsbury Town Shops, then owned and operated by the *"Renaissance Man,"* Charlie Rice.

I picked a day when I would be in town going to job interviews. It was fortunate that I was able to schedule my interviews with Lou's availability as we had not seen each other in almost four years. I was pleased with my good timing, and I had a good feeling. That odd type of good feeling you get in anticipation when you sense something really cool is about to happen. Something that would have an impact on my life.

The date was Monday, February 12, 1973. The 20-degree temperatures and biting wind cut through me like a machine. The sky was milky white. A chance of snow persisted. I arrived at the *Herald* about 10 AM and waited for Lou, sitting in the storage area atop a pile of papers that were last week's edition. One of the production girls offered me a cup of coffee.

I watched the crew go through their Monday actions on the print floor while listening to Elton John belt out the words to "Crocodile Rock" on the radio. I leafed through Sunday's *Hartford Times* to the sounds of the Cornelius Brothers and Sister Rose belting out their hit "Too Late to Turn Back Now".

I read a story about high school basketball by a wonderful writer, the late Dennis Randle. It was informative and well-written. I recall wishing I could write like Dennis. During the ensuing years, I would have the good fortune to come to know and work with Dennis on projects.

News of day was stark. North Vietnam had just released the first 116 POWs. Ohio became the first state to post metrics on its state signage. At Cincinnati's Riverfront Stadium, home to the Reds and Bengals, the traditional distance marked on the outfield walls, from home plate to centerfield, had been 404 ft. It was now marked, 123.2 m. Yeah, that was not going to work for me.

In China TET, the lunar New Year had just begun, and this would be the year of the Monkey. I recalled my year in Vietnam. My involvement with the infamous 1968 TET Offensive. For me, stuck deep in the Mekong Delta with the 9th Infantry Division, it felt more like the year of the asshole!

Lou appeared. He was his typical effusive self. Coffee cup in one hand. Glasses hanging from his neck. Bushy eyebrows. A hearty laugh. Handshake like a driving piston. A greeting that froze you in place. And a question that sounded more like an order. *"Want to Work for the Herald! I'd like you to work for the Herald! Start today!"*

Well, I would be lying if I said I wasn't a little blown away. WOW...was my first thought.

I had to catch my breath. I was tentative but excited about his offer. I answered, *"Yeah, OK. Because I feel like I belong here, so, I'll give it a try. Six months."*

Lou made some comment like it was a good decision and it will most likely be one that changes my life. At that moment, I couldn't even begin to grasp the profundity of that statement or where, over the ensuing years, my time at the *Herald* would take me.

At 10:33 AM on Monday, February 12, 1973, I became, the second-ever, officially named *Sports Editor* for the *Farmington Valley Herald*. It became the day in my life when I took the fork in the road I was destined to travel. I believe Yogi Berra would have been proud of me. During the preceding years, others had sat in the SE chair. Lou made sure I understood that I had just become the first officially named SE for the *Herald* since 1956. Honestly, it would take a few years before I came to understand the honor of the position I had just accepted.

I was now a part of what would become the happiest, most carefree and fun-filled five years of my life. I called my girlfriend with the news. She lived in Western Massachusetts. She sounded happy yet, I could sense a distant chill in her voice. Not in what she said. But in what she didn't say. I would be lying if I said I wasn't concerned, or a bit sad. I knew our relationship was drifting.

My acceptance with Lou was a handshake and the usual Social Security and required unemployment paperwork. Lou agreed to my six months saying there would be no hard feelings if I chose to leave. His plan was for me to take 60 to 90 days to learn the business of the *Herald*. After all, the games and the writing of stories is just a small part of a newspaper's heart and soul.

There's planning and scheduling of what the next edition will be. Size of the paper and its layout. Revenue-generating sales of advertisements and page placement. There is town news, individual columns, editorials, photography, and darkroom production. The constant networking with resources. There's composing room production and the on-going editing of, well, just about everything. I came to know it as, *"The Juxt,"* short for juxtaposition or the relationship of a newspaper's components and how they are placed together in contrast for effect. When all is said and done, there's still the activities of distribution and supporting administrivia that accompanies any business.

Spring and summer passed by quickly. I was now out and about covering Little League and Babe Ruth League baseball. I wrote about the American Legion baseball team. Slow-pitch softball, bowling leagues and a fishing derby. I did independent pieces on locals playing college and professional sports making a few trips to Yankee Stadium, Shea Stadium and Fenway Park. Covered stock car racing at local tracks. I took photos for the Herald's correspondents and a few advertising promos for our sales staff. Developed film and printed screen-print pics for every edition. I was the *Herald's* multi-tasker long before that term became chic.

I liked what I was doing. I earned every penny of my $66.27 weekly paycheck. It certainly wasn't much of an income, and I was not living very large. My apartment cost me $50 per month. Gas was free. Food was purchased at a reduced rate. I often fished for my dinner and worked a second job in a liquor store for a few extra dollars. The idea of leaving the *Herald* and heading back out into the workforce of interviewees...like selling insurance or used cars. Not for me, baby! Hell, I'd rather shoot myself in the foot. My only twinge of discomfort was the continuing sense of uneasiness with my girlfriend, Deb. Though still together and happy with each other. We seemed to be drifting. Not so much apart...just aimlessly drifting.

My six-month window of time with the *Herald* was upon me in what seemed like a few heartbeats. It was August and I had a decision to make. The decision came down to a Wednesday evening. A late-night conversation with Lou after the paper had been put to bed and mailsacks sent on their way. As I approached his desk, he smiled and nodded. He knew what was coming.

Then again, Lou Ball had no idea of what I had in mind. That's why he liked me. Probably the reason he hired me. I sat down across from him and said that I wanted to stay at the *Herald* for the following reasons. He uttered his hearty laugh. Drained his coffee cup and said, *"Let's hear it."*

My terms were simple. I wanted to be a fulltime employee.

Nothing less than a 45-hour workweek. I would work my own schedule. I would begin covering the Farmington Valley's seven high schools. Girls and boys. That would be 47 sports teams during fall season, alone. I would cover whatever college or pro sports I could find time to do. Lou nodded and said okay.

Currently, I was filling one full page with sports and a second page with 40-50% copy due to ads. Now, I would need a full-page front page in the *Herald's* B section and at least three additional pages with no less than 60% of sports, meaning ads would have to be adjusted or an additional four-page leaf section would have to be added.

That would add cost to the paper's production. A cost that could easily be offset if the ad folks found one more client per month. I would continue to take all my own photos and do the darkroom activities. I had more items but decided that I had presented enough for one evening. We agreed to continue talking the next evening.

Lou smiled. He asked if I wanted more money. I said no. Again, he just nodded. As I rose to leave, he smiled with that sly grin. Quietly, almost in a solemn manner, he said thanks. A week later in my pay envelope I had been given a 50% increase in pay. It truly was one of those *"aha moments"* in one's life.

So, it was on that late night in early August of 1973 the fortunes of the paper and my life would begin a romance that I still cherish today. In Lou's own words it became the day the *Farmington Valley Herald* changed and once again came alive, becoming a full-service newspaper to all...men and women. Girls and boys. And for the girls, field hockey, Ole Connie Applebee's baby from 1901, was the first target in my sights.

The awakening for many souls, including me, was about to happen.

5

"*Ken King here,*" his voice coming over the line clear and strong.

It was my first call as I began putting my plans into action. I needed sports schedules and the Athletic Director at Granby High School is my opening bid. Ken assures me he will put the boys' schedules into the mail that day. I say I want girls' schedules, too. There is a brief silence and then, with what sounds like a renewed gusto, King replies, "*You bet!*" I had vaulted over my first hurdle.

A half hour later I make my second call to Bob Summers, Athletic Director for Avon's schools. When Summers comes on the line he announces, "*Rob. I've already put all my schedules in the mail.*" Before I could ask how he knew what I was calling for he adds, "*Just had a call from Kenny King at Granby.*"

Later that afternoon, I answer a call from Farmington's

Athletic Director, John Grocki. He says his schedules have been mailed because he wants to get a jump on his TO-DO List. I'm pretty sure he also received a call from Avon's Bob Summers. The word is beginning to spread like a cascading waterfall.

The next morning East Granby's AD, Herb Neuhauser calls to say his schedules have been sent. He's looking forward to seeing me visit the school. Though he's not sure if anyone will come out to see games at Connecticut's smallest high school. Dave McConnell from Lewis Mills High School in Burlington returns my call assuring me schedules will be in the mail.

Canton's Bill Modano has a secretary call saying fall schedules will go out in the afternoon mail. She pauses. Then, in a monotonous drone reads to me words Modano has written on the note, *"Why do I want girls' schedules."* Do I plan to print them in the paper! I let it pass. Hey, in every group, there's always one!

That leaves me with one school to contact. Simsbury, the largest school in the valley. Athletic Director Bob Broderick is not in his office. So, I venture into more familiar territory, the boys' athletic office. Seated behind his desk is Russ Sholes. Simsbury's resident thespian of athletics for more years than I have been alive.

He is called "Mister Sholes" because he has earned that respect. He's coached football, basketball, baseball and soccer teams. Taught gym classes at the high school, junior high and grammar schools. Ran the town's summer camps at the old town pool. Painted houses during summers. His lore is ubiquitous to Simsbury. He's been my athletic guidepost since I was old enough to know sports was fun...and hard work. He's taught us exercise and competition. How to jump on a trampoline. Hidden strategies of crab soccer. The art of dodgeball. Effective positioning and rotating in volleyball.

And three very memorable points of sports. The first, in any sport, if you keep moving nobody gets a clear shot at you. Second, in baseball, never hit to the pitcher. And finally...when

Mister Sholes blew his whistle, that meant **STOP, LOOK** and **LISTEN!**

He is to the town what Connie Mack is to baseball's Philadelphia Athletics. What Red Auerbach is to the Boston Celtics or George Hallas, Old Papa Bear, to the Chicago Bears. He is Simsbury's un-bearded Father Time. Carrying the scythe to assure the seeds and growth for living life are carried on. The hourglass to assure no deserving soul gets cheated out of time. Always, ready to do battle with the unannounced arrival of the Grim Reaper's sniping probes. And he possesses a patented stare from behind dark glasses that can melt ice and ignite a campfire in a windstorm.

He greets me with that smile and booming voice I have known since I was five years old. Once you learn, you never forget. Like when he blew his whistle.

We share amenities and I ask him for schedules. When I ask for girls' schedules, he smiles and says, *"It's about time somebody asks for them."* To my surprise he has recently talked with Lou Ball at the *Herald*. Learned that my job is to rebuild the paper's sports section. I am humbled when he says if anyone can rebuild the once-famous section, *"Robert you're the guy who can do it!"* I thank him for his kind words.

Mister Sholes says he thought I would have been a good halfback, or wingback. I tell him that I really don't care for football. Playing outside when it's wet and cold is not on my need-to-do list. He mentions I could have been a decent point guard in basketball. I shake my head saying I was too slow and not strong enough to run the show, despite my averaging 15.3 per game in junior college. He adds, *"You were a good second baseman. Pesky bat and a good rally starter."*

I break into a weak smile. Nod and say, *"Perhaps!"* All the while thinking that my pesky bat he's referring to produced a meager .231 career batting average. Not really all-star material. But I feel a renewed blast of adrenaline as I drive back home that evening. Humbled at his vote of confidence about rebuilding the *Heald's* Sports Section and his simple words that I was the one who could do it.

For the first time in weeks, I have a good, relaxed feeling that maybe, just maybe, I can do this. I laugh out loud when I recall those dodgeball games. *"Just keep moving, baby. Don't give anyone a good shot at you. Don't think of this as work. This is fun."*

I turn up the volume dial on my AM car radio. Del Shannon bellows out the words to his biggest hit, "Runaway."

Hey, I'm going to be watching high school sports, college sports and whatever professional sports I can worm my way into. The opportunity to write my thoughts and opinions of what I see. And to get paid. Not much pay. But how many of my friends and peers wake up every morning with that wonderous feeling of anticipation for the day's activities? Every day when I awoke my first thoughts were, *"OK, what fun can I get myself into today!"* The next step is simple, but a little scary.

It was time to jump into the deep end of the pool. To see if I can swim.

6

A combat medic in Vietnam taught me there are two rules during war. Rule number one is simple. *"In war, people die."*

Rule number two is an absolute. *"No one can change rule number one."*

Along the route, I learned there were a few more rules of war. Like rule number three. *"There are no rules!"*

Rule number three! Widely misunderstood and misperceived. Always, surreptitiously applied, usually in a mean-spirited way and without empathy. And, often, deeply institutionalized. In late summer of 1973 during my travels around the valley, it didn't take long for me to see all three of those rules of war were evident in varying degrees, some metaphorical. I guess that I knew the rules existed. Still, it was a sad and rather painful lesson for me to again see and re-learn. Right in my own backyard.

I expected to find some of the old established rules in place. Those subtle abuses of policy and procedure wrapped and disguised in carefully planned cultural biases. Those long-accepted inequities falling within the boundaries of what is tolerable. And, obviously, what is not. Those situations where one exists within boundaries of institutional racism, anti-semitism or homophobia. Denied by those in charge who always claim they are not aware the situations really existed. Like I witnessed during my military years in almost every location where I served.

Then, I found one of those rules of war right in the middle of the fields where I was working. One of those deep-rooted, unwritten prejudices with stone wall supports. Those unspoken denials that begin at the top of the organizational chain. It ran the gamut from the simplest levels of thought to deep-rooted applications to young people who just wanted to be a part of sports.

Slightly out of breath after running through a stick-handling drill, she introduced herself to me, *"Hi. I'm Kent Walton, co-captain of the Simsbury girls' field hockey team. And you are...?"*

I guess that I had been standing a bit too close to the action and got noticed. I introduced myself and the purpose of my visit. It was late August. School and the 1973 fall seasons would begin in about 10 days. These were pre-school informal practices engaged in by most schools. Then, I noticed something I wasn't looking for. Those perceived, but unwritten imbalances of justice. Those battles between the norms and the mores. One of those rules of war.

The Trojans football team, one of the top-ranked teams in the state, worked out on the school's football field. The boys' varsity soccer team went through drills on their regular season field. The field hockey team worked out on the high school's front lawn along the main thoroughfare, Farms Village Road. Their practice field was a series of gentle hills and valleys. Like rolling turkey hills complete with small trees and drainage grates.

Not your everyday hockey field.

I asked why they were practicing at this location. Walton toweled away the sweat from the heavy humidity of that late August evening. She took a couple of swigs from a cup of lemonade and said matter-of-fact, *"Pre-school practices. No formalized drills. No coaches permitted. Can't be on the regular season field."*

I pointed out the football and soccer teams practicing on school fields. Walton's reply was quick and right to the point. *"No Shit!"* Her answer came right down the middle of the strike zone. Yeah. Muddy waters sometimes have a habit of clearing, quickly. Walton then added in a satiric manner, *"You tell me why. Then we'll both know."*

Subsequent visits to neighboring schools produced mirror images. Led by their co-captains, Sue Hebert and Pam Sproull, Granby's girls worked through informal drills on the school's front lawn while the boys' soccer team worked out on their regular season field.

To the blaring sounds of The Doors "Love Her Madly," Avon's football team hollered in unison during calisthenics on their football field. The field hockey team practiced on a grassy area pigeon-holed next to West Avon Road. That also appeared to be the norm for informal get-togethers at Farmington High, Lewis Mills and for the first varsity season planned for Canton High School. I was beginning to see life *"Down in the Weeds."* At the lower levels of that accepted ethical prejudice.

At each school, it was like listening to someone read from the same script. Each with its own subtle nuances to the epidemic and their own way of pushing back and not rationalizing the need for compliance to those *"Asinine Rules."*

Others likened the situation to *"playing at a public reform school,"* while others believed girls' teams were perceived and treated by the school and town administrations like, *"Bad little girls. Little bitches. Little needy bitches."*

On one visit, I stood in the rain and listened to a young girl, a field hockey player, speak softly and openly. *"They think we're all a bunch of lesbians. Chasing each other around a field with wooden clubs. Can't wait to get back to the locker room for a little action!"*

I wrote down the young girl's thoughts in my notebook. Still writing and with my head down, I started to ask the question. Then, I hesitated. But the tea leaves had been read. The question was out there to be asked. I looked at her while gently biting my tongue.

I asked, "Are you...a bunch of lesbians with wooden clubs? The locker room...and all that other stuff."

She pondered my question, and I could see she was deep in thought. She inhaled deeply and looked directly into my eyes. Her face was stoic, rainwater running down from the bill of her baseball cap. She was 16-years old and suddenly, I felt bad that I had asked the question. Putting her in that position. Like I was being invasive and had no right to know the answer.

Her answer, like her self-observation, was soft spoken, and I believe the answer came from her heart as she spoke, *"Some are. Yes, some are!"*

It was past 10 PM. I was sitting at my desk in the *Herald's* newsroom. My clothes still wet and clammy. Lou Ball came in wearing that concerned look on his face. He asked why I was here at this late hour. My explanation was a bit static and admittedly, I had not yet worked out all the thoughts I had encountered that day. Lou patiently listened as I shared with him the stories of the day. His words of guidance were like an oasis in the desert. You had to know Lou to understand the meaning of what he was saying.

"Leave 'em happy. Leave 'em sad. But leave 'em something," were his words.

Lou said that if I wrote what I saw, what I heard and the truth that was in my heart, I would be OK. He wanted me to know and understand, even with the best of people and situations, I wasn't going to please all the people all the time. Some people are always going to be hurt. Be thankful there will be those people who will see something in me they trust...and will share powerful emotions. Like that 16-year-old field hockey player had done earlier that evening.

That informal conversation with my boss, my friend, Lou Ball, on that late Thursday evening would walk me through a critical portal perhaps even I had avoided. It allowed me to shed so much weight of indecision, opening me up to the ambiguities I would soon come to better understand.

If I saw a wrong, it would be OK to say something trying to right it. Not be ashamed to do so. Politically correct, hell, after Vietnam I didn't give a shit about being PC.

I remembered a poem I had written when a bad situation left me standing at a fork in the road and I needed to make a critical decision before going forward.

For if that old metal stop-sign at which I spat
when I was ten years old has rusted and faded,
*   why then I, too, have aged.*
And if my sanctuary of forgetfulness has robbed me
*   of the more intimate emotions and understandings*
*   of this and other worlds, then come, today or any day,*
I am a better man for admitting my neglects.

Honestly, I was not sure what my struggling attempt at poetic words really meant. Yet, I had a strange feeling they were needed now. For me to better understand. Of the anguish and frustrations to what that 16-year-old girl was saying to me. Her calmness of frustration. Her trust in me. The obstructions that would be a lifetime.

I had written those words many years before to the Young Rascals singing "People Got to Be Free." In Vietnam, during war. As if one day I would need them. Like on this day. Perhaps to right a wrong. The day I again revisited and re-learned all about the rules of war. Especially, rule number three.

There are no rules in any war.

7

Sometimes you need to get hit by a brick before waking up to see all the controlled turmoil going on all around you.

Farmington Valley high schools had damn good field hockey programs. Just ask the pros who ran the sports books in Las Vegas. Granby's girls were coming into the 1973 campaign riding a 33-game unbeaten string that stretched back to 1969. No need for a rebuild, here. For the Bears it would be another case of reloading an already potent team.

To my surprise, I learned from a Vietnam vet I had served with who worked the floor in the Vegas casino's betting rooms. In early September, Granby's field hockey team had a short life on one of the supplemental betting boards in Las Vegas. And, in Reno too. How they got to the betting boards is a mystery. Even my in-the-know friend, *"The Mortarman,"* had no idea who established the lines.

Their betting line opened at $20 and their odds were 7-5 they would go unbeaten during the regular season. There was nothing about winning any tournaments. Just the fact they had a Las Vegas and Reno betting line was freakin amazing.

Simsbury's field hockey history dated back to the mid-1950's. Despite the loss of key stars from a strong '72 team, they appeared to have the players to produce another winning season. Farmington had created and maintained a legacy throughout the state as a quality program and tough to beat. Avon had developed into a winning program. A team capable of beating any opponent on any given day and coming into the '73 season, they were on a ten-game winning streak. Lewis Mills was entering its third varsity season and Canton would enter its first varsity campaign with a gang of girls finally getting the opportunity to show off their skills.

There persisted an on-again-off-again rumor that following the regular 1973 season the CIAC would hold its first-ever post-season field hockey tournament. Initial notifications, or teasers, had been distributed to state high schools beginning in June. Subsequent distributions of tournament-type information and protocols had also been made. Nobody held their breath. The CIAC had tried this before. Efforts had not gone well.

Talk of a true, post-season tournament went all the way back to the late 1950's with proposed sponsorship by the New Haven Register and Waterbury Republican newspapers. And the 1960's with sponsorship by Raybestos, an automotive brake company in Bridgeport since 1902. A company with a world-wide recognition in sports, both with its women's and men's teams.

The late Joan Sullivan built the field hockey program in Simsbury during the 1954 and 1955 school years. Sully was in her 20th season and had suffered just one losing year. She had a good pipeline of players coming into the program, many who began playing in gym classes, town feeder leagues and then in junior high. Simsbury teams were typically well-balanced, leaning towards defense, always with a gang of all-state level fullbacks. They usually had a couple of speedy wings and good goaltending. Her 1973 team mirrored those components but were untested. Sully said they would be good. I had to believe what I heard as I had no baseline of measurement in which to gauge this squad verses the successes of previous years.

What I did notice was the game of 1973 was played at about the same speed as it had been played in 1963. Though, slower than is played today, especially games played on artificial surfaces. Throughout lineups, overall field hockey skills were noticeably better. Players were more athletic, bigger, faster, stronger, quicker and more aggressive.

Holly Burk, co-captain, could play every halfback position. Kent Walton was a co-captain and anchored the halfback line. She was also asked to do double duty as a go-to on the scoring line. Sully had experienced front liners in Amy Johnson and Kathy Hudson.

What the Trojans knew they had was defense, and they wore it like a blue ribbon. Pat Hoskin was the leader. She was quick and liked to play an aggressive one-on-one style. Few opponents got past her on her stick side. Burk was joined by another veteran in Sue Marshall. Shelly Armitage, Wendy Menzel and Mary Ann DePattie were also found roaming the middle of the field. Simsbury's defense was a brick wall. Maybe, the best defensive unit in the state. Scoring would be the challenge for the Trojans.

Kent Walton and Holly Burk
1973 Simsbury Co-Captains

The two questions needing answers: who would become a back-up scorer to support

Walton and how effective would the goaltending be, which was iffy and untested. I had watched Joan Sullivan coach since 1956. You could read her face like the lines in a textbook. She sounded a bit nervous speaking in her nasally B-flat voice. The last words of her sentences rising higher in tone sounding like she was running out of oxygen. Then the quick head nod.

When I asked Sully about the fortunes for her team she quickly shot back, *"Why, what have you heard about us?"* I walked away wanting no part of that conversation. There were lots of unanswered questions about Simsbury's 1973 team.

My first meeting with Farmington's coach, the late Jean Hunt, was as close to a religious experience as I could remember. Mainly, because it scared the hell out of me.

I kind of expected another Joan Sullivan-type personality as she and Sully were close, personal friends. Both graduates of Boston University's Sargent College of Health and Sciences. They had known each other for over 20 years.

Hunt said she would meet me on the field at 4 PM. Practice ended early due to rain. I stood at the far end of the field. I was reading notes when I heard an echoing voice boom out, *"You. Penfield."* I looked to one side. Nothing. Again, the voice from the abyss. *"You, Rob Penfield. I want to speak with you!"* I could feel my heart beating.

Honestly, it sounded like the voice of God calling out to me.

I looked up and saw a woman at the far end of the field. Like the guardian at the Gates of Souls, she stood erect, pointing at me. *"I want to speak with you,"* she bellowed. Her arm wavered as she continued to point towards me. Jesus, it felt like I was being called home to the mountain!

I started jogging towards her because I didn't dare walk. I came face-to-face with this new stranger. She stared into my eyes. She smiled, introduced herself and thanked me for coming. She walked me into the locker room. The girls were in various degrees of undress and I felt uneasy. Hunt saw my uneasiness. She smiled and said, *"It's OK Rob. You'll do just fine. You're among friends."*

Thus, started my relationship with Jean Hunt. Despite the gruffness and her old school approach, I came to know her as someone with a heart of gold. A person I would want standing guard at those Gates of Souls. The person who, on my last night in Simsbury before moving to Baltimore in 1978, called me at 11PM. Clinked the ice cubes in her glass and said, *"Rob, this one's for you and all you did for us."*

Hunt's teams continued to produce quality players and winning teams, year after year, beginning in the early 1960's. Many of Hunt's players were ready for varsity action as sophomores but couldn't break into the lineup because of the solid corps of well-trained juniors and seniors who had put in their time and were playing ahead of them.

She was confident her 1973 team would be successful. Perhaps seven or eight wins. But was quick to say, *"We're not as good as we think we are."*

Hunt begun her career at Litchfield and was now in her 15th year at Farmington. Her '73 version had one of the best players in the Valley, team Captain Abby Walsh. She was one of the smoothest, most graceful players in the state. Opponents all tried to stop Walsh. Often, double-teaming her. That was the kind of respect her game had earned. She was a good leader and often had to re-group her team as they had a tendency to play out-of-control. Walsh, a quiet leader, was one of the best-ever to play for Hunt.

Patty Lavoie, a junior, was a goal scorer in support of Walsh. Another skilled junior, Loretta DiPietro had developed into a stable force at left halfback. Jeanie Scarrozzo and Mary Ellen Seravelli were experienced frontline players.

Goaltending was a huge strength for the Indians. Missy Saxton wore the pads between the pipes and may have been the best goalie in the valley. She had a positive and daring aspect to her goaltending and liked to come out of the net and attack on-coming foes. Mix it up with those who got too aggressive. She stopped tough shots at key times in many games. To the admiration of her teammates, she was the last line of defense. She was Farmington's China Wall!

Avon had all-stater, Heidi Zacchera. To the casual eye that would seem to be all they needed. From her center-forward position, Zacchera scored goals, created corner hits and dropped back to play defense, a rarity for a scoring line player. Avon did win games because of Zacchera. Their success, though, was due to the overall performance from a group of key players.

As many games as Zacchera's aggressiveness won at one end of the field, Avon's goalies, Mary Ann Hollfelder and Betsy Curtis, won games for the Falcons at the other end. Hollfelder was smallish in size and as quick as a water bug. She was a nervy darter who would fearlessly come charging out of her goal screaming at opponents. Scaring the shit out of anyone within earshot. If you got too close to her, she'd bump you. Hard!

I once watched her yell at an opponent loud enough for all to hear, *"You get your boney ass outta here or I'll whack it with my stick."* The girl cowered and backed off with her head bowed.

Alice Yokabaskas was one of the best and beloved officials in the state. Alice was working a contest at Farmington where one particular play became the epitome of Hollfelder's style-of-play. After being bumped

Holly Blacker, Marsha Maines and Caryn Bray of Avon

off the play, a disgruntled Farmington player turned to Yogi, as she was often referred to, and pleaded for a penalty which fell on deaf ears. The player's second request to Yogi for a penalty was more vocal and a tad more sordid. Yogi stopped the player in her tracks and did some quick educating as the game continued on around them.

Alice put one had on the girl's shoulder and one finger in her face and said, *"You were offsides. The ball hit one of your feet. The backside of your stick. And you threw the first elbow. Which of your penalties would you like me to call against you!"* The complainer went silent.

After the game I asked Alice about the incident and Hollfelder's elbowing the player. Why no whistle for her elbow? Alice laughed saying she just didn't have the heart to call a penalty on anyone who played with that kind of passion. It's what made Alice Yokabaskas special. Why you liked and respected her whenever she was assigned to do a game.

Coaches are always clamoring for those special players. Bonnie Tyler had two of the very best. Caryn Bray was a leader on the halfback line. I watched many Avon games and I never saw Bray play out of position. She played her lanes skillfully, harassing opponents into mistakes resulting in goals for Avon. The other was Marsha Mains. As a fullback she had skills and abilities of a halfback. Opponents stayed away from her side of the field. Tyler called the two, her coaches on the field.

Holly Blacker and Mary Jo Capitani were experienced starters. A young sophomore, Karen Poirier, was gifted and skillful. Her flashes of athletic power and brilliance were punctuated by her bouts of lackadaisical play. When Karen Poirier wanted to play you could not stop her. She was that good with unlimited potential.

I would quickly learn that Lou Ball's words of support were true. I couldn't please all the people all the time. No matter how good or how badly they played. As new as it was for me to cover girls' sports, it was even newer for the girls to be the primary targets in the sports pages. It was unnerving for some. At times, just as confusing as that ambiguously written law, Title IX.

The girls wanted newspaper coverage. The good kind. The warm and fuzzies. Since I didn't know how to write *"Warm and Fuzzy"* I wrote what I saw. When an individual or team played a good game, I said so. When they played like horseshit, I said that, too. Many struggled with that aspect of notoriety. Including their parents who flooded the *Herald* with phone calls demanding I not write the bad stuff. I dealt with it in the best way I knew how. I said to the folks, you wanted it and now you've got it. Pick a lane and deal with it. It had become a case of be careful what you wish for. Ironically, the coaches felt my stories, observations and perceptions hit the targets, dead center.

It was going be a bumpy learning curve for everybody.

8

Sometimes, I like to think big. I had this belief that one day one of the girls playing for Lewis Mills or Canton High School would become President of the United States.

Yeah, I know that sounds a tad hokey. Hell, what did I know about politics? I didn't trust politicians in 1973. Still don't trust 'em today.

I would, however, trust one of those girls who played field hockey. They had nothing to hide. They were honest with their thoughts and efforts. Cared about what they did and their teammates and they wanted to learn. After years of having no stage to show their talents, they came to play. With enthusiasm and honesty, the type of person I look for in people I want on my team. Supporting me when I need it. Somebody I would vote for to be my President.

I watched those girls learn their lessons and grow as

quickly as the famous tobacco stalks from our valley. It was easy to see many of the girls would soon be trekking on the path to success in their adult lives. Perhaps to the White House. Silly me. But that's the quality of young lady that I was watching develop. The ones who had waited so long for the opportunity to show off their stuff.

Both schools' field hockey programs were still in their infancy. Mills would begin its third varsity season. Canton would be swan diving into its first. Mills would be led by coach Linda Hamm who had that special gift of training and transferring the skills and knowledge onto her players. Janet Beck would lead Canton's very inexperienced gang. Both had built their programs from scratch.

Hamm would have the support of her Athletic Director, Dave McConnell in Burlington. Her early varsity teams had been able to scratch out a few wins over bigger, more experienced programs. Beck did not have that support. Her combined JV and varsity team was coming off a 3-9 season. The AD, Bill Modano, was overheard talking with a school board member. *"When (if) they win, we'll make more resources available."*

I never received a clear or concise explanation from Modano to what was inferred by, *"Make more resources available."* As Bill Modano would often do, he'd remind me that perhaps I had not really heard what was being said or had taken his words out of context. I liked to remind him that his words explaining a circumstance were usually given to me already out of context.

The difference between the valley's successful programs and the ones just getting started was a living dichotomy not lost even on my inexperienced eyes. In Granby, Simsbury and Farmington, I was watching field hockey players performing skilled athletic moves, as individuals and a team, to the rhythmic and subtle beat in my head of Paul McCartney & Wings cooing through a version of "My Love." A sound that was smooth, experienced, and established.

At Mills and Canton, I was watching girls who were wonderfully athletic, learning to be skilled field hockey players as they traveled the path to whatever beat that happened to be the song of the day, be it Jim Croce singing "Bad, Bad LeRoy Brown" or Pink Floyd oozing lyrics from "The Dark Side of the Moon." It was rough and edgy. But getting a little better every day.

Mills had a two-year head start on Canton and took on a full slate of Northwest Conference games plus an aggressive non-conference schedule. The Spartans were a formidable opponent. There was a base of talent. They just did not have enough of those well-skilled players and they lacked the depth of established programs.

Senior Candy Thierry was a front-line scorer and the inspirational leader. She was respected by many players from opposing teams who evaluated her performance saying, *"That girl can play!"*

Michelle LaVigne was one of the most athletic players in the valley and a scorer when called upon. Karen Summers, a winger, may have been the fastest runner on the team.

The deep defense was getting better with each game. Melanie Gibson's play at fullback was being noticed through-out the league and Mills had good goaltending in Deb Nettleton.

I recall a practice when Hamm, upset that a play was not working and frustrated with the performance of a few of her key players, turned to me. *"You know something, Rob. We're one player away from not only going to the tournament, but from going deep into the tournament."*

I wasn't sure if I agreed with her. But then, this was Linda Hamm. And she saw more field hockey with her eyes closed than I did with mine wide open. Did she need another scorer? Or a fleet-footed wing who could sprint down the sideline and make crossing passes? Nope! She had scorers. Good wingers.

Strong inners, a good halfback line and a good deep defense.

"What I need is one more athlete who is a field hockey player in the middle of the field. Someone who understands the discipline and flow of the game."

Hamm was like a world class chess player who was six moves ahead of the competition and simply looking for the gift of discipline. And if Linda Hamm said she was that close to having a team go deep into any tournament, you could damn-well bet the farm on that observation.

Canton's road to success and more benefits from the athletic budget would be a little bumpier. Let's not underestimate the '73 team. They were raw and not expected to win many games. But as an opponent, if you came to play the Warriors and didn't bring your A-Game to the pitch, you were going to lose. A few good teams waltzed into Canton with thoughts of romping to an easy win over a new team. What they got was bitten in the ass and crawled home with a loss. And a few other teams of renown got the shit scared out of them as that young, inexperienced Canton team took them right down to the final seconds of the game.

You could almost feel the Canton groundswell coming to life.

The Warriors had limited skilled players but did not want for athletes. They had plenty. Cindy Bahre and Debbie Davidson were the lone seniors in the starting lineup. At fullback, Bahre teamed with junior Margie Crandall. Shelly Grace played in goal forming a good deep defense. Davidson an aggressive player, anchored the halfback line between Mary Raftery, Joan Lally and Deb Keyes.

There were shortcomings. Coach Beck had seniors playing ahead of others who were more skilled and talented. That would cost Canton a few early season wins, which in turn, would cost the Warriors a shot at the tournament.

The scoring line players were young but athletic. Sophomores Darcy Johnson and Carol Stefanik would become three-year starters. Nancy Moulton, Mary Ann Grinvalsky, Mary Jane Hinman and Linda Bahre filled out the lineup. Each getting varsity starts during the season. Lynne Bouchard, a sophomore, could play on the scoring or halfback lines and became one of the steadiest players.

Now it was time to learn. What this group needed was to convert that pool of resources into field hockey players. To learn field hockey skills and the strategies of the game. Ensure the right people were playing in the right positions. To maximize their athletic talents. Then, manage and hone those resources into a competitive unit complete with strategy, compliance, and discipline. A timeline typically of two, maybe three years.

The talent was there. What they needed was leadership to take them to that next level of learning. How to play field hockey. How to survive and play another day. Learn how to climb the ladder and win. Establish a legacy.

They were a year away from finding that person who would take those resources up the next rungs on that ladder. If 1973 was to be the year of learning, then 1974 would be the year of new coach, Gail Juday.

Her presence would send Canton's field hockey fortunes on a forty-year joyride.

9

Granby just beat you in every possible way they could.

The Granby team was the epitome of field hockey skills. They were skilled and aggressive when it was needed. They knew the game. They were in shape. Hated those days when they had to *"Run the Hill"* for punishment when set plays would fall apart. And their practices, well, that's where they learned how to win. Granby's practices were more demanding than most of their games. They were riding a 33-game unbeaten streak and had not lost a game since September 1969.

Their field was not the best. When you stood watching Granby's girls atop the hill that overlooked the hockey field, the playing surface resembled the uneven topography of a pepperoni pizza. Some days the playing surface was a test of survival. Practices were situational, as if the conference title were on the line. Every possession and scoring rush like trying to end a sudden death OT game. Every defensive stop being the most important play of the game.

Some days it flowed like a graceful dove on the horizon. Other days, hell, it looked like they were trying to put out an ugly dumpster fire. Practices were conducted with the same intensity of a game. Players became ornery. Short-tempered. Curt and terse with their language. Skirmishes on the field. Stick jousting. Threats of revenge. Most players admitted that the toughest games were less physical, even more enjoyable, than most of the practices.

But don't think for a minute this team didn't know its place and position. Its strengths and weaknesses. Yeah, they were that tiny school. Those barefooted farmers and ugly duck-lings...well, upstate somewhere. Whose dads were blue collar workers. Lots of stay-at-home moms. That tiny school who year-after-year would rise up from the farm pastures, taking on all challengers, big and small. Out-play them on the field. Out-defend them in key situations. Embarrass opponents with elevated field hockey skills and beat the living shit out of everyone.

Their coach was Dottie Johnson. Now, if I were a football coach, I would want Dot anchoring my offensive line, playing center on my team. Perhaps playing middle guard on the defensive line. Dottie was tough and solid, like a fire hydrant.

I would come to know her as the most prepared leader ready to take her team into a competition. That's how she showed up to her first job interview at Granby. How she conducted gym classes. How she coached her field hockey team. She didn't yell or belittle players. Nor did she rant and rave about mistakes. Dottie didn't throw things or display uncontrolled disgust. Her disciplines and motivations were what I would come to call, *"Tweeners!"*

No, she didn't yell, but she didn't coddle, either.

Dot used a series of hand gestures with her players. She

knew how to heighten anxiety and create expectations in players. Players who knew they had not met expectations with their play. Her unique sign language was received and understood as if it had been conveyed via a bullhorn. Her facial gestures added to and punctuated the hand signals. She would flash a look, sometimes as bland as vanilla ice cream. Other looks ranked right along with award winning drama on Broadway. And, if she wanted to deliver that look with extra authority, she'd quickly run a hand through her blonde hair a couple of times while exhaling with a low growl. You'd hear a murmur run through the players like a chain reaction. *"Wow...I screwed up. Boy, did I mess up that play. What the hell was I thinking!"*

I marveled at the responses. At her unspoken language. It was absolutely, uncanny.

What Dot Johnson did have were field hockey players. Lots of 'em! They played the creative, yet challenging, 4-4-2 formation. Demanding to play with multi-responsibilities, confusing to opponents and at times, indefensible. It created gaps, confusing the teams who played the standard 5-3-2 formats. It forced opponents' best players out of their comfort zones. It gave Granby's more-skilled players lots of room to roam and perform. You might slow Granby's approach down a bit, but opponents could not stop it.

The 4-4-2 needed talent to be effective. Granby had the people to run the show. It started with the center-half position, co-captain, Pam Sproull. Pam had the athleticism, quickness, cockiness and hockey skills to make the complex formation work. Offensively, to lead the attack inside the 25-

Sue Hebert and Pam Sproull
1973 Granby Co-Captains

yard line. Defensively to get back and cover her lanes. The omnipresent responsibility to control the tempo of a game at midfield.

Pam Sproull was not the best field hockey player in the state. She was absolutely, the best field hockey player to run Granby's complex formations.

The 4-4-2 needs a running mate on the halfback line. That responsibility fell to a junior, Lynsie Wickman. She was a dynamo who would explode in and out of situations, reminding me of the Peanuts Cartoon character, Pigpen. That visual of swirling dust that would cut a swatch though the field leaving skid marks, stunned opponents and wide-eyed teammates gasping for breath. When Lynsie's radar focused on the goal, she was on a mission. It was best to just get out of her way. Including teammates. Otherwise, you were going to get run over.

The spread formation needed speed on the outside fringes. Sharon Schneider would usually outrun anyone who tried to defend her. She was an attack inner by formation but played on the fringes like a wing. She had the ability to reach the ball and stop on a dime while opponents went sliding by trying to put on the brakes. She made strong crossing passes into the scoring zones. Break down Granby's offensive scoring stats for the '73 season and you will find that Schneider was involved in most of the team's goals.

Every 4-4-2 needs a scorer on the front line. Granby had a dandy in Val McCord. A real sniper who would quietly cruise into the scoring circle. Find one of her favorite spots. Dig in and snap off wrist shots so fast defenses had no chance of setting up for a block without committing a penalty. McCord was fiery. Bump into her and she'd come right back at you. And after a score, Val was a pretty good trash talker and she could back it up. More than once officials had to pull her apart from an opponent after a tete-a-tete evolved into a joust with sticks or a shoving match. And sometimes those jousts were with her own teammates.

Senior Sue Hebert was a co-captain. She teamed with junior Sue Jensen as a formidable duo at fullback. Hebert was quick to the ball and had good stick handling skills. Her Mom and Dad are both deaf and graduates of the Clarke School in Northampton, MA. They are not a sign language family. They are oralists. They read lips and speak. Hebert would often be seen mouthing silent directions to teammates. All seemed to understand and carry out the movements in her messages.

Jensen came from a tough home environment. You could see that anger in her play. She played hard and had a booming shot when she teed off on a ball. When she played angry, nobody got past her without feeling her wrath. A few attacking inners who tried to challenge her ended up on their asses. The only real question still to be answered was the last line of defense. Granby's goaltending.

The Bears would be breaking in a new one in sophomore Joanne "Jo-Baby" Sproull. She had size, skills and although untested, showed an aggressiveness and savvy of an experienced netminder. The first time she came charging out of her goal area attacking a scrum some 15 to 20 feet away from her net, Dottie Johnson almost choked on her Bazooka chewing gum. Johnson made both a hand and facial gesture that said in no uncertain terms, *"Don't ever do that again!"*

Sproull blocked the shot. Kicked the ball away. Nodded at her coach agreeing not to do it again. She would, however, repeat that move numerous times throughout the season including a memorable play in the state championship game.

Linda Dewey was a tall, long-legged inner on the scoring line. She had a strong upper body, a good stick with a wicked hard shot from within the scoring circle. At times, it appeared she wasn't running hard. Until you saw the opponents trying to keep up with her long-legged strides. Nancy Hutchings joined her on the scoring line at left wing. She wasn't flashy. Just a steady performer who did her job at both ends of the field. Mary Byrnes was another frontline performer with a steady game, a good stick, and a goal scoring threat.

Jody Wickman played right halfback. A good hockey player with all the standard skills, Jody had one dominant skill that many of the era did not have. She could run backwards. Not fast, but effectively. It made it tough for attacking lines as she did not have to turn her back on anyone when running to a spot. She was able to adjust her defensive stands quicker than most.

Ellen Burbridge played mostly on the front line, but she could play any position on the field and was a whole different breed of cat.

She had arrived at Granby at the end of her sophomore year and now, as a senior, was playing in her first-ever field hockey season. She was an athlete through and through. A perfectly proportioned upper and lower body and field hockey skills that seemed to just happen as she moved. She knew what to do and when to do it. Had that sense and uncanny ability to know where to be at the right time. Knowing where her teammates would be or where they were supposed to be. Almost as if she had eyes in the back or her head. And she played as if this field hockey thing was more fun than work.

Burbridge was as close to a natural at this game as I would see in the valley during my five years at the *Herald*. Granby's 4-4-2 set would not have worked without Sproull running the show from her center-half position, supported by Lynsie Wickman. And, Granby would not have won their state championship without Ellen Burbridge and her on-field athletic skills.

The Bears played in the NCCC. The weakest conference in the state. Suffield had a competitive team. Beyond them the remainder of the league were cream puffs. They did play a wicked non-conference schedule. Simsbury, Farmington, E.O. Smith, Avon and a home-and-home series against Enrico Fermi.

Granby didn't deceive you. They didn't try to hide anything. They came right at you with their skills. Their simple challenge was come beat us. The only ones who came close were those teams who played that in-your-face brand of defense. Farmington and Simsbury. And even those much larger schools could not beat the Bears on the scoreboard. Nobody could. Because Granby beat you every way possible.

Perhaps Las Vegas and Reno should have kept Granby as a betting line on their supplemental room betting boards. Despite having insider information, I might have taken the odds and put down a few bucks on them.

Nothing like a sure thing when using house money.

10

Sleep! It just never came easy for me. Not after Vietnam.

On November 17, 1973, I awoke from a restless battle with nightmares. It was now early Saturday morning. The clock on my old Motorola radio read 2:03 AM. I was flushed and my face was hot. I was having bad dreams about Vietnam and I was antsy. Breathing hard. My t-shirt was soaking wet. My head hurt and I could feel a pounding behind my right eye.

The darkness in my apartment was softened only by the din of the streetlamp along Hopmeadow Street almost 200 feet away. I wiped the sweat from my face with the sheet. My clock radio played softly. Jim Croce sang, "I Got A Name." The Elegants followed with their soft flowing melody "Little Star". The soft quiet of the music had an odd deafening sound. Kind of a loneliness with an eerie echo.

I got out of bed. It was cold in my apartment, like it usually was in late fall and winter. So, I kept my sweats on. I hardly ever turned on the 1960's baseboard style heating elements because the cost was too expensive even for my small apartment. I made a cup of Maxwell House instant coffee. So-named for the Maxwell House Hotel in Nashville where it was first served in 1894. Used a big cup like the ones you see in today's coffee houses. I sat on my daybed. Put my floppy Vietnam boonies hat on my head. Covered my legs with a blanket and lit a Winston cigarette, one with the new, improved charcoal filter.

There was a sadness to my being. I was tired and battling a nagging cold. I had a cough and body aches. My nose kept running. And I had awful dreams that wouldn't go away. Took a deep drag on the Winston. Blew the smoke out, slowly. Sipped my coffee and let my mind wander. Another nightmare about Vietnam. They never went away. Always, it began the same.

Outside the small hamlet of Gho Denh. It was Christmas Eve, 1968. I had been blown out of a truck by a mine hanging from a tree. Blown about 15 feet into the ruins of a building and knocked senseless. As I regained my wits, I could feel the pain in my lower back where I had hit a tree and landed on cinder blocks. My legs bled and burned from shrapnel wounds.

I cleared the cobwebs from my head only to hear the thumping sounds of percussion from Russian made AK-47's. I was taking fire from three sides. I could hear the enemy yelling at me. *"You **die today, GI!"*** I could hear rounds whizzing past. An infantry rifleman once told me if you can hear rounds whiz by, they're within 10 inches of your head. It was freakin scary.

I was bleeding and kind of figured these were about to be my final minutes of life on this earth. Not being stoic or brave. I was just too goddamned scared or stupid to know any better. I closed my eyes tightly. Shook uncontrollably for a few seconds. I could feel tears running down my cheeks. Then I began returning fire with my M-1 Carbine. A rifle squad from the 9th Infantry Division came to my rescue. I made it through the ordeal. As GI's will often say...guess it wasn't my day to die.

I thought about my Saturday. Hey, I was going to New Haven. The field hockey championship game. I wondered if any of the Granby girls were awake. Couldn't sleep, like me. Thinking about their game and their opponent, Guilford High School. Or thinking of other things that had invaded their lives. Did they have nice dreams or were they scared and struggling with awful nightmares? Maybe they went to church and were praying. I wondered if there were any field hockey gods. Nah, stupid thought. I took another gulp of my instant coffee.

My mind continued to churn. Memories suddenly crashing in like a tidal wave. My senior year of high school. Simsbury. Henry James Memorial High School. Sully's 1963 girls field hockey team. My classmates. Good team, 9-0 that season. No tournaments. Visions of games in my head like that of grainy black-and-white movies of that era. Images of names, some remembered. Some forgotten.

The speed of Pat Schaller as she breaks up an opponent's two-on-one break. The strength of Elaine Crosscup as she bullrushes past a defense. Judy Shaw stickhandling in open field. Bonnie Bogus breaking free down the sideline. Outrunning her defenders. Her stick being waved in the air hollering out unbridled shouts of joy as she cuts across the goal mouth towards the post. B J Lewis, deftly stickhandling through a maze and putting a perfect pass on Bogus' stick as she flicks a rising shot under the left elbow of the goalie for the winning score. Simsbury shuts out E.O. Smith and completes an undefeated season.

If there had been a field hockey tournament in 1963, those girls would have won that competition. No doubt in my mind.

That had been only ten years ago. Damn, just ten years,

yet I had lived a lifetime.

I thought of my girlfriend, Deb in Western Mass. We'd met at college almost two years before during my senior year. I liked her. But, since I started working at the *Herald* our relationship had suffered. And like any cliché one can resurrect, most of the reasons were my fault. I was working 50 hours a week at the *Herald*. Another 20 hours at the Corn Crib liquor store next door to my apartment. I also put in time in the paper's dark room printing pictures I would sell for extra pocket cash.

We were now seeing each other just once a week. There were fewer phone calls and conversations. I had made a feeble attempt to explain my feelings. Writing her a poem to supplant my inability to deal with a verbal explanation. Try and explain what was going on in my life...in my head. Oh, I struggled with those written words as I was struggling with my spoken words. Mis-understood and confused emotions. Afraid of what I knew I must eventually do. *"Pick a Lane!"* Break-up.

I pined over my sad menagerie of words.

Foolish nonsense now and then
> **perceived as noble within the best of men**
> **but not in me as I learn how to live.**
Aching at what I cannot say,
> **and seemingly wrong in almost every way,**
> **because it's only like and not love**
> **that I dare enough to give**
> **and I am a coward.**

I closed my eyes thinking, holy shit, is that really lame. I took another deep drag off the shortened Winston. I could see its glowing ember in the darkness. A small bit of light in my life. I thought of the *Herald*. The real light in my life. The *Herald* kept me going. Kept me alive. It had become my love. I wiped away tears with my sleeve. Wish I could wipe away the memories. Goddamn you, Vietnam. I finished my cigarette and crushed it out in an over-filled ashtray. I finished my coffee that was now cold.

My mind wanders. On this day in 1928 The Boston Garden opens hosting a full card of boxing. The infamous 1968 NFL TV blunder known as *"The Heidi Game"* between the Jets and Raiders is played. In 1960, Andre Charles is born in a San Diego hospital during a power outage. He will become known to the world as Rupaul.

Today, I will go to New Haven and watch a girls' field hockey game. I have this strange, overwhelming feeling, that I must be at this game. That this day will have a significant place in history. I must be there because I feel its impact is going to resonate within me, too, for the rest of my life.

It was early morning, November 17, 1973. Perhaps sleep may come to me tonight.

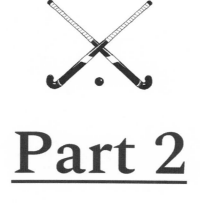

Part 2

"The 1973 Regular Season"

11

The 1973 girls high school field hockey season in Connecticut would truly be one for the books. And I do mean books. From its first game in September to the championship game in November.

It's a time when hardcopy documentation of scorebooks, game results and supplemental information will be stored on shelves in stiff plastic notebooks and cardboard boxes. No floppy disks or thumb drives. No CDs or memory chips. A time in our lives when we looked at clouds in the sky for a momentary reprise from the blaring sun or to see the rolling thunderheads of an oncoming storm. Certainly not for pricey airspace of today's cloud, inhabited with electronically stored alga-rhythms and endless tidal waves of data.

You know that oft-repeated lament. If we had only kept more of that original hardcopy information and not discarded it, like when our Moms threw out all our baseball cards in the 1960's. Then again, in 2030, like those long, lost baseball cards, I may see a 1973 field hockey scoring book for sale on eBay at $229.99.

It's mid-September. Regular season high school athletic schedules roll to the starting line. One of the early, interesting games that fall includes Simsbury. It will turn out to be a doozy. Albeit for Simsbury, the game will deliver as much early season joy as it will provide anguish later in the season. The Trojans will get a chance to try out their untested offense as they travel to Enfield to take on the improving and high-scoring Enrico Fermi High School. The Falcons are beginning their second varsity season.

It was one of those Indian Summer days in New England. Temperatures in the mid-80's and humid. Joan Sullivan watches her team as they run through pre-game warm-ups. It's the season opener for the Trojans. She looks nervous, doesn't say much. She bites her fingernails. At the other end of the field Fermi coach Carol Albert hollers out her commands like a drill sergeant conducting marching orders at a military bootcamp.

The diverse gap in coaching styles is obvious. Sullivan looks to the ground, tight-lipped. Her hands and fingers knotted together as though she is praying. Albert's resonating voice cuts through the humidity in staccato bursts like a machete. You can feel waves of heat emanating from the hardened ground. The Jackson Five's high pitch sounds and thundering beat blares one of their early sing songy hits, "ABC" from a tape player on the scorer's table.

Fermi takes early control charging into the Simsbury end of the field, hammering away at the Trojans' goal. Eight minutes into the game they have already amassed four penalty corners and a half dozen good shots on goal. Simsbury's goaltending is shaky, and Sullivan is pacing the sidelines. She mumbles words about her goaltending.

Then, as dominant as the Fermi attack had been, Simsbury's vaunted defense comes to life and shuts them down. They stifle the Fermi team every way possible. Play defense and ram it down their throats. Over the next 40 minutes the Falcons will mount only a few minor threats.

Simsbury's Kent Walton answers the questions about the offense. In a five-minute span she scores twice, both goals set up by the Hoskin, Burk and Marshall defensive lines. Their defensive play will dominate the remainder of the game. Fermi goalie, Deb Bourque, is screened on the first goal and is overpowered by Walton with the second score.

"We just couldn't stop them" remembers Fermi's fullback, Debbie Teske.

Fermi responds and cuts the lead in half on a goal from senior Donna Teske. Coach Albert yelling, *"About Damn Time!"* Teske does not respond to the remark or look at her coach. She accepts congratulations from her teammates and her sister. From her sweeper position, you can hear Simsbury's Pat Hoskin yell to her teammates, *"Let the bitches enjoy It. Because it's the last one they're going to get."*

Sullivan urges her team to get one more score before halftime. Her words, still echoing, are answered in a heartbeat as Beth Anderson controls a loose ball in front of the goal, lifts a wrist shot in the right corner giving Simsbury a 3-1 halftime lead. Coach Albert's voice is almost hoarse. She stalks the sideline. Stops, bends over with hands on her knees her head slowly nodding. Further up the sideline, Joan Sullivan has stopped biting her nails.

The second half passes slowly. Simsbury's defense continues to be as stifling as the Indian Summer heat. Kathy Hudson adds an insurance goal and Simsbury closes out their season opener with a rather stunning and surprising, 4-1 win over Fermi. Walton answers some of the questions about the offense. The goaltending is Ok. And Sullivan knows that. Simsbury won the game. Despite four goals, I had concerns about the offense. How will the Trojans do against a defensive-minded team?

Midway through the second half, I'm walking the sideline focusing on individual Simsbury players, their skills, and reactions to situations. I hear voices call out to me, *"Hey, mister photographer."* I turn to see a group of girls sitting on a hill. One is pointing at me and says, *"Yes, you. Can we talk with you!"*

As I approached, I recognized the young lady who was calling to me. It was Pam Sproull, one of the Granby co-captains. The group was half of Granby's starting lineup. They had taken a day off from practice to scout Simsbury and Fermi. Granby would be playing both schools during the ensuing weeks.

We compared notes for what we all had just seen. The Simsbury and Fermi teams. The offenses and especially, Simsbury's defense. Not surprising, we agreed on most points. Especially, how each coach had handled situations during the game.

It quickly became clear why Granby played at a level above their peers. It was this type of pre-games preparation. These girls made it clear. They were willing to go that extra distance. Like using their own time and expense to make a 50-mile roundtrip to scout teams they would be playing during the season. These were the early days of field hockey rivalries. Nobody did live, pre-game scouting. Except Granby.

In return, the Granby girls expected nothing less than success.

12

Friday afternoon, Granby opened its season with a 7-0 whitewash of a weaker conference foe, East Windsor.

Pam Sproull kicked off her senior year with a hat trick. Her running mates on the halfback line, sisters Lynsie and Jody Wickman, accounted for three more goals. It was one of those games that could have ended up 12-0. Coach Dot Johnson had backups in the lineup for the entire second half. A nice game for egos. Not a good prep for an upcoming game at home against high scoring Enrico Fermi.

Saturday morning, Fermi's Falcons came to town with a 1-1 record. They had beaten a talented E.O. Smith team, 2-1, then got smoked in a surprising and sloppy 4-1 loss to Simsbury. A game that had been personally scouted by half of the Granby team.

Granby's scouting of Fermi paid off right from first

whistle. Linda Dewey, a junior, scored twice, one a whistling shot that had opponents ducking to get out of the way, and the Bears rushed out to a quick 2-0 lead. Granby's 4-4-2 formation was confusing the Falcons. Luring front line players out of position. Fermi's coach Albert stood along the sidelines, speechless. Pacing the sideline throwing her hands into the air and shaking her head.

A few of the Simsbury players were in attendance and one commented, *"Wait'll she starts yelling. She'll bust an artery."*

Val McCord started the second half with a quick score and Granby's lead swelled to 3-0. Albert began yelling. The Simsbury players began applauding. Granby's Dot Johnson hollered encouragement to her mid-fielders, *"Don't let up... Don't let up. Don't let Teske get loose."*

Johnson was referring to Fermi's high scorer, Donna Teske. She did get loose and mid-way through the second half picked up a goal off a penalty corner. Moments later, she just missed a second goal with a shot that went wide-right on a pass from Sharon Benoit. With just over five minutes remaining, Sara King exploded through the Bears' defense and sent a quick wrist shot into the Granby net.

Goalie Jo Sproull never moved on the play. She stood just outside her net and said, *"Okay, that one's my fault."*

Time ran out on Fermi, dropping a 3-2 game and falling to 1-2 on the season. Asked about her team's performance, Coach Albert, visibly angered, spoke loudly saying,

"We got outplayed. That won't happen again."

Despite the terseness, I sensed the anguish. Not in losing a field hockey game. It was more than that. Went beyond what happened on the field. She wanted her girls to be successful. Fermi was a new school. A new team trying to build a legacy. They were learning how to survive. Now in sports and in what they would face during the ensuing years as adults.

She was teaching discipline and compliance. How to understand commitment to each other. How to be a team and how to practice. Having her girls wear dresses to school on game days. You could almost read that emotion in Albert's face. She cared deeply for what she was doing, and for her girls. Albeit she did it in a brusque and very loud manner.

True to her words, Fermi would not lose another game during the remainder of the regular season. They will become one of the most potent-scoring offensives in the state. Teske will become a prolific scorer with 18 goals. With her line mates, Benoit and King, the trio will score 39 of their team's 43 goals during the regular season.

Granby's Pam Sproull said her team was tired after playing two consecutive days. She believed they should have won the game by a larger margin, but said they let Fermi get back into the game. To my observation, Fermi had out-hustled and out-played Granby during the final ten minutes playing themselves back into the game.

Said Sproull, *"Hey, we won!"*

Overheard by her coach, Dottie Johnson said with a serious face, *"No, we survived!"*

As I left the field heading for my car, I spied the Granby AD, Ken King, who gave a cautious smile. The kind of cautious smile that says, "Phew, that was a close one." His words are dead center on target, *"A lesser team loses that game."* I nodded in agreement.

I had also noticed some goings-on with the Granby team. Those funny, quirky things that happen to teams making them who they are. During the game I heard those on-field jabs at each other. Internal trash talking. *"You're out of position."* *"Move your fat ass faster."* *"Gimmie the ball. Pass the ball."* And the occasional, *"Shut-up!"*

I jotted them down in my notebook and put a plus-mark next to the notes. I had played enough sports to know that these were those signatures that make a team into who they are, as opposed to the negative connotations of who they are not.

I made one more note on that page. *Makes no diff - Granby can play!"*

Avon won its opener running their winning streak to 11 games only to be upset 1-0 by Lewis Mills in Burlington. Candy Thierry scored the game's only goal in the first half. Goalie Debbie Nettleton made it stand up behind fullback Melanie Gibson and an inspired Spartans' defense.

Says coach Linda Hamm, *"Candy Thierry is one of the best players in the state nobody knows about."*

Avon had its chances. They got off a dozen shots at the Mills' goalie and out cornered the winners, 9-7. *"We couldn't get that one breakout play we needed,"* said Avon Coach Bonnie Tyler. *"They outplayed us and won the game."*

Mills had pulled off a nice upset of Avon and now had a date at Canton. They were accompanied by a large group of fans. Mostly moms and friends. They sat about 100 feet away from the large group of Canton fans.

Canton had its own contingency of moms who came to games. There was Duffy Grace, Jonie Bahre, Liz McKenzie and others. The *"Moms Mafia."* They'd sit along the sideline in their folding chairs. They knew more field hockey than most of the coaches. They'd smoke cigarettes and keep up a running chatter with anyone who dared to come near or engage them. That included opposing players, coaches, and town officials. It was best if you just didn't mess with them. They were a tough bunch of broads who didn't take crap from anyone.

The dads usually showed up during the second half, always complaining about officials. They couldn't understand why officials blew whistles and announced a violation with hand signals. But never vocalized what the violation was. I had to laugh. They just didn't take time, or care to learn what those hand signals meant. Hell, there were hand signals in football, baseball, and basketball. I saw no difference in the applications.

From a Canton fan came a vocal comparison that both teams were likened to, *"A bunch of stinking gerbils learning their way through the mazes."*

It turned out to be one of those classic games between valley teams. A game where each team pushed its opponent around in a battle of attrition. A day when Canton's young Warriors would make history.

Linda Bahre and Candy Thierry traded first half goals. A second half defensive struggle ensued. Debi Davidson earns respect from all with plays deep in the Canton end of the field along with her halfback mate, Mary Raftery. Mel Gibson is a force on defense for Mills, often taking on double-teams to break up a play. Late in the second half, sophomore Carol Stefanik scores off a penalty corner after being set up by Lynne Bouchard. The Warriors defense makes it stand up. Canton wins, 2-1 for its first-ever varsity victory.

As the Mills contingency moves towards their bus, that familiar voice from the Canton crowd yells out, *"Gerbils, well now we're freakin rats! Deal with It."*

Farmington opened its season hosting Hall High of West Hartford. Jean Hunt has concerns. She knows little about the visiting Warriors. The game turns into a titanic defensive affair eventually won by the Indians. Senior captain, Abby Walsh, slams in a rebound off the post with less than a minute remaining. When asked if she will celebrate this win, Hunt laughs. *"Celebrate, no time. We've got E.O. Smith coming in this Saturday."*

Her words were never truer about Smith. After chasing the Panthers all over the field for most of the game, Indians junior Loretta DiPietro knocks in a shot for a 1-0 lead. The goal is waved off due to an offsides. The game ends in a scoreless tie. The Indians are now 1-0-1.

If plaudits are to be handed out, they should go to goalie Missy Saxton. Some of her saves defy explanation. For one save she comes 30 feet out from her net to take on a breakaway by Faith Witryol. She blocks the shot and makes a game-saving pass.

Early the following week, I was at Farmington High School covering a soccer game. I ran into Jean Hunt who was on her way home. I asked for an overview of her first two games. She started to speak, stopped and held up one finger. *"Rob, talk with me tomorrow. Right now, I need a drink!"*

You had to admire the emotion and her honesty.

13

The Farmington Valley was well-known for its field hockey teams. If you wanted to gauge how good valley schools were compared to the rest of the state, you had to go roaming. Watch a few games. Give it the real eye test. As I often did while traveling the state for my weekly assignments.

Cookie Bromage is one of the calvary that has come to the rescue. She builds the field hockey program at Enfield High School. Starts with a few broken sticks, lots of begging for new equipment and that blind energy needed to climb tall mountains. Carol Albert had done the same at Fermi. Now it's time to play each other for the town's bragging rights.

The game is a contrast to be sure. There are birds. Falcons and Eagles. Attitudes. Albert is effusive. Bromage is laidback. Styles of play. Fermi is a high-flying offense. Enfield is cautious. There is history, of sorts. Fermi is the new kid on the block. Enfield the established homestead. Fermi is the new world atomic scientist. Enfield the old-world town named after a location in Middlesex, England.

So, whose field hockey team will find that little extra to win the game? While Bromage runs her practices to prep for the game, a little-known story is taking shape at Fermi. One of those *"Under the Radar"* stories you never hear about. A story that never makes the front pages. In fact, field hockey stories rarely make it onto any pages in the local Enfield publications.

Eddie Mantenuto is the new ice hockey coach at Fermi. Mante, as he is called, is a Needham, Mass native. He played college football at American International College just over the border in Springfield, MA. He was hired as a teacher at Kosciuszko Junior High School. I had known Eddie during our years at AIC and recall many conversations we had at sporting events or sitting on the Campus Center steps in the Quad between classes.

The story begins with a casual conversation Mantenuto is having with Albert. She mentions the struggles of her team. Manti says he can help. Albert doesn't seem to mind. So, off to field hockey practice he goes with that blind enthusiasm that is so much a part of his life.

Mante shares the story with me in his enthusiastic manner with the usual effusive embellishments. After two hours of intense observation, he tells Albert he has figured it out. He believes the attacking line needs to create wider splits to spread the defenses, like in ice hockey. He is adamant in pointing out that the best player he sees, Donna Teske, needs to touch the ball every time Fermi goes on the attack.

Says Mante, *"When she touches the ball, good things happen!"*

He adds that set plays, like give-and-go passes, need to be made sooner with more crispness, so defenses can't clamp down on any one player. He draws up two plays in the dirt and calls them, Play One and Play Two! *"Why Not,"* says an amused Albert.

Mantenuto's approach...keep it simple. In retrospect, they're not really plays, but more situational approaches. Play One is for Teske leading the attack with the ball. Play Two is Teske leading the attack without the ball. Either way, both plays are going to work if Donna Teske touches the ball.

Game time has all the hoopla of a match between arch-rivals. During warm-ups a tape player is heard. Elvis Presley sings "Suspicious Minds" and Marvin Gaye croons "I Heard It Through The Grapevine." Family members and fans turning out for each team. The Fermi football team parades past the field hollering out cheers for the girls. And, to the surprise of many along the sidelines, including Albert, there is Eddie Mantenuto.

From the opening bully, Mante runs along the sideline behind Albert. When the pass needs to be made, he hollers out, *"ONE!"* Albert also hollers *"ONE."* The pass is made. The next possession the yell is, *"TWO."* Albert also yells out, *"TWO."* It's like an Abbott and Costello movie. The show goes on for the first half and then, Mante disappears. Knowing Eddie as I did, I'm sure he figured he'd done what he could for Coach Albert. His job was done! Time to go.

The Falcons outplay the Eagles. Teske scores both goals in a 2-0 Fermi win. It will be the start of a seven-game unbeaten streak that takes them into the first-ever state tournament. Teske, now feeling the freedom to roam the field with her wonderful skills, appears to be enjoying the game more. And despite wearing a dress on game days, she's listening less to the intense bantering of her coach.

Mantenuto will go on to have a successful coaching career leading Fermi's ice hockey team, never having a losing season. Later that fall, I ran into Ed at a football game. When asked about the field hockey support, he answers in that wonderful and jolly way I have come to know during our years at AIC. *"Hey, I just gave 'em the old one-two."*

In a footnote to the game, Enfield co-captains, Kate Mullen and Nancy Beauregard, bruised and beaten, tearfully promise their coach that Fermi will not win the return game scheduled for mid-October. They also promise they will qualify for the tournament. Cookie Bromage smiles. She knowns her girls mean it. She sees the emotion and the depth of that promise in their eyes.

They kept that promise to their coach. In the final week of the regular season, they would tie Fermi in the return match and beat Simsbury to qualify for the post-season tournament.

Cookie Bromage never had any doubts.

14

Lorraine Splain is what is often referred to as a player's coach.

She coached field hockey at Old Saybrook High School and was part of the school's athletic activities for almost 40 years. She became the iconic standard bearer to how one achieves success in the Shoreline Conference, perhaps the toughest league in the state. She is a field hockey hall-of-famer. I once asked her a simple question, why her teams were competitive, and always ready to play.

There are the usual standard answers offered. Not with Lorraine. Her answer hit the target dead center. It taught me a lesson about humility.

"In this league if you're not ready to play the game, you're just a week away from a three-game losing streak." She added, *"Wins don't always show up as results on a scoreboard. They*

come as a part of living and learning."

She had shared that observation with me on a cold November day in 1973. Her Old Saybrook team had just been eliminated from the first-ever tournament, losing in the Elite Eight round to eventual state champion, Granby.

When I mentioned they had just lost to one of the best teams in the state Lorraine smiled and said, *"That's how we get ready to play in our league. Guilford, Westbrook or East Lyme. Whoever we're playing that day is the best team in the state. Today, it happened to be Granby! Tomorrow, for these girls, it will be the rest of their lives!"*

I looked out over the now-empty Ether Walker field in West Simsbury. Her words reverberating in my thoughts. What sets a team apart from its peers? Why do some teams win those close, gut-wrenching games while others become the victims, coming up a little short on scoreboards?

In just about every game, results typically come down to any one of many reasons. A bad possession. One mis-directed pass. A simple mental error. Or a situational play where a player is out of position by a few feet. Nuances so subtle they go unseen by most watching the action. And most games such as these are typically won because of the efforts and dedication put in during those long, arduous days of practice. The repetitions and the coach's resonating voice yelling out, *"All right, let's do it one more time."*

Getting ready for the next game. Or getting ready for life after the games.

All those lessons learned that go unseen and don't appear on scoreboards. Those ethical mores solidifying who we are and where we're from. Lessons that we end up using every day amid friends and loved ones for the rest of our lives. Splain taught her players about discipline, roles, and responsibilities. Lessons they would use in field hockey. Oh yeah, they would use those learned lessons in the way they would live their lives, too. Her words were prophetic. Results are not always measured just by numbers on a scoreboard.

That was life's approach for Lorraine Splain. Her '73 team was young, yet already with varsity experience and off to a 5-1 start. Sophomore Ann Salz and junior Margie Clynes were strong on the scoring line with support from two fleet-footed wings, Deb Tareila and Mary Dohna, both juniors. The Rams' forte was strong mid-field play, and Splain had one of the best in the state in senior Leslie Collier and good goaltending in junior Lynn Caley.

Guilford was again bulldozing its way through their early season Shoreline Conference schedule with a 4-0-1 record, outscoring opponents 15-1. Mary Bunting, Dawn Sprague and Sharon Farquharson led a vaunted attack. Lindsay Taylor at center half and Amy Cunningham at fullback anchored a stingy defense. Leslie Gribus was a shutdown goalie. This was a team that looked to go deep into the playoffs. A 1-1 deadlock with upstart and conference foe Westbrook was the lone blemish on their schedule to date.

Westbrook's Knights, coached by Gail Perzanoski, were a young team sporting a 4-1-1 record, coming off wins over Daniel Hand and North Branford. They were led by a terrific goalie and co-captain, Rose Weisse. On offense, Lynn Clements, Rae Hirst and Tammy Hustud were good front liners and center half, Chris Rackcliffe controlled both the offense and defense with her mid-field play.

As coach Splain had pointed out. *"Everyone in the conference is your rival. If you play a team whose record is 2-4 and you take them lightly, you will lose. You must bring your A-Game every day. You play your opponent as if they are the best team in the state."* What Splain had referred to as, *"That looming and terrifying three game losing streak."*

As Lorainne Splain left the Ethel Walker Field that day after being eliminated by Granby from that first-ever tournament, she reminded me that one should never be ashamed of results, good or bad, if you have given your best effort. I asked about Granby. Splain said, *"Today, they were the better team."*

I asked, *"What about tomorrow?"*

Her answer to me, *"Ask me tomorrow!"* I already knew what her answer would be. Her girls would be using, for a long time, the lessons that were learned today.

Lorainne Splain really was a player's coach.

15

Arlene Salvati threw everything into building a successful program at Cheshire High School. Sweat, tears, time, and anything she could bargain for or manipulate, including the kitchen sink.

Pleas for equipment, uniforms, facilities via formal and verbal requests, notes and letters, some never opened by the town's Board of Education. It appeared that the BOE had a different agenda and field hockey, girls' sports in general, were not on a short or long-range list to be a part of that agenda.

Despite the lack of interest from the town's leaders and with limited resources the Lady Rams get off to a good start in the fall of '73 in the competitive Housatonic Valley League. Anne Cumpstone, Patty Williams and Sue Kantor are the able tri-captains of an experienced and senior-laden team. They open the season with a 3-1 win over a good Amity team. Shutout a good North Haven squad, 3-0 before staving off Branford for a 3-2 victory. This is followed by another shutout of Lyman Hall and a surprising easy, 5-1 beatdown of an experienced and skilled Sheehan team.

Cheshire is 5-0 and suddenly finds themselves in the tall cotton of field hockey programs being rated as one of the top ten teams in the state. They generate quite a following, and large crowds, including students, begin showing up for home games. Salvati and her girls set their sights on winning the tough Housatonic Valley League title.

Following their loss to Cheshire, Judy Samaha's Sheehan squad is floundering at 2-3 and riding a three-game losing skein. They need wins and have a daunting schedule ahead of them including key games at Amity, North Haven and a return home date with Cheshire.

Darien gets off to an unassuming 4-2 start. They explode for two late goals in the final three minutes in beating off a scrappy Roger Ludlowe team. A tight 1-0 win over Danbury is followed by a close victory over Andrew Warde. The big game comes against arch-rival, Staples, ending in a scoreless tie. Coach Becky Strominger's Blue Wave is thought to be a pre-season top five ranked team. To date her team has performed sluggishly in the first half of the season.

The Blue Wave has a strong and skilled team and their annual demanding schedule against the best of the downstate teams. They have an aggressive and experienced front line. The team is led by co-captains Jennifer Barrett and Deb Carella, and a fine player in deep back sweeper Leslie Milne.

Strominger sums up her team's performance to date saying, *"Good wins. Bad losses!"*

The CIAC is playing a waiting game before they will announce plans for a tournament. Most of the Darien girls are not aware they are now playing for a spot in post-season play. Strominger can't wait any longer. It is time for the tournament speech. Prior to their game against Andrew Warde, Strominger assembles her team and informs them about the planned tournament. *"We didn't know there was to be a tournament"* said co-captain Barrett.

The season now takes on a new sense of urgency. Darien still has a tough schedule to play and the tournament information infuses a tidal wave of enthusiasm. It energizes the Blue and White into a spirited run that will eventually take the girls to the tournament semi-finals. Remembers Barrett, *"The tournament sounded like a second season."*

New Canaan was coming off the 1972 mythical WFCIAC state championship with another well-stocked and experienced team from along "Preppy Corridor." Since 1968 this team has produced a record of 46-3-5. Perhaps the highest winning field hockey percentage to date in the history of state public schools.

They have experienced frontline players in Laurie Canada, Janet Zucco, Jane Stoddard and Betsy Blackwell. Sue Fulton, Jenny Smith and sophomore, Elaine Banko anchor the defense. Amy Buchalter is the team's all-conference goalie backed up by Kay Pennington. Sue Swerdetle's team will again find themselves ranked as one of the state's top ten teams.

New Canaan can score, but as the coach laments, *"We go into scoring funks."*

They waste little time before strutting their game, sprinting to a 5-0 record including wins over Stamford, Wilton and Roger Ludlowe, outscoring opponents 15-1. They fall into a mid-season swoon tying three straight games including deadlocks with rivals, Darien and Staples. Against Darien, a goal by Blackwell with 30 seconds remaining knots the game at 2-2. A third and surprising tie, 0-0, is against Trumbull. What Schwerdtle refers to as, *"Our horseshit game."*

Greenwich returned key players from a successful 1972 team and is also looked at as a top ten competitor. Coach Bea Walko's Cardinal has a strong front line led by Priscilla

McClung at center-forward and Ann Sneath at center-half. Sue Michaud and Nancy Duke are impact players and Joan Holman is a strong fullback. Beth Long will become one of the first in a long line of all-conference goalies.

Early wins over Staples, Andrew Warde, Brian McMahon and Roger Ludlowe send loud messages to future foes that Walko's Cardinal has another strong team and will be a real player and hard to beat during the regular season.

Surprisingly, it's not just the usual suspects grabbing all the headlines during early season games. In the Berkshire League Joan Bulmer's Nonnewaug Chiefs, led by co-captains Patty Wright and Cindy Bartlett, race out to a 3-0-2 record ahead of rivals Shepaug Valley, Litchfield and a senior-laden Coginchaug team. E.O.Smith begins 3-2-1 with a challenging schedule against Granby, Simsbury and Farmington. Newington, behind the leadership of Lisa Meucci, starts off with 4-0-1 record after thoroughly beating down Avon, 4-0, in a stunning upset.

In the Western Connecticut Conference, Weston has been the class of the league and 1973 is not a rebuild year, just a reload. At mid-season the June Olah-coached Trojans stand at 5-1-1. They lost to a good New Milford team and played to a surprising tie with Joel Barlow. Dale Thomas is playing with broken fingers and CB Tomasiewicz at center halfback makes the offense go for a team that will, at times, overwhelm and outscore its opponents during the regular season, 30-3.

Stamford wins its opener over Rippowam behind the scoring of Sue Mihalik and Penny Rickel and defensive play from Toni Rinaldi and Brenda Baxter. They set their sights on winning their first city championship and earning a tournament bid. But Pat Bradbury's Black Knights hit a roadblock with losses to New Canaan, Norwalk, and a heartbreaking loss to Greenwich in the final minute. At mid-season they stand at 3-3.

Cindy Wilson's Windsor Locks team takes a few games to

find its rhythm, then reels off wins over Enfield, Simsbury, Glastonbury and Bloomfield for a mark of 6-2 led by the scoring of co-captains Nancy Shapiro and Marie Duwell. It's Fermi's coach Carol Albert who alerts opponents to the abilities of the Raiders even after her Falcons beat them, 2-0. Cautions Albert, *"They're good and will surprise you. Nothing fancy. Don't go to sleep on them."*

In Meriden, Maloney's girls play an up-tempo and physical game as they explode onto the scene with wins over Southington, Conard and Platt. The Spartans are coached by Sandy Piantek and led by front liners Shelia Mihalek and speedy left winger Deb DiGiandomenico. Word spreads quickly among the teams on their schedules. When you play Maloney be prepared for a track meet and a physical game of bump and elbows. Remembers junior winger Joyce Allgaier, *"Our success is to play an up-tempo game and we liked to play physical."*

Says a player from Hall High, *"Physical, like hell. Those girls from Maloney play down, dirty and want to kick the shit out of you."*

If there are any questions about Maloney's style of play, they are answered in a game against crosstown rival, Platt. Maloney runs out to a 4-0 lead running the Panthers team into the ground. Not just beating the crap out of Platt but increasing the intensity as the game progresses. Loose officiating lets the massacre continue.

Late in the second half a Platt player just throws up her arms and walks off the field. She'd had enough. Others follow her to the bench. She had played the second half with a fractured wrist that had blown up to the size of a circus balloon. Two fingers on her other hand had been dislocated. The Platt coach then pulls her team off the field. Eventually, calm is restored. The games' final minutes are played out with no further incidents. Platt finishes the game with eight players on the field.

When I heard that story from a friend who had seen the game, my only thought was of the rules of war. Specifically, rule number three. There are no rules.

Perhaps carrying guilt, neither official signs her name in the home team's scorebook following that game.

16

Rumors. CIAC tournament rumors. They were spreading like a wildfire in the dry Montana grasslands.

Who was going to be a part of the first tournament! Who was going to get left behind? Suddenly, lots of middle-of-the-pack teams are beginning to feel a new type of pressure that came with a surprising itch. It now had a name. It is called, "Tournament-itis."

West Hartford's Hall High School has been in town since 1924. For a mid-week game, the Warriors made the five-mile trip to play the newer kid on the block, cross-town rival, Conard High School. They played lethargically with no emotion, looked confused and lost to the Chieftains, 2-1. They fell to an embarrassing 2-3 record.

Coach Sally Ann Warren figured it was time for that in-your-face pre-game pep talk using lots of adjectives. She read the riot act, loud and clear. Her girls still controlled their own destiny. It came down to a simple equation. There really was going to be a post-season tournament. If they wanted a shot at post-season play, they had to win-out the five remaining games on the schedule.

It was a demanding schedule including games against teams that were about to qualify for the tournament. Remembers Janis Gustafson, one of the co-captains, Coach made it clear. *"You're better than this. Get off your asses and start playing."*

The Warriors responded.

It began on a sun-drenched field in Burlington. Co-captain Gustafson led a spirited attack during the final eight minutes to tie Lewis Mills 1-1, scoring a goal in the game's last 20 seconds. Linda Kendall scored a goal in the final minute to beat Newington. Then, avenging a previous loss, Hall scored a major win, its biggest in years, dominating Avon 5-1, behind the defensive play of Sarah Minor and goalie Judy Wincze. Hall was now 4-3-1 with four games to play. Home to Avon, at Manchester and a home-and-home series against up-and-coming Canton.

As the final seconds ticked away at Avon, Hall's coach Warren stoically stood along the sidelines, hands on hips slowly shaking her head and wondering as she indirectly spoke to the wind. *"Where the hell was this intensity earlier this season."* The Warriors were now just a win away from producing their best ever varsity season.

In Woodbury, Nonnewaug continued to surprise everyone. Opponents, their fans. Even themselves. Their record was 5-0-1 and the Chiefs found themselves in first place in the competitive Berkshire League. Joan Bulmer's team had a good scoring line led by Carol Wright and Liz George and a strong defense anchored by Carol Cassidy.

It was turning into a typical season. One of expectations and surprises.

17

The wonderful fall weather continued into the second week of October. Surprisingly, all six of the Farmington Valley teams were still in the running for a tournament bid.

Avon makes two trips to West Hartford and comes away with a pair of 1-0 victories. Heidi Zacchera's first-half goal at Hall holds up behind the goaltending of Betsy Curtis. Holly Blacker scores a second half goal against Conard and Marsha Mains repels late rushes into Avon's scoring circle.

"The best hockey we've played in two years" said coach Bonnie Tyler. The two wins give the Falcons a little breathing room with a demanding schedule ahead during the ensuing weeks.

Farmington's Jean Hunt had concerns. Who would step up as another scorer to support Abby Walsh? Hunt's girls were coming off a surprising 2-1 loss to Newington. She found that extra scoring when her Indians steamrolled past what had been expected to be a competitive Watertown team, 6-0. Two sophomores, Mary Ellen Seravelli and Peggy Streich combined for four goals. The Indians added another blowout win over Bloomfield, 10-0. Emily Miser, Jean Scorrozzo and Jean Balazy were another trio of scorers, accounting for six goals.

On a chilly Saturday morning Farmington would play their third game that week, hosting its bitter arch-rival, Avon.

Avon vs Farmington. Now that's a real rivalry. Hell, anybody on the schedule against Farmington is a rivalry, but when you're the town next door, it's not going to be a friendly game. And it wasn't.

Farmington would prevail, 1-0. The game would end as controversially as any conspiracy we choose to embellish: UFOs at Roswell, New Mexico. Who shot JFK. Where's Jimmy Hoffa's body. How'd Farmington win this game!

A huge crowd was on hand atop the hill across from the Farmington River. The home team did not disappoint, taking a 1-0 halftime lead on a goal by Patty Lavoie. Loretta DiPietro made the play setting up the goal. Her hard shot from the top of the circle skipped along the ground, bouncing off the goalie's pad onto LaVoie's stick who flicked it, waist-high past the Avon goalie Betsy Curtis.

You couldn't help but hear the trash talk coming from both teams. The Falcons were usually a low-key group. But this was Farmington.

At halftime, both teams made adjustments. Hunt moved Peggy Streich from the scoring line to fullback providing more speed to cover a wider area in front of goalie, Missy Saxton. Tyler's adjustment moves halfback Caryn Bray, giving her a wider area to defend. It looks as if Avon is playing a 4-3-3 format. The move neutralized Farmington's attack and the game becomes a battle to control the center of the field. Whoever wins that battle will have a good run at their opponent's net. For most of the second half, Avon wins that battle.

The timekeeper hollers out, *"Five Minutes to Play!"* Avon's Karen Poirier slices between two defenders, picks the ball off Walsh' stick. Poirier shifts through gears and speeds off toward the Farmington goal as if she were on a mission. She stickhandles inside the 25-yard line, side-steps two defenders. Teammates Blacker and Zacchera trail the play, staying back about a half step to stay on-sides.

At the top of the scoring circle, Poirier and Farmington fullback Streich collide with such force they both carom off each other in different directions due to the impact. There is no whistle for obstruction. The ball seems to have a mind of its own and goes airborne before dropping into what I call, *"The Dead Zone."* That small parcel of land just inside the scoring circle, behind the deep fullback and to the left of the goalie.

Avon's Zacchera, staying on-sides, sprints across the open spaces in front of the goal and is on it before the defense can react. Before the ball rolls outside the scoring circle, she switches her stick to her left hand. With an athletic move that seems almost impossible, she swipes at the ball with a grunt while falling away from the goal and tumbling out-of-bounds. At such a peripheral angle, the ball just a few feet off the end line, her shot has maybe a 1% chance of finding its way into the net.

But it did find its way into the net.

There was a brief period of muffled silence. Goalie Missy Saxton turned back to the field. The look on her face was that of, *"What the hell just happened."* Once it registered with folks that the ball had gone into the net, the Avon crowd exploded into cheers and they began spilling out onto the field.

Zacchera never saw her shot go into the goal. Standing on the end line she has that faraway look on her face, wondering what happened. When she sees the ball in the back of the Farmington's goal, she flashes a wry smile and lets out a laugh, wiping away the dirt from her uniform. She had done the impossible and with four minutes to play the game was tied, 1-1.

Just the way a heated rivalry game should be.

That's when the euphoria in the Avon throng ended. When the controversy began. The conspiracy was born.

The lead official is a good one, Bonnie Maskery, whose husband Paul is the head football coach at Farmington. Initially, she had yelled to the scoring table to stop the clock until the fans were cleared off the field. No whistle had been blown. She again pointed to the scoring table and instructed each school's scorer to not make any inputs in their scorebooks. Yeah, you could sense it. That creeping feeling like something bad was going to happen.

And it did.

From my vantage point, I heard Maskery tell coaches Hunt and Tyler she had blown her whistle and called-out, *"No Goal. No Goal!"* Odd, nobody on the field or along the sidelines heard a whistle or remembers Maskery making any on-field call. Not the Farmington players or their goalie. Not the second game official. Not the Avon fans or players. I was standing near the goal. I heard no on-field whistle nor did I hear either official make any calls.

The official explanation is Zacchera was outside the scoring circle when she launched her impossible shot. What made this observation just a tad iffy in the eyes of many, Maskery was on the far side of the field, over 40 yards away from the play. She didn't confer with her officiating partner. And her view of the ball she said was outside the circle, was blocked by a crowd of players.

It was an impossible call to make...and took away an impossible shot that was made.

A little more salt was added to the wound when play resumed the game clock was set at one minute and forty-five seconds. Coach Tyler held up her arms and in a pleading voice said softly, *"Where the hell did the other two minutes go!"*

Her pleas went unanswered. The phantom call would stand.

If prone to do so, one could use any or all the clichés to describe this one. You've heard em all. Like taking a shower with your socks on. Or, going to the prom with your cousin. Or words that were a little more biting as was heard throughout both crowds as they migrated slowly towards the crowded parking lot exchanging vocal salvos.

This was a ghost call. One where a call is made, most likely in error, the official then defending her call. Even when she knows the call was a bad one, yet she's too embarrassed to admit the mistake, letting the bad call stand. Be you a player, coach, fan or even a sportswriter, this is one of those game endings that leaves you feeling slimy and pissed off.

An Avon policeman was holding court in the parking lot amid an agitated and vocal group of Avon fans. He had formulated his MO for what he believed was truly, a crime of emotional theft. I stopped to listen. When I heard some of the evidence, I had to admit his observations had merit. That is, if I was going to investigate the results as a real crime, which after the evidence was presented, began to sound like one. His voice rose, precipitously, as he pointed out each piece of evidence as a good member of any constabulary should.

He began, *"Let's See, the official, Bonnie Maskery is from Farmington. She's officiating a Farmington game against Avon. The game's being played at Farmington. Her husband is the head coach of the Farmington football team. She's just made a critical call, that shouldn't have been made, allowing Farmington to win the game."*

He paused, *"You know the line. If it sounds like, smells like, walks like and quacks like one, It's probably a fucking duck!"*

Oh yeah. Now, a new conspiracy had been born. The bitter rivalry lived on.

18

The Somers girls arrived in Granby for a conference game and were getting off the bus. Their mannerisms and talk were like listening to a funeral dirge.

Yes, on this beautiful sunny day, they were most likely going to get smoked by the Bears who were undefeated in 38 straight games. Said one of the Somers players, *"Let's go out and get a little sun and have some fun."*

I wrote down the salty responses to her words from teammates, hoping they would become part of my post-game story. That evening, I showed the quotes to my editor, Lou Ball, who laughed and politely said, *"Nope! Can't print those words."*

Granby did stroll past the Spartans on this day, 5-0. A third consecutive shutout for young goalie, Jo Sproull. For the Bears this was a game of goals by committee. Ellen Burbridge and

Val McCord scored early. Lynsie Wickman and Mary Byrnes added second half scores, and Dottie Johnson had many of her reserves and underclassman in the lineup for the second half. Two days later Granby ran into a hot goalie in Avon's Betsy Curtis, but hung on to win, 1-0 on an unassisted goal by Burbridge, running their unbeaten streak to 40 games.

The Bears were now into the last few games of the regular season and a high ranking in the tournament. Still, you could sense the concern in Coach Johnson as she looked over the schedule's final games. They would play their toughest conference rival, Suffield, and had a road date at Farmington. She eventually came to the season's final game. It was a home game. She tapped the page with her finger. She quietly spoke, *"Oh yeah. Simsbury!"*

Granby shutout Suffield, 3-0. Sharon Schneider and Val McCord doing the scoring. The Bears then went on the road for a demanding game at Farmington. Neither team liked each other. The Indians dominated the game as they outshot, out cornered and outplayed Granby in almost every aspect of the game. Said Granby's Lynsie Wickman, *"I don't like Farming-ton. Especially their halfbacks."*

Remembers Farmington halfback, Loretta DiPietro, *"We hated Granby. They had a center (McCord) who was nasty and a halfback (Wickman) who talked too much."*

Mary Ellen Seravelli and Val McCord traded first-half goals. Beth Hackett put Farmington ahead, 2-1 with a goal that caromed off Lynsie Wickman's stick. Granby's goalie, Jo Sproull, appeared to have the shot covered. The play ended with Sproull and Wickman glaring and jawing with each other in front of the Granby net. Their exchange did not appear to be pleasantries and had to be separated by teammates for the game to continue.

Wickman got a sense of revenge as she knocked in a goal off a Farmington stick with four minutes to play. The game ended in a 2-2 draw. She made sure Farmington players knew her name as she called it out and pointed at players following her goal. Her actions were the classic emotions of Lynsie Wickman. That wild and whirlwind driving passion she exhibited every game.

Canton was still clinging to life on the vine. The Warriors were coming off a tough 1-0 loss to Simsbury. The game was a gigantic defensive struggle and would have ended in a scoreless tie if not for an obstruction call. Three minutes remained when Debbie Davidson made the strong defensive play to stop a three-on-two break. But Simsbury's Kent Walton cut left, running into Davidson's lane. There was nothing the Canton halfback could do.

Simply, she had done her job well, but was in the right place at the wrong time. The whistle blew. She was called for one of those unfortunate violations of obstruction. The call could have gone either way. Walton smiled as she had used her experience to engineer the violation, putting Canton on the run.

The call allowed winger Amy Johnson to catch up to the play and during the ensuing free hit she ran a wheel route and swooped in taking a pass from Walton and rolled in a score from 15 feet out. Goalie Shelly Grace was screened on the play by a wall of her own players camped out in front of her. She never saw Johnson's shot coming. The shot was almost blocked by Lynne Bouchard who made an all-out diving attempt, getting her stick on the ball just as it crossed the goal line.

"I have a new respect for Canton," said a relieved Simsbury coach Joan Sullivan following the game. As she spoke you could see the stress of the game in her face.

The Warriors rebounded with a 4-1 win over Bloomfield, getting key scores from Carol Stefanik, Linda Bahre and a strong performances from Bouchard, Mary Ann Grinvalsky and Joan Lally. They still had a slim shot at the tournament but would need to win out the remainder of their schedule.

That challenge started the following week against rival Lewis Mills. The Spartans, too, were still alive for the tournament. They were coming off a tie with Hall High and would need to close out their season with wins.

On a beautiful autumn day atop the mountain in Burlington, Mills and Canton played one of the most fun games for any fan to watch or any player to be a competitor. Karen Sanders had a first half goal for Mills and that would stand up for the win. The defenses were the stars. Canton's Darcy Johnson had what appeared to be a clear shot at the goal, only to have Mills' fullback Melanie Gibson get the tip of her stick on the ball to flick it off course. Moments later Mary Jane Hinman put a hard shot on goal, kicked away by Mills' Nettleton.

At the other end of the field Mills' Candy Thierry, moving right, fired a laser across the goalmouth that was headed for the open corner of the net. Canton's Margie Crandell stepped in and took the shot in the right leg just above her shin guards, falling to the ground in pain. Thierry's shot would surely have been a goal had Crandall not taken one for the team. Mitch LaVigne had what looked like a goal only to be repelled by Grace in Canton's goal. The game came down to the play of goalies, Deb Nettleton for Mills and Shelly Grace for Canton, both making huge saves, time after time. Many at point-blank range.

The win kept Mills' slim post-season hopes alive. The loss ended post-season hopes for Canton. At game's end Lewis Mills coach Linda Hamm walked off the field and was heard to say with surprised enthusiasm, *"Now, that's entertainment!"*

On the way to my car, I ran into Canton's Athletic Director, Bill Mudano. It was obvious he did not want to run into me. I posed a quick question about the efforts of Canton's first varsity season. His answer was confusing and went something like, *"Well they worked hard. Need more discipline. They're not a tournament team."*

Ironically, I shared most of his opinions, but I wanted to know more why he felt they were not a tournament team. He mumbled a few thoughts about being a young team needing a higher level of coaching and really didn't deserve a spot in post-season play.

Whoa! Deserve...! What the hell did he mean by that?

I was a bit flummoxed and wanted to know more why Canton *"Didn't deserve to be in a tournament."* He shook his head saying he didn't want to answer that question. I asked, *"Why. Afraid I'll get it wrong."*

As he turned and walked towards his car, I heard him say, *"No Rob. Knowing you, I'm afraid you'll get it right."*

His words made me feel like I (*The Farmington Valley Herald*) had arrived in the valley.

19

As surprising as Simsbury's early season successes were, their offensive capabilities and frontline effectiveness had now dissipated with the suddenness of a winter's sunset in the Northwest Territories. Disappeared beyond the horizon with a thud.

They had started the season with a record of 4-0-1 but the Trojans were a team with lots of unanswered questions. Defensively, fullback and halfback lines, they were perhaps the best unit in the state. The concerns focused on all-around offensive capabilities and goaltending. The scoring line was slow to the ball. They were being outhustled and outplayed within the scoring circle. Dominated by opponents quicker and tougher between mid-field and the 25-yard lines.

Their record stood at 4-3-2 with three games to play including games vs Avon and Granby. To the casual fan all looked OK. To the folks with an eye for hockey, they were teetering on the edge of the great abyss, needing only a slight nudge to go into a free fall. Concerns were serious and Joan Sullivan knew it.

Their losing skein would soon present me with a most uncomfortable situation. A question of balance and of ethics. I would turn to the most effective decision-making tool in my life. Using my gut feeling to make decisions. I had no idea at the time of the impact my eventual decisions would have on me and others. Or the long-term ripple effects. Absolutely none. Zero, nada, nil, zippo.

But I would come to realize my gut opinions of that day would prove to have a profound impact on the lives of many people and their futures. Including mine. Simsbury was in trouble. They needed to make changes or there was a good chance they may not make it into the post-season tournament. That ate at the soul of Joan Sullivan, and she wore that pressure on her face every day. Even in her gym classes. She seemed stressed, short-tempered. Not a fun person to be around.

Just when Sully thought it couldn't get any worse, Enfield came to town needing a win for tournament consideration. Cookie Bromage and her Eagles dealt the Trojans a crushing blow, shutting out the home towners, 2-0. Sue Herter scored the clincher for the Eagles in the game's waning moments. Simsbury looked lethargic on offense. If not for the workhorse type effort of Simsbury's fullbacks, the score could have easily been 4-0. Or worse.

I had been at Sperry Park watching an Avon soccer game. I arrived at Simsbury as the game was ending. Wow! Talk about a funeral march as Sullivan's team trudged back to the locker room. Walking slowly, dragging their sticks behind them. The crowd cleared. Sully was standing alone near the middle of the field. I did not want to interact with her, so I turned and began trundling off to my car. I got about 30 feet when I heard Joan call out my name. I slowed but kept walking. Again, I heard my name called, only this time it was hollered out in a crisp and nasally, C-sharp tone. Like when your Mom is going to scold you.

My thoughts, "WHOOPS, didn't quite make a getaway."

I had this uncomfortable feeling. What was about to go down was not going to be fun. I gritted my teeth and turned towards Sully. Slowly she walked towards me. Both hands buried deep in the pockets of her jacket. Her shoulders pulled in tightly to her head. She was looking at me. I did not take my eyes off her as she approached. I didn't dare. I knew what was coming and I wanted no part of it.

Sully stopped, abruptly, about 10 feet from me. She exhaled, loudly. Closed her eyes and tilted her head back as if stretching her neck. She opened her eyes and glared at me. Her stare burning through me, she said in a mechanical way, *"I need to talk with you."* She hesitated and again spoke. *"Rob, we need to talk,"* her voice rising with each word spoken. One thing I did know for sure. I didn't have any outstanding issues with Joan Sullivan and certainly didn't need, or want to be here, at this moment.

But, I had known Joan Sullivan since I was nine years old watching games on the old slanted pitch at Memorial Field. A little kid who chased field hockey balls hit out-of-bounds. So, I decided to give her all the courtesy, concern, consideration and respect I could muster before my patience ran out. Before stupidity would become a virtue...or before I died. Whichever would come first during the ensuing moments.

So, there I was. Standing on a spot where, as a kid 15 years earlier, I had herded stray cows from the back pasture towards the main barn for afternoon milking at Holly Farms on Firetown Road. Now, I was a little lost in a time warp, herding my emotions. Tensions which in a short while would be exposed and standing naked in the wind. But nothing was going to get in my way. Something deep inside was driving me forward. I dug my heels in as I had done years before herding those strays back to the barn. I was once again 12 years old. Or maybe I was 27. It made no difference.

I nodded and said in a brash though subdued way, *"OK. You called this meeting. Start talking."*

20

You know, nothing good ever lasts.

Good health, good fortune. Winning streaks. Relationships. They begin and they end. They re-start and end again. They run their course and then they just slowly fade. Often with heartache and pain. Life changes. Always changing and evolving. You react and adapt to the changes in your life. Or you let it eat away inside...as it slowly destroys you. You decide what you want to do. It's your choice, sometimes.

My relationship with Joan Sullivan was about to change, and I wasn't sure if I was going to have any choice in the transformation. Will our relationship end? Or will it survive?

Following a rather long silence the words seemed to explode from her mouth, her body quickly swaying back-and-forth. Her arms flailing in the air performing in an animated fashion. Her words came out in a low scream, ***"What's wrong*** *with us? What happened to this team! Is it me!"*

Her nasally voice rose another octave. I dared not say a word. She droned on with a litany of thoughts. I knew she was loathed to be telling me her thoughts. Asking me...for suggestions and recommendations about field hockey. Asking me...about her sport. Her life. She was the coach. The woman. I was just a man. Asking me...a lowly sportswriter. What the hell did I know? Now, she wanted me to answer her questions, solve her problems. This was extremely dangerous territory to tread.

In the world of sports there is a line drawn in the sand separating our reasons to co-exist. Opposing souls are not allowed to cross over into the other's zone. Lou Ball had taught me about that line. He was adamant I understand the only time you cross the line is at the Alamo when Colonel Travis draws that line in the sand with his sword and you choose to cross it. To stay and fight. Sully and I were not at war...not yet. But between us, there was now a line drawn in the sand.

Joan wanted to know what had happened to her team. Where the offense had gone. Why her team could not score goals. She (her team) was now losing to teams Sully believed they should be beating. Whose fault is it? What needs to be fixed? What changes need to be made? The list droned on.

My silence continued. Then, with her hands on her hips in a defiant stance, she fired that one final, nasty, heat-seeking missile in a slightly obnoxious tone. Sully's tone reminded me of a pitcher sending me a message with a fastball being thrown at my head intending to cut me to the quick.

"C'mon Rob. You're supposed to be that smart ass guy who knows all about us. Girls' games. Tell me, smart ass guy. What do we need to do!"

Well now, Joan Sullivan had just stepped over Travis' line drawn in the sand at the Alamo. Now she was daring me, too, to step over that line. I was surprised. This was unlike her. I figured she must have really felt out of control. She didn't need to be coddled. She needed to hear the truth and justice. At that moment, that's what I planned to deliver.

Now, a benchmark of any successful society is the quality of the justice dispensed. More swiftly dispensed the better. Sully had fired the first shot. Then, launched that nasty heat-seeking missile. Despite everything Lou had taught me about not crossing that line...it was time for me to do so. Choose to stay at the Alamo and fight. Time to walk into her zone. Walk the tightrope leading her into that valley of change. Step over that line so my justice is not delayed. If I did not do this right here and right now, about the only thing that I may ever accomplish is proving to Joan Sullivan my stubborn stupidity has no backbone and is a misunderstood virtue.

Throughout my life, I would often refer to these times and circumstances as, *"Sliding down the razor blades of life."*

I stepped over the line.

I closed the gap between us, standing face-to-face with Sully. Close enough that my breath told her I had eaten a cheeseburger with mushrooms for lunch and washed it down with a Pabst Blue Ribbon. At that moment I wished I were someplace else in another time. Perhaps at the Alamo. Chasing stray cows back to the barn. Or perhaps sitting at the bar having another Pabst Blue Ribbon.

I did not, nor would I ever presume that I was smarter than her about field hockey. I did presume it was time that I defended my reasons for crossing that line in the sand and dispensing my justice. The quicker the better. Hey, she had challenged me. She had crossed that line. Dared me to do the same. I now know she didn't expect me to and was quite surprised when I did.

It was one of those moments in my life when I felt comfortable at being slightly uncomfortable. A rubicon of sorts that I did not fear. Just jumped in with a little nervousness. Like my old Aunt Fay had taught me years ago, *"You'll never know what it tastes like...until you're willing to take a bite."*

This was a big deal. Remember, there were lots of emotions at the Alamo. Those folks who crossed that line in the sand, choosing to stay and fight...in case you've forgotten, they didn't make it out alive.

So, I spoke in a matter-of-fact manner and did not mince words. I extended the index finger on my right hand and waved it just inches in front of her face. *"Joan, this one's on you. You threw the first stone. You started this and you put me in a position where I have to finish It."*

I took in a deep breath and continued. *"Dammit, you know what to do Sully. You've always known what to do. You don't need my recommendations. If you want them, sure, I'll give them to you. Whether you want them or not!"*

To my complete surprise she said, *"I do want them, Rob,"* in a voice so soft I could barely hear them on her lips.

I dispensed my justice in a sharp, pejorative tone. I said her scoring line was too slow. Opponents were beating her players to the ball. Beating them off the ball. Her wingers were quick but were being outmuscled. Not quick enough around the net. Too slow in mounting their attacks.

I caught my breath and said, *"But, you already know that. Don't you?"* My eyes burned into her face.

My voice heightened. I said her offense was predictable. Ineffective, easy to defend. Too slow getting back to play defense. I pumped my finger in her direction like a piston telling her she needed quicker people. More elusive attackers who had no fear of mixing it up with opponents. I made sure she understood that mixing it up meant tossing a few elbows and not being afraid to piss-off a few opponents. Play quicker and meaner. Send a message and show no fear.

Her halfback line was good but needed more speed. Opponents had exposed this weak link, game-after-game. I was sure Sully had seen the same thing but had not taken any action to correct it. I made sure she heard every one of my opinions as I used some salty and obnoxious adjectives.

I stopped. Took in another deep breath before pointing out one more of my concerns. One I felt was so obvious I felt embarrassed even to bring it up. She needed to upgrade her goaltending. Someone who would not be afraid to play between the pipes. Aggressive enough to rap a few girls in the ass with her stick if they got too close to her.

She already had that person...sitting on the bench. I said loudly, *"But you know that. Don't you. So, it's time to deal with it!"*

There was silence. We stared at each other. Neither of us spoke.

I softened my tone and told her that I had recently watched the JV team play. They had a gang of players I thought could play on any varsity team I had seen. Two girls on the attack line. Smallish in size but much quicker and more aggressive than some players currently on the varsity's scoring line.

Playing on the halfback line was one of the best young athletes I had seen in the valley. I asked why a talent like hers was still laboring away on the JV's. And goaltending. Hell, she had a good one already sitting on the varsity bench. Capable, athletic and aggressive. Put her between the pipes... her energy, alone, would be an upgrade over what she had now.

I wagged my finger at Sully saying, *"Dammit. You know what to do. Just do it!"* When finished, I touched her on the elbow. I mouthed the words, *"I'm Sorry."* Turned and quickly walked away.

Wow. At that moment I really wished that I was again 12 years old and herding stray cows back to the barn. When I looked through the trees, I saw that old barn. Now the main building for Hopmeadow Country Club. Yeah, nothing good ever lasts. Change! Always evolving. Adapt to it or be consumed by its creeping challenges of critical mass. Be an agent of positive change. Or be its victim. Your choice.

But oh god, had I ever crossed that line. I had delivered the full megillah. Nothing sweet about the content or its delivery.

I had made sure the message hit the target, dead center. My fear was that it may have hit a bit too dead center.

During the drive back to my apartment, I listened to WACE, 730 on my AM dial. During the early 1970's it was a small oldies station in Chicopee, MA with a daylight-only license. James Taylor sang, "You've Got A Friend." My response was something like, *"Not anymore, Jimmy baby!"*

That evening, my conversation...argument with Sully, ate at me. I didn't sleep well. I was embarrassed with my words and actions. Sully didn't deserve some of my retribution. Then again, perhaps she did because she pulled me across that line in the sand. I wasn't going to cross that line until she fired that nasty heat-seeking missile. And now there was a response factor. What I referred to as waiting for the molasses to move.

If I had not crossed that line in the sand, I would never again be able to face her within the ethical requirements of my work, let alone our personal relationship. I kept telling myself to use that logic as the justifications for my actions. I wondered if Sully was at home, sipping a glass of wine, thinking about our conversation.

The following day I returned to Simsbury to pick up some info from the new basketball coach, Ray Schwarz. As I walked along the back of the school near the athletic fields, I spied hockey practice. Something caught my eye. Something was different.

Playing on the varsity's frontline were two diminutive players. Sophomores up from the JV's. Denise Lamb, or "Lamie," as she would be called and Eileen O'Conner, known as "Pinky." Playing on the halfback line was another sophomore, Kim Longo, who I felt was a terrific athlete and budding star. In goal was athletic and aggressive sophomore Elaine Marcil. Sully had listened to my words. She had pulled the trigger.

I marked the date in my notepad. October 17, 1973.

I had one of those gut feelings. Field hockey at Simsbury

High School was, like so many relationships, about to change, dramatically. I didn't know it at that moment, but that base cadre of sophomores would breathe new life into the '73 team. Providing that needed kick in the ass.

Subsequently, that group of sophomores would become the base force carrying Simsbury to two straight state championships in 1974 and 1975. Today, I laugh at that fact.

Perhaps, I should have created a healthy Las Vegas betting line. Put a few bucks down on the Trojans. Boy, wouldn't that have been the real kick in the ass.

On my way home, I stopped at the Maple Tree. I sat at the bar thinking, *"Oh my god. What have I done!"* Questioning my own gut reactions. Only time would tell. I gulped down my cold Pabst Blue Ribbon.

My relationship with Sully had changed. In some ways, we were now more distant. In others, much closer. I discovered a different person other than the Joan Sullivan I had known. One whose world of success came with a monster. I recall asking her if she feared anything. *"Nothing,"* she snapped at me. Then following a silence with tears in her eyes, solemnly admitted she was deathly afraid of failure. Once in a conversation she broke down and started crying just talking about the possibility of failure.

She had a new respect for me. For my life and for my work at the *Herald*. My strong opinions and forthright thoughts. My not being afraid to fail. She admired me for my time in Vietnam and my injuries. I was no longer that little toe-headed 10-year-old kid she once knew who chased hockey balls hit out-of-bounds at Memorial Field. No, I wasn't a close, trusted friend. But I wasn't an enemy, either.

Joan once shared with me a wish and desire. A lifetime belief. That one day her white stallion would arrive. Honestly, I wasn't sure what she meant. Some believed her white stallion meant scoring a special goal. To others, finding love. I knew it had to do with the fire that burned inside her. Her friendships. Her relationships. The desire to win. Her fear of failure. And what drove her to be a successful leader in whatever she chose to do in life.

Developing young girls into women. A ragged bunch into a winning team. That extra time and effort she'd put into her teachings. Often going undetected by those who would end up benefitting from her lessons. The stories about Joan Sullivan people didn't know about. Those who were the recipients of that warm and soft side of her quiet caring. That new pair of hockey spikes that showed up in a player's locker. Or a paid trip to summer hockey camp for those whose families couldn't afford it. It would not have happened if not for her benevolence. That was the caring side of Sully many folks didn't get to see.

Because with the late Joan Sullivan, that was part of the deal. Her passion was her legacy! She wanted to win...right to the end. And her thoughts of the everlasting day, when she would stand at the gateway to Valhalla, her life judged fairly, ready to be received by her warrior peers, perhaps even coming to peace with her white stallions. Because Joan Sullivan would be ready for her next challenge. Without any fear of failure or obstructions!

Yeah, like I said. Nothing good ever lasts.

21

As I said, sleep just never came easy. Not after Vietnam.

The darkness of the early morning hours of November 17, 1973, had been another restless night for me. More bouts of back and neck pains along with terrible nightmares.

Horrible recollections from Vietnam. Over and over. Screaming into my head. And I couldn't stop them. Still can't, today.

A long, hot shower brought a sense of being and focus back into my life and readied me for the day ahead. Soon I'd be on my way to New Haven for the first CIAC girls' field hockey championship game. Granby's girls would take their high-level skills and a 49-game unbeaten streak against the number one ranked team in the state, unbeaten Guilford High School from the powerful Shoreline Conference.

Held together by masking tape my Motorola clock radio

played "Top of the World" by the Carpenters. Ringo followed with "Photograph." Jack Scott did, "My True Love." As I shaved, out-of-focus pictures and memories of war traipsed through my mind. Tiny hamlets ablaze. Thick black smoke. Like a Cape Cod fog. Lots of dead bodies. Women and children. Kathy Young and the Innocents melded voices in their 1960 hit "A Thousand Stars." I finished shaving. My reflection in the mirror looked so sad.

A quick weather insertion from the DJ shook my cobwebs telling me the day was predicted to be cool, so I dressed in a heavy pair of jeans, a turtleneck and a weathered blue woolen boatneck sweater that looked like it had been woven on the old looms during the Industrial Revolution. I wore thin sanitary socks under heavier wool socks and an old pair of double-thick, canvas-lined Keds.

For outerwear, I donned my soiled and battered olive drab green army field jacket with warming inserts. It still had my name tag and the long-established 9th Infantry Division patch, *"The Octofoil"* stitched on my right shoulder. A large *"Squared A"* patch for the First Army was sewn on the left shoulder sleeve. I would also bring along a scarf, a pair of lined gloves and a wool cap for the chill of the early day.

The music resumed. Shelby Flint sang her haunting ballad, "Angel on My Shoulder." The Bobby Fuller Four followed with "I Fought the Law."

Scott McKenzie lazily cooed "San Francisco," his voice cracking slightly from the torn paper speaker inside the old clock radio. The song, reminding me what to wear in my hair if I choose to go and be a part of what had been 1967's Summer of Love in San Francisco. I snorted a laugh thinking out loud, *"Scottie, I'll betcha you don't want me to wear my 9th Infantry Division patch."*

I carried my equipment in an old olive drab colored army shoulder bag. Three cameras. Zoom lenses. Lots of film, a note pad, a light rain poncho and at least a half-dozen Paper Mate pens. I always carried snacks. A sandwich. Bag of cookies. A Snickers Bar, before they became a bigtime snack. Or a Chunky bar whose TV pitchman, Arnold Stang would advertise, "*Chunky-What a Chunk o' Chocolate.*" Also, a couple of Cokes, ginger ale or maybe a few cans of beer.

I wore a can opener on a leather strap around my neck. A small, hinged tool known by every Vietnam vet as a P-38. Unlike the weapon of American troops, the M-16 rifle, that often jammed during combat, the P-38, a can opener, was the only piece of individual equipment the military ever made for the troops in Vietnam that actually worked every time you needed it. I still have my P-38 today, hung on a chain with my dog tags.

I had gassed up the night before and was ready to go. I drove a 1967 Chevy Camaro. Candy Apple Red, chromed mag wheels with slightly larger, wide tread, F-70 Cooper Tires. No power steering. Nice looking car and fun to drive. It had a great radio with extra speakers I had installed. I enjoyed listening to music during the many hours I spent in my car.

As I left my apartment the clock radio read 3:34 AM. It was early, but I felt something tugging at my soul. Calling out to me. I traveled cross-country through Granby and East Granby, onto Route 20 near Bradley Airport and picked up Interstate 91 South in Windsor Locks. The trip would be about 60 miles and would take about an hour and twenty minutes.

Traffic was light, mostly semis, as I cruised onto I-91 south towards Hartford in the early morning darkness. I tuned into Springfield's WHYN, 560 on my AM dial. They were playing an extended cut of oldies. Buddy Knox sang, "Party Doll." Bobby Darin did, "Dream Lover." Dobie Gray warbled through his blues classic, "Drift Away." I had fallen asleep to that song on those nights when memories of life and war camped out in my head abusing my thoughts. Randy and the Rainbows bounced through their airy 1963 version of "Denise."

Tommy Edwards sang his slow, infamous bump-n-grind

ballad, "It's All in the Game." The original melody to Edwards' song had been written by an amateur pianist as a lark while he was on a vacation. It was an instrumental of soft melodic tones, written in two keys for strings and titled, "Melody in A Major."

On this day, November 17, 1911, the songwriter is issued a copyright for his little-known composition. The music afficionado is Charles Dawes. He will become a future Nobel Peace Prize recipient for authoring the "Dawes Plan" for reparations to European countries following WWI. In 1925 he will become the 30th Vice President of the United States to Calvin Coolidge. During his VP years, "Melody in A Major" will be played at many of his official functions.

In November 1951, songwriter and lyricist, Carl Sigman, will put words to the melody, change the upbeats and meter to the music, and it will become a pop-charts hit for an up-and-coming young performer from Tennessee, Dinah Shore.

And, again, on this very day, November 17, 1958, the song, "It's All in the Game," words and music, will become the number one hit in the United Kingdom for Tommy Edwards, and will remain on the Top 100 charts for months. The song will end its charts run on April 23, 1959. Eight years to the day of Charles Dawes' passing in 1951.

As Springfield's WHYN slowly faded, I heard a newer oldie, "If You Could Read My Mind," by Canadian Gordon Lightfoot, ironically, born 35 years ago today, November 17, 1938. Del Shannon finished off the set accompanied by the big Hammond Organ screeching out the hard-driving beat to his song, "Little Town Flirt."

I continue hurtling south in the early morning darkness. Wondering what fortunes and unknown experiences, now tugging on my soul, are waiting for me in New Haven, beckoning for me. My body shaking and tingling to the anticipation of the unknown.

New Haven. The Elm City. Nicknamed for a public tree

planting program. Sponsored by the city council and supported by the Edward Malley family. Begun 102 years ago on this very day, November 17, 1871.

"Come Softly to Me" a 1959 classic by the Fleetwoods, is playing on the radio.

22

So, how did I get myself involved with field hockey? As I recall, it was easy and very painful. I had to break some bones. Unfortunately, they were my bones and more than 50 years later many remain broken and painful to use.

It was spring 1967. I was in the army, my duty station was Fort Sill, Oklahoma. Company clerk for B Company, 225th Heavy Equipment Maintenance. On a whim and a dare, I decided to attend an open tryout for one of the post's four baseball teams. Baseball had been a part of my life from the earliest days playing on sandlots, Little League teams, high school and college teams and the occasional forays into picking up a few bucks playing for a semi-pro or a company team. I wasn't really much of a ballplayer. I was borderline OK. I was a good, dependable teammate.

To my surprise, I was notified by the officer in charge, a

Colonel Williams, that I had made the C-Team as a utility infielder. I was surprised. Thought about the best I might get was being an alternate on the D-Team. The C-Team were high school and college players from around the country. These guys had game and were considerably above my level of play. But the Colonel said he liked my attitude, and the choice was his.

He introduced me to the coach. A leather-faced Sergeant First Class. An E-7-NCO level, or what we called a five-striper. His name was Turner. He was a grizzled lifer from Mississippi with 25 years of service. A WWII, Korean and Vietnam war vet.

He spoke with a mush mouth. A wad of chewing tobacco packed into his left jaw about the size of a small animal. I barely understood what he was saying. Except when he talked about the Ku Klux Klan. Of which he was a proud member in good standing back home in the infamous Neshoba County. I would learn to follow his hand gestures. And, from our very first meeting, he never remembered my name. Not once. I was many names. Pinehead, Rebar, Robot, Pinfall, Roper, Paulfield, Petsky, Pearlman, Feldman or J for Jew, which I was not and made no sense. And of course, my personal favorite, *"That goddammed Yankee from up North."*

I do not believe Turner was able to clearly spell or pronounce the words, Connecticut and Massachusetts. But when it came to calling me a Yankee, he was really good at that one. The word seemed to have four or five "e's" on the end of it when he spoke it.

In early July we traveled to Oklahoma City. A doubleheader against Tinker Air Force Base. We would be playing at All Sports Stadium, located on the Oklahoma City Fairgrounds. At game time the on-field temperature was 118 degrees. In front of a surprisingly large crowd the home team won the opener, 1-0 in a snappy 1:43, a quick game by any standards. It's what happened in Game One that would hasten my exit from baseball, a game that I knew...into field hockey, a game that I did not know.

Tinker's pitcher was a former major and minor league hurler. These were the days where folks were still affected by the Selective Service Draft. To avoid combat duty, most pros and college stars joined army reserve and national guard units. They did their six-month commitment and summer reserve duty, usually playing sports, lessening their chances of being sent to Vietnam.

He could throw over 90 mph. He stood about six-foot tall and weighed a slight 160 pounds soaking wet. He had a slingshot arm. A fastball that was fast. A curve that really curved. A knuckler that slowly knuckled and a screwball that screwed. It was easy to see what made the difference between a good pitcher I had faced in high school and one with major league qualities. In my first two at-bats I struck out each time on three fastballs. I heard 'em go by. Never saw 'em. Their catcher and the home plate umpire just laughed at me.

After eight innings, had struck out 16. He had a perfect game going...24 batters up and 24 batters down. Nobody had reached base. And, he had been tossing down a few beers on the bench between innings. By the eighth inning, he was certifiably drunk.

In the home half of the eighth inning, Tinker's first baseman, Bobo "The Bomber" Robinson hit a homerun over the 365 mark on the right centerfield fence. The ball just exploded off his bat and disappeared beyond the bleachers. I watched the ball fly out of the ballpark and believe it probably landed in another area code. The newspapers would report the ball traveled 487 feet.

Robinson is a large black man from central Louisiana, standing about 6' 7" and went well over 300 pounds. You kind of wondered what he was doing in the Air Force. Or if he was in the Air Force at all. We joked he was a disguised B-17 Bomber.

That large black man will later come to my rescue.

In the top of the ninth our first two hitters struck out on six pitches. Sergeant Turner looked at me, made a hand gesture and said, *"Go get em you goddammed Yankee!"* My own teammates were humming this death dirge as I dragged my bat into the batter's box. Both the umpire and their catcher were roaring with laughter. It was funny.

Now, I'm figuring, let's just get this over. I tell the catcher throw three over my head because I'm going to swing at them. The catcher says, *"Kid, three right down broadway,"* meaning I was going to get three fastballs in the center of the plate. The pitcher's ego would allow nothing less. Now that's real baseball.

It was so hot that the pitcher, just 60 feet away, looked out of focus. So, I started swinging when he went into his windup. I never saw the release point or the pitch. But I hit the ball on the sweet spot sending a line drive right past the pitcher's ear into centerfield for a clean single, breaking up his perfect game.

Standing atop first base the pitcher yelled every foul word in the book for ruining his perfect game. My own teammates yelled at me. *"Bad thing to do Yankee."* And stuff like, *"Hey, thanks for making this game longer."*

Coach Turner was the most unhappy of the bunch. *"It's 200 fucking degrees out here and you want to make this game longer."* He finished by spitting a huge wad of slimy chaw onto my glove. About the size of someone's lunch that had been puked up.

The pitcher threw over to first, three times, aiming at my head. Hell, I wasn't even leading off the bag. The big first baseman, Robinson, put a stop to this nonsense. He walked over to his pitcher. Picked him up by the front of his uniform, had a few words with him and dropped him on the ground. The pitcher struck out our next hitter on three fastballs. Game over.

As I walked off the field a ball went whizzing past my head, just nicking the bill of my cap. It was the pitcher, screaming and yelling at me and coming at me with a bat. First baseman Robinson stepped in. Hit him with one punch to the jaw. Down and out cold. They carried him off the field. I looked at Robinson and nodded. He pointed at me and said, *"Hey peanut. Watch your back in the next game."*

The seeds had been planted and irreversible actions had been set into motion.

23

My exit from baseball and entrance into field hockey was less than an hour away. And, like so many occurrences in my life, I didn't even know it was happening. That is until I got knocked out and came to...and found myself in a new world.

Game two was tied 1-1 in the fourth inning. The on-field temperature was 126 degrees. With one out and a runner on first, the batter hit a hard groundball to short. I cut towards second to cover the bag for the frontend of the double play. I caught the flip barehanded and pivoted across the bag for my throw to first. That's when first base and lots of landscape behind it just disappeared as a very large person about the size of a small locomotive was barreling in on me screaming, *"You little shit. You're dead!"*

That's the last thing I remember.

I regained consciousness in the dugout. When I came to, I

was groggy. Sick to my stomach. Sounds and visions were fuzzy. My head was on fire and lots of my body parts hurt like hell. I had been knocked out, driven about 15 feet into leftfield. The team doctor from Tinker AFB was examining me and talking with Colonel Williams. The Doc had a cigar in the corner of his mouth and was drinking from a long neck bottle of Lone Star Beer.

Diagnosis of my injuries were blunt and delivered as the doc gulped down his beer. I had a cracked knee bone. Broken elbow. Maybe a dislocated shoulder. My left cheekbone was the size of a golf ball. I had been spiked. Multiple broken bones in my left foot. Kicked in the crotch. My left wrist was broken. Two fingers on my left hand were pointed in the wrong direction. I, most likely, had a concussion. A long and painful bus ride back to Lawton, loomed.

The doc gave me a shot of morphine and the alarms and bells going off in my head stopped. The colonel joked that it could have been worse. I could be on my way to Vietnam. I looked away and let the morphine take over my body.

I rode back to Fort Sill with the Colonel in his air-conditioned Buick Riviera. I drank beer and washed down a pain pill the Colonel gave me that was about the size of a nickel. I was soon in la-la land. He took me straight to the hospital. Hush-Hush conversations took place with a few doctors. I was admitted, tended to, and cared for until Thursday evening when I was released. There were no charts on my bed. No documentation was ever carried by doctors or nurses. I was instructed not to sign any paperwork.

It took a few weeks to learn my hospital stay was not on any records or in my Personnel 201 File. I felt a little like the company clerk that never was. I was aware of a non-written protocol that if you played sports, your daily workload was less. In some cases, waived until your season was completed. When released, Colonel Williams picked me up at the front door and took me out to dinner at a Chiricahua-Apache restaurant on the Fort Sill Reservation. He told me no records of my hospital stay were filed and I was not to talk about it. Even with the NCOs at my permanent duty station, Company B at the 225th HEM. Those folks would receive no documentation.

Over dinner, Colonel Williams asked if I wanted to continue playing sports. I was surprised since I had been banged up pretty good and the idea of playing baseball at any level was out of the question. He cut into his medium rare T-bone, chewed slowly savoring the tasteful piece of reservation-raised beef. He washed it down with a healthy gulp of a dark red Zinfandel.

He looked at me, smiled and said, *"Would you like to play field hockey?"* I was dumbstruck.

The Colonel explained that the post did, in fact, have a field hockey team. Unknown to most, it was stocked with some active-duty personnel. A few civilian vendors and a couple of civilian employees. The team was made up of 16 women and four men. That was the stipulation. Since the government was sponsoring and paying for the team, the roster had to be 20% military male. He said they were rather good and if I chose to play, I would not have to work a full day in the orderly room. Initially, I thought he was kidding. Thought about it a little longer and said yes. I had nothing to lose.

We finished dinner and he took me out to where the team was practicing for their next game. Ironically, the next game was against the field hockey team from that same Tinker Air Force Base from Oklahoma City. We walked out onto the field towards an introduction with the coach. My only thought was, *"How in the hell did I end up here! Field Hockey!"*

"Call me Bitchie," said the coach as she put out her hand to greet me.

She looked as if she could have played football on Fort Sill's traveling A-Team. The activities of practice were going on around us. I asked where the other men were. The coach laughed and shot a glance at Colonel Williams. She said their names were on the official roster, but, they never showed up. Colonel Williams assured Bitchie I would show up. A little condescending in tone she replied, *"Good for you, Rob!"*

Again, I couldn't help but think, "What the hell am I doing here?" But, unlike the baseball coach, Sergeant Turner, Bitchie remembered my name.

As the weeks passed, I did some digging for information about Colonel Williams and the field hockey team, coming up with some rather surprising finds. There were none.

There were no records for a field hockey team in the Support Services & Activities groups. No line items for operating expenses in any budget sheets. Nobody in the General Accounting Office would say a word when asked about costs or show interest in my inquiries. An admin corporal in the army regulations office was the first person I heard use the words, "Black Ops" and secretive initiatives when I posed my inquiries.

And Colonel Williams. Seems nobody knew exactly who he was or what his job was at Fort Sill. Didn't know his responsibilities or what his presence was being used for within the wide vista of 4th Army operations. Wasn't even sure if Williams was his real name or if he was actually in the US Army.

Yup. Everything sounded normal to me.

24

My injuries mended, somewhat. I began practicing with the team.

The Colonel was right. The ladies on the field hockey team were good athletes and from my limited knowledge of the game had good field hockey skills. It was easy to see they were most likely good at any sport they chose to play. Make no mistake, folks. I was in rather good shape and it took every ounce of energy and the best use of my limited athletic talents just to keep up with the women in practice.

Bitchie was a player-coach from her center-halfback position. The left half was Cathy who was called Muffy by her teammates because of her looks and her pedigree. She came from a well-to-do New England family and had played field hockey at private schools. The right half was Cuzz, and she played with a toothpick in her mouth. At practices I could see under her jersey, she carried a gun.

The scoring line was a zoo-like menagerie of personalities punctuated by the left inner known as Puss and the right wing who was called Boots. One fullback was a stunning-looking woman, Casey, who liked to bowl, lift weights and play guitar. The other fullback was Miss Gertie who was a 45-year-old civilian worker and the mother of four.

It took a week to learn a little information about our goalie. During games, she smoked cigars and nipped from flasks she kept in her back pocket. She also carried a long knife strapped to her left leg. And a pistol strapped high on her right thigh. She had a slit in her sweatpants so she could reach in and remove the weapons when needed.

Folks just called her, Killer!

I practiced at left halfback. It was Bitchie who came up to me on my first day with the team. She tapped my crotch with her stick and suggested I should wear protection. For the rest of that night's practice, I found a small plastic bowl in one of the trash bins, wrapped it in a towel and stuffed it down my pants. For the rest of the year, I would wear the standard cup worn by most male athletes.

The rules of the game were different. In designated areas you could use both sides of your stick. Sometimes the directing of a ball with your foot was not called a penalty. A free hit meant you could use your stick or pick up the ball and make an underhanded throw to a location.

Sticks were viewed as weapons. Not a violation. Obstruction was hardly ever called. Instead, they were promoted and practiced as if they were set plays. Third-party obstructions were treated like setting a screen in basketball. Body checking and elbowing was permitted to whatever limit you could get away with per that night's official. It was a very rough game, even without the knives, guns, and elbows.

We won games and I occasionally got to play during the times of free substitution. Another loosely applied rule. The team compiled an impressive record of 12-3-3. I developed a great respect for my teammates. For their athleticism and their field hockey skills. I came to believe that in their heyday a few of the players had-been world-class athletes.

The girls treated me as a teammate because I put in my time and didn't slack in my practice efforts or my commitment to them. I learned so much about field hockey and peoples' lives in my 14 weeks on that team. Funny, not one of them gave-a-damn for Constance Applebee. Even Cathy, the purebred. She had once met the legend when Applebee visited her private East coast school. *"Stuffy old English bitch,"* remembered Cathy.

I had that funny feeling that Connie Applebee would not want to be a part of this team or caught alone in a dark alley with our goalie. Truthfully, I had no desire to be caught there, either. Whenever asked, I would refer to my time on the field hockey team as playing for the *"Fort Sill Zoo."*

At times, my teammates could be flat-out scary.

25

We completed our season in November beating a Tulsa club, 7-2. The game ending in a stick-swinging fight between their top player and our left inner, Puss. Honestly, it was the first time I heard her speak any words in my 14 weeks with the team. Including every freakin curse word I'd ever heard in my life. And a few I had not heard.

She won the stick fight, hands-down! I shuddered at the thought of having to do hand-to-hand combat against her. You know, with a 12-inch bayonet on the end of our sticks. Let me tell you. I would have followed that woman if she led a banzai charge in the darkness.

We settled into our 1941 Greyhound Silversides Bus for the three-hour ride back to Lawton and Fort Sill. Prior to leaving I had been handed mail by one of the headquarters workers. I decided to wait for the ride home before I opened it.

During road trips, I always brought a book to read and a writing pad. I would jot down thoughts or interesting things to remember. Unique happenings or words that were intriguing and I wanted to learn their definition. I wrote poetry, or at least made a poor attempt at it.

My mail was fun to read. A letter from a college friend who was serving in the navy somewhere off the coast of Spain. A nice note from a girl I knew back home who said to call her the next time I was back in town. A letter from my banker saying my small investments were doing well. And an official-looking envelope from the Department of Defense saying my name had come up in a Military Occupational Specialty Code, or MOS review, for possible deployment to Vietnam. Jeez, that letter took the air out of the balloon.

We rumbled through the Oklahoma darkness. Hank, our driver, lit up a smoke. An unfiltered Chesterfield. Buck Owens and his Buckaroos were singing "Sam's Place" on his Emerson Eight Transistor radio that hung from the ceiling and swayed gently with the movement of the bus.

Bitchie stared into the darkness as if searching the universe for answers. Loud snorting and snoring emanated from Cuzzy. I could hear soft cooing from Casey as she sang softly, beautifully, gently strumming on her guitar.

In the next row Puss and Boots were also singing and cooing, wrapped together as one...and they appeared to be gently strumming each other.

I won't try to describe the sounds coming from others, like Tootsie who's probably having a bad dream. And Skipper who's mumbling out loud, perhaps fondling herself. I took in a deep breath and closed my eyes. I leaned my head forward and with both hands began rubbing my forehead. I felt someone plop down in the seat beside me.

It was Killer.

Reacting to the suddenness of her appearance, I flinched back. In the din of the coach her face had that wide-eyed look or scary look of all those characters you remember from those black and white, B-rated horror movies we used to watch on Saturday nights. My first thought, *"Oh Shit! I'm down in that alley with Killer."*

To my surprise, she smiled, put her hand on my shoulder and said to relax. I tried to, somewhat, but I could still feel my heart beating. She was smoking a smelly cigar and nipping from her flask. Though not a hard liquor drinker, I took a hit from her flask. **YIKES!** My eyes bulged. Tears streamed down my cheeks. I fought for a quick breath.

Holy shit. Whatever it was that went down my throat, I'm pretty sure that's what a lit cigar would feel like if I tried to swallow it.

As my body shook trying to recover, she spoke softly, unlike her language on the field, thanking me for my efforts and contributions to the team. I responded, my voice still kind of scratchy, saying I really didn't do much. She reemphasized her words, saying, *"You did more than you know."*

It's what she said next that captured my attention.

"Rob, For the rest of your life, you're going to be doing things that will have a positive effect on lots of people. People like me. I know this. You won't even know you're doing It. That's just who you are." Wow, a little of that lost air from the DOD letter, went back into the balloon.

As she rose from her seat, she said it had been a pleasure to have known me. She hoped I felt the same about her. She gave me a big smile. A pretty smile. Then, she leaned in close to my face. I could feel her warm bourbon breath on my cheek, and in a voice almost too soft for me to hear she whispered in my ear, *"They call me killer...because I have killed people."*

She gently kissed me on the cheek and disappeared into the darkness of the back of the bus. My face was flushed. Heart pounding. My hands were shaking in my lap. Still recovering from the bout with her flask. In an eerie way, I knew that after this day I would never see her again. And I have not. Hank's transistor radio filled the quiet coach with a 1962 song by Claude King about a mountain man, Clifton Clowers and his pretty, young daughter up on "Wolverton Mountain."

So, there, that's how I got into this field hockey thing. Or whatever anyone wishes to call it.

Recollections from that night so many years ago, still burned into my memory. In an old bus with others, yet all alone with my thoughts...scratching them down on a yellow legal pad using my stylish Paper Mate Pen with the new, long-lasting refills. Precious thoughts of my life. Of tomorrows. Killer's words. And Vietnam. Thoughts that went on and on. All while rolling down those bumpy backroads of Oklahoma enveloped by the surrounding darkness and the complicated intricacies that are the lives and deaths of those around me.

Our old 1941 Greyhound Silversides Bus, spewing a diesel fuel cloud behind us like an alien cloaking device. Me the kid from that small town in Connecticut, hermetically sealed inside this old rattling coach. Alone with my thoughts, my fears, and my teammates. Bitchie and Muffy. Tootsie and Cuzz. Puss and Boots. And the Killer.

I closed my eyes and locked the memories of the moment into place. I then noted the date on my yellow legal pad. November 17, 1967.

26

Time is an uncontrollable resource. It doesn't really care what we think or how we feel. It's cold and has no empathy or conscience. It's sudden and absolute. Time tells us when it's ready.

On Friday, October 5, 1973, CIAC President John Daley officially announced what had been rumored since early spring. The CIAC would be, for the very first time, sponsoring and conducting a post-season field hockey tournament beginning in early November. It was time to begin trusting that canary in the cage from deep down in the mine shaft. Make a critical change or die as that canary will do without oxygen.

The announcement was somewhat less than monumental. The CIAC office and its tournament committee had been sending out tournament protocols and instructions to high school athletic directors since late June. Many ADs and coaches believed this was going to be another practice fire drill. So, schools continued to prepare their teams to play regular season and rival games. Not tournament games. After all, they'd been down this road of empty promises before.

News coverage for the announcement was light in weekend papers throughout the state. A few daily papers ran the story on Monday to lowered readership as it was Columbus Day. To say I was rather flummoxed at the timing of the announcement would be an understatement. Lou Ball had taught me it was OK to run a big story on Saturday or Sunday. But never...never announce a major story on Friday. Especially a Friday followed by a holiday on Monday.

The impact is a little like standing on a downtown Hartford street, yelling a warning at someone to watch out for that on-coming bus as they step off a curb...a warning to someone in downtown New Haven, 40 miles away.

Lou said we would run the story in our next Thursday edition. Or, when we had all the facts. We did run the official announcement in our October 18th, 1973 edition, two weeks after the CIAC's announcement. Honestly, though, I believed the tournament really would happen since my first conversations with CIAC folks in early May.

Despite the questioning attitudes, rotary dial phones were sparking to life throughout the state. Announcing the news. Passing on the info. The ping-pong ball effect. I tell you the news. You call two others, pass it on to them and then, they pass it on to more folks as the network widens. And on and on it goes. What I liked to refer to as, *"HONK-HONK, Ad-Infinitum."* This was the communications mode of the day. A 1973 version of what is today's wide-area-network (WAN).

Again, it was 1973. There were no emails, texts or tweets. No downloading from the cloud. It was landline telephones. Rotary dial or touch tone of heavy bakelite or lighter plastic. The Pony Express of the times for passing on breaking news.

Those were the days when Southern New England Telephone Company, or SNETCO, made money from people who dialed telephones and made calls. Especially when calling outside their calling area. What we referred to as long distance or toll calls.

And somehow, it all got communicated. It's an utter surprise for today's populations who cannot live more than an hour without some form of electronic communications. Of course, that's not to belittle today's products of modern communications. But for 1973, this type of communication was the Cadillac of the day.

Pat Mascia, the field hockey coach from Amity Regional High School in Woodbridge, was named Director of the Tournament Committee. Typically, an edict from the CIAC's Director, John Daley, who most likely made a strong suggestion to Mascia that she take the job. Remembers Pat, *"I was on lots of committees during those years."*

Pat Mascia was a dedicated and tireless worker. She'd surround herself with good committee people and always deliver a quality product. The rationale for why a tournament was coming to fruition in 1973 was the unanswered question with multiple choice answers. You could pick one of the choices or you could pick 'em all. Finally, in 1973, it was a question of *"Why"* with no wrong answers.

Daley kept a close eye on the cost of running the CIAC and the outside influences. The most impacting influence came in a dramatic turn of events having occurred the year before. In July 1972, Texas Senator John Tower's camp surprisingly pulled back their attempt at adding the troubling and unfriendly *"Tower Amendment"* as a supplement to Title IX. Its removal temporally eliminated one roadblock for the CIAC. Within hours, a supplemental amendment was penned by Senator Birch Bayh and Congresswoman Patsy Mink that would affectively keep Tower's amendment from reappearing for at least eighteen months.

But questions persisted. Why had Tower's camp pulled the plug? The brief explanation from the committee heads explained nothing. Just one of those *"Gift Horse"* things. So, it was best that folks just went their own way and stayed away from searching for a definitive answer. At least for now!

The supplement from Bayh and Mink was as confusing as the original Title IX wording, but it did the job blocking Tower's plans. Once completed, it was attached to already approved legislation and passed through congress at the late-night hour of 11:50 PM on a Saturday night when about the only things stirring were the local nightclubs and TV re-runs of old black and white horror movies. Nobody there to block passage. By early Sunday morning, girls' sports and related educational opportunities were back in business. Safe from Senator John Tower's amendment for...well, nobody knew for how long.

With the Tower roadblock temporarily out of the way, Daley began focusing on his next moves. Revenue generating needs from towns and schools registered as CIAC members. He now had more confidence and lots more wiggle room in which to work. It wasn't just field hockey being planned. Girls' basketball was about to hold its inaugural tournament in late winter of 1974. And softball, too, would have a tournament in the spring. This was a huge announcement. Daley was rolling the dice.

For Daley it was now a case of how to present the revenue increases to each municipality for the widening vista of the CIAC's proposed services. A timeline for the changing infrastructure. Specifically, the procedures for Daley's cost applications, had begun a phased-in, critical mass implemen-tation some eight months earlier. Some accused Daley of having insider information. Made no difference now. Daley's plan, just push the pedal to the floor and let's see what happens.

Daley's targets would be athletic directors, school boards

and local congressmen. His formula and message was simple. The CIAC needed revenue to generate revenue. If the girls wanted to play...town budgets, boards of education and boys' sports would have to pay. He had started his phased implementation in early March. By October, revenues from towns were committed. He couldn't wait any longer. It was time to announce the CIAC's plans.

And the Tower amendment. Perhaps his politicos saw that their canaries in their cages had stopped singing and were struggling for air in the vacuum of their own soiled environment. Said a writer from an emerging Austin gay rights group, *"Old Johnny T and his cronies got caught out in the hog barn with their pants down!"*

Still, nobody was laughing yet. Time was still the enemy.

Part 3

"Bubble Week"

Strange Times and
The New Frontier

27

Bubble Teams. A part of today's sports language.

Who's in. Who's out. Bracketology. Teetering on the edge. Language that has become a part of our culture. But, not in 1973. In fact, the first time I heard the term was from a longtime respected sportswriter working for the Springfield Massachusetts newspapers, the late Jerry Radding.

Radding was a WWII vet and a 1951 graduate of American International College. During my junior year at AIC, I met Jerry prior to that year's AIC-Springfield College football game. He stopped by our fraternity house, Theta Chi. We sat together in the upstairs kitchen and over coffee shared pleasantries. During ensuing times, I would often run into Jerry on campus and sporting events. He was a supporter to our fraternity, a real jock house, as many of my frat brothers went on to play in multi-levels of professional baseball, the

National Hockey League and the National Football League. They also appeared in a number of Hollywood produced sports movies.

Jerry was nice to me, especially because of my Vietnam service. He always had time to stop and talk and was receptive to my thoughts and aggressive approaches to sports.

In October 1973, he was scheduled to be the keynote speaker at a luncheon for a group of students and local sportswriters from Western Mass high schools and newspapers. I had not seen Jerry in over a year. The event was to be held at the Ole Storrowton Tavern and Carriage House located on the fairgrounds at the Eastern States Exposition on Memorial Drive in West Springfield. I called the Springfield Republican asking if I may attend. For no fee they signed me up. Ironically, my name would appear on the guestlist as, *"Penny P. Penfield."*

His interesting talk delved into the changing times and faces of sports.

Radding emphasized sports was no longer exclusive to New York, Chicago and Los Angeles. Now it was Kinshasa, Reykjavik and Bangkok. The politics of the Olympics after the Tommie Smith and John Carlos black-gloved fists at the 1968 Mexico City games. The 11 dead Israel Athletes during the 1972 games in Munich and the end of the men's basketball game. The game, won by the Russians, after the final three seconds were replayed three times to get the desired ending of overcoming a USA lead, engineered by the Russian game officials. A game that even today, 50 years later, members from the US team have refused to accept their Silver Medals.

One of those Olympic results that became the bane of my gallows humor when talking about Olympic judges and officials. My formula was simple. To determine an event winner, *"Throw out the highest score. Throw out the lowest score. Then, shoot the Russian judge."* Problem solved! Yes, it's a little raw. Lou didn't mind me using it in one of my columns.

Jerry Radding laughed heartily.

Radding spoke about the emergence of women's sports and compliance to the Title IX and the subsequent loosely defined, poorly written, six-year programs of compliance. Or, as he referred to it, *"The political joke known as Title Eight and a Half."*

He spoke definitively about the emergence of women's sports. His critical points zeroed in not only on issues of sports but our society and culture. How the media can, and eventually did, affect an event like the Billie Jean King-Bobby Riggs *"Battle of the Sexes"* event at the Astrodome in 1973. How it would affect the pending battles between the NCAA and the AIAW. The many slippery slopes that lay ahead. He even used the words, *"Fake News."* But he made sure all understood that the news was not fake. It was real. Fake only to those who did not want to hear the truth, because it had a nasty habit of biting them in the ass.

His talk completed, he returned to his table and his lunch of the Inn's famous pot roast, mashed potatoes and green beans. He had seen me in the audience and called me over to his table. I was surprised, thrilled he remembered me. Remembered that I was a Vietnam vet and had been twice wounded. He was thrilled when I told him that I, too was writing sports and asked if I needed anything. I told him about my involvement in high school sports, especially the girls' sports, and interest in the upcoming first-ever field hockey tournament. I talked about the teams teetering on the edge of qualifying for post-season play and a chance to be a part of history. And how hard it was to write about girls' sports.

"Ah Ha. The ones sitting on the bubble" said Jerry. *"Not knowing if they'll ride it to glory, or if it's going to pop."*

I asked Jerry, *"Bubble. What's that?"* He said it was an old descriptive term he had used in the early 1950's for a team that's still alive in the playoff picture, but in a precarious position. Where one wrong move bursts the soft balloon-type bubble they're sitting atop and all opportunities go down the toilet in what he described as, *"One very ungracious flush."*

"Bubble." The first time I had ever heard that term. That's all I needed to hear because the visuals in my head were clear and I could see teams. Boys and girls. Hanging on by a thread. No wiggle room for errors. Survive, or disappear with no honor or respect. I was sure there'd be those who would hate the term. I was already battling with some folks who believed I should be much gentler in my reporting because it was girls.

Well, that's not me. It made no difference. Boys or girls. And, I will say it as many times as I have to. As I admitted to. If you played well, I said so. It you played like horseshit, I said that, too. It pissed off folks. I simply said to people, *"If you don't like what I'm writing, don't read it."* I had no fear and the backing of my editor. So, when it came to living on the bubble, well, that really got to the real crux of the situation in a hurry. A perfect description. Ungracious flush or not.

During his professional career, Jerry Radding covered 43 NCAA men's basketball tournaments including final fours and 31 NIT finals at both Madison Square Gardens. I shared with him the displeasure of some of my readers. He smiled, put his arm on my shoulder. His thoughts were like a quick jab from a boxer.

"When you worry about what people will think of you, find another profession. Because, like Edmond O'Brien in a 1949 film noir, you're DOA, baby...Dead on arrival. And never let a coach intimidate you."

That made me think of my crossing the line and defending my position and honor with Joan Sullivan just a week before. Crossing that line at the Alamo and doing battle in the middle of that old cow pasture. It really was defending myself...or being DOA.

Radding's words were never truer. And now the final weeks of the 1973 field hockey season awaited with building anticipation, like the shoot-out at the OK Corral. Three of the

Farmington Valley's six teams were close to or on *"Jerry's Bubble."* Throughout Connecticut, another dozen teams would be playing for their survival. Oh yeah, it was going to be one hell of a week watching teams ride the bubble. Into tournament history. Or, ingloriously flushed down the drain of shame. Because that's the stark suddenness of a *"Single Elimination Tournament."*

On the drive home, I had to laugh when the Drifters conjured up memories of Saturday night dances in the high school cafeteria with, "Save the Last Dance for Me." I thought of Jerry's *"Bubble."* Wondered..."Yeah, if you're still around for the last dance."

The bubble was like time. It doesn't have any empathy and doesn't give a damn what happens to you.

28

Bubble Week came rolling in like a surging tsunami. Even though everyone knew it was coming, its impact was stark and sudden. For some teams, players, coaches, even their fans, the impact would be emotional and overwhelming. And since most had not been down this path before, the pain of those emotions would go far beyond the expectations of what one simple tournament game could ever be.

Early in the season coaches had made comments about the possibility of a post-season tournament. Their consensus: *"Yeah, a tournament will be nice. But our focus is preparing for games against our arch-rivals."* Their tone to the possibilities of playing in a post-season tournament remained secondary to playing their school's rival just down the road.

I remembered my aunt saying that folks don't think about water until they're thirsty and need a drink. Her message to those who listened. Hey baby, plan-ahead. Be ready, just in case. A single elimination tournament is not another game or two you play. It's a whole new season.

Many established programs had already qualified for post-season play. Their goals now were to hone their game and stay away from injuries. For those schools struggling near or at the .500 mark, that early season aloofness to the priorities of games verses rivals, suddenly shot to number one on *"TO-DO Lists"* for many coaches.

I was rather amused with the whole scene. Finally, there would be a tournament to declare a true champion. A wonderful, long-awaited and overdue opportunity. A second season.

Yet, a multitude of coaches and players were treating the possibilities of being a part of the inaugural tournament as no more than playing in just another game against a longtime rival. It was hard to put an emotional mark on such a game since nobody had been down this path. That is until "Bubble Week" arrived. When the urgency of survival and the real possibility of peer embarrassment by nervous coaches became the priority.

Fake news was now very real.

What better day to kick off the week of holy terror than on a Monday. It started in Madison, Connecticut. Daniel Hand High School was hosting North Branford needing a win or a tie to keep its hopes alive for a spot in the post-season field. The Black and Gold was riding the bubble with a record of 4-3-4 heading into the season's final. No wiggle room there. Lose and they were out. Even a tie might cost them a bid as they had but four wins.

Tigers coach Wili Roz' simple assessment. *"We need to win the game!"*

Every coach will tell you. When you need a win...what you don't need is to play a game against a team that has nothing to lose. What a college coach I had called, *"A Cow Shit Game."*

Because no matter how it came out, it was going to stink. North Branford's Thunderbirds were in the first years of their budding varsity program playing in the demanding Shoreline Conference. They were coached by Babby Nuhn who, in subsequent years, would go on to establish a 50-year legacy in North Branford, building her program into one of the most respected in the state.

Neither team was known for offense and that fact was on display after a scoreless first half. Midway through the second half, Tigers co-captain Cindy Horn emerged from a crowd in front of North Branford's goal and flicked a shot into the net and the home towners had a 1-0 lead. A second goal in the final minutes put the lid on a 2-0 victory. Daniel Hand had weathered the bubble and now had a record of 5-3-4. They had now become the first real bubble team becoming tournament eligible.

Avon was teetering and needed a quality win to sew up a tournament bid. Farmington was shaky but looked good for the tournament. Simsbury on the other hand, was perilously atop that thin-lined bubble and had a wickedly hard, end-of-season schedule. The Trojans' fortunes were now riding on the backs of four untested sophomores. Nobody knew that more than Sully. And me, of course. With what I would come to call, *"My Pabst Blue Ribbon Philosophy."*

Simsbury entered *"Bubble Week"* with a record of 4-3-2, having to play three games in four days. Avon would be the next opponent. Nothing would be easy for either team. This game was a dogfight. The Falcons had never beaten the Trojans and now had them on their own turf. With a tournament bid on the line and a chance to beat Simsbury, Avon's girls came out for a light practice on Sunday. It meant that much to the girls, and the memory of that *"Conspiracy Loss"* to rival Farmington was still fresh in everyone's thoughts.

Bonnie Tyler made a few subtle changes. Caryn Bray

would again cover a wider area from her left halfback position. Mary Anne Hollfelder was back in goal. Mary Jo Capitani appeared to be playing a *"Tweener"* position. Operating as a rover between the scoring and halfback lines. It looked as if Avon was playing a 3-5-2 format. Forcing Simsbury to play outside the realm of its standard 5-3-2 alignment.

But the Trojans were up to the task. That new cadre of sophomores were a quicker, faster and more aggressive group and not intimidated by the Falcons. It truly was a bitterly fought game. Bumping, pushing, sticks being slammed together. Trash talking and a few shoving matches. Avon was ready. Joan Sullivan had finally made her needed changes.

In the final seven minutes, it was Avon's frontline athletes, Heidi Zacchera and Karen Poirier along with their halfback line that proved just a bit too much for the vaunted Simsbury defense. Avon's Carter Jordan split two defenders and Zacchera found her with a nifty pass. Jordan scored the game's only goal. Avon won the battle, 1-0. Their first-ever win over Simsbury. Their record was 6-4, and they were now tournament eligible. Simsbury stood at 4-4-2 with two games to play.

Simsbury's Pinky O'Connor Against Newington

In the words of Avon's Bonnie Tyler, *"Perhaps the best game we've ever played."*

No time for rest. On Monday, Simsbury hosted Newington. Another team on the bubble. Like Simsbury, the Indians had started well, but were now in a freefall and needed a win. Newington grabbed an early lead when co-captain Lisa Meucci scored on a whistling blast from the top of the circle. One of those goals where the ball just has a homing device and finds its way through a menagerie of legs and bodies. Simsbury goalie, Elaine Marcil, saw Meucci take the shot from the top of the circle and never saw the ball until it was wedged in the netting behind her. Marcil held out her arms, palms up, that pleading statement, *"I never saw it!"*

Simsbury's sophomore experience came alive. Denise Lamb, playing in just her second varsity game, scored by outhustling the defense, beating the Newington goalie with a quick wrister to tie the game. Early in the second half, Kent Walton gave Simsbury a 2-1 lead only to see Newington again fight back to tie the game 2-2 on a rebound by Mary Bonigsegna. But, in the end, it was another young sophomore, Eileen O'Connor, who scooted through traffic coming face-to-face with the goalie and scoring on a shot that ricocheted off the goalie's foot.

Simsbury survived, 3-2. Their record was 5-4-2. I saw Sully standing alone at the far end of the field. I chose to leave her alone and walk in the opposite direction. They were still atop the bubble with a tournament bid on the line. They could not afford to lose a game. They had one more regular season game looming on their schedule.

Wednesday. Halloween. At Granby!

29

My family ancestry is English and Scottish. I can still painfully recall when my mom would dress me for Halloween in a costume that made me feel like I was trying out for a picture on a cereal box. My elderly grandparents in attendance, long with European traditions, would then remind me of how I was to go on my appointed rounds of the neighborhood.

"The Sky is Blue/ The Grass is Green/ May we please have/ our Halloween" was the hearty plea as I held out my plastic jack-o-lantern to be filled with candy.

Or, if you lived in the 16th century, the Glasgow version of begging to *"Hand us our Thruppence,"* or three pence reward for services. A less than glorious way of begging for money. An extra reward payment for what workers believed they were owed for their sweat, toil and tears working for the masters within a feudalistic environment.

It was Halloween. Simsbury went knocking on Granby's door. Begging, clawing, fighting for anything they could come away with. Their *"Thruppence"* because they believed they had earned a shot in the tournament. More importantly, their season was riding on this day. A tie or a win over the 9-0-2 Bears would make them tournament eligible. Of course, Simsbury wanted to win the game. Beat Granby and, as was heard being hollered by a few Simsbury players during warm-ups, *"We want to stuff that winning streak up their asses!"*

Hey, nothing like a little town rivalry to fan a Halloween inferno.

Surprisingly, a large contingency of the Granby student body showed up for the game. En masse, they wandered across the end of the field with the subtleness of a herd of buffalos stampeding around fine china. Walking through the rows of Simsbury players as they warmed up. They would ring the field two and three deep. As would teachers, custodians, school bus drivers. Police officers. Lovers and other strangers. For the pride of Granby. Even the usually subdued Dot Johnson and her Granby team took notice of the crowd.

Val McCord, Granby's frontline sniper walked to mid-field. She warmed up but would not play in this game. Unavailable due to a leg injury. She stood with her stick in both hands. Staring at Simsbury players. I could see her mouth moving. Couldn't hear what she was saying, but it certainly caught the attention of a few Simsbury players.

I'm pretty sure her words would have been unprintable in the Herald. Val had a way about her. Of goading her opponents into mistakes with language I referred to as, *"Strong enough to hang your laundry on"*. Then she'd swoop in taking advantage of that opportunity. She was one of the most officious trash talkers in the game.

Two of Simsbury's young sophomores, Lamb and O'Connor, stopped to take in the McCord show. They looked at each other, then looked back at McCord. Both smiled. Returned to their warm-ups. When I saw their actions, I knew I had made the right decision in stepping over the line to do battle with Joan Sullivan. She knew it, too.

The area had turned festive and loud. The Granby boys' soccer team massed atop the hill overlooking the crowd below. Led by their coach, Bill Stacey, they hollered out a series of cheers urging the girls to, *"Kick Ass."* I spied Athletic Director, Ken King, standing along the sideline. He turned towards me, a stunned look on his face. He smiled and uttered just one word, *"Yikes!"*

Tony Romano, the boys' basketball coach stood near the field. He was munching on an Almond Joy candy bar. I offered greetings. His answer, *"Damn...those girls keep winning. Puts too much pressure on the rest of us to win."*

My comeback was, *"Really, Tony. That's it."* He flashed a wry smile and took another bite of the candy bar.

The day was cool. The sun popping in and out behind low puffy clouds. Joan Sullivan stood near mid-field. Her head bent slightly forward. Hands buried deep in her jacket pockets. Sully spied the activities going on around her. She felt surrounded. Like she had just walked into an ambush. She inspected the playing field. Kicked at it with her toe, mumbling, *"Terrible field...Terrible field."* It was no worse than her own field.

Granby coach, Dottie Johnson stood about 100 feet away. She saw Sullivan evaluating the field. Johnson chuckled. Their eyes met. It was the newer kid on the block against the wily veteran. The preppies against the farmers. Johnson flashed her famous huge smile. Sullivan nodded in respect. The wheels of thought were turning. You could feel the emotion in your chest. There was tension. And there were two teams ready to go at each other like nasty alley cats with attitudes.

Standing along the sideline, I felt a nudge from behind. Turning, I saw the familiar face of Alice Yokabaskas, who would be the lead official for the game. She stood beside me and looking out over the pitch said, *"Rob, this one is going to be a dandy."*

Halloween. I panned the area taking in the unfolding activities. I had this odd, eerie feeling. Today...this game. There would be no winners.

Just survivors.

30

As Alice had predicted, the game turned into a dandy.

Not fast-paced, but steady. More tentative in style and execution. No individual shining stars. Instead, team efforts. Every player on each team seemingly touching the ball as the foes swapped possessions and control of mid-field. Two teams playing as if each was afraid to make the first big mistake. A dangerous way for Granby to play. This type of strategy was not their game. Especially against a longtime and hated rival. A team who, proverbially, had their backs against the wall.

The game was scoreless at halftime.

As the second half began you could sense the large crowd getting anxious...louder, more antsy and boisterous. Their Bears responded. Driving the ball deep into Simsbury's end of the field. Pam Sproull and Lynsie Wickman got off hard shots on goal. Simsbury goalie, Elaine Marcil kicked them away.

Nancy Hutchings rolled a dangerous-looking shot at the Trojans' goal. Marcil did a pop-up slide, kicking the shot away less than a foot from the goal line. Penalty corners ensued, but the vaunted Simsbury defense beat back wave after wave from the Granby attack. With ten minutes remaining the game was still scoreless.

Then, in a heartbeat, the flow of the game changed, dramatically.

Simsbury came alive in a way that had not been a part of their attack during previous games. Suddenly, the Trojans were faster, quicker to the ball. A little meaner. Nastier. Hungry for action and seemingly pleased with the aggressiveness and corporal punishment they were now dishing out.

Lamb and O'Connor were untouchable. With water bug-like quickness, they darted in and out of Granby's defenses untouched and began firing shots at goalie Jo Sproull. Shots on breakaways and from corners. Simsbury's offense was now muscling up and physically fighting off Granby's front liners. The Trojans had become the determined road warriors. They hungered for their *"Thruppence."*

During the game's final five minutes Simsbury's pressure kept the play near or inside their opponent's 25-yard line. Usually within the scoring circle as Granby had to play on its heels. Kent Walton sent a whistling drive that hit the goalpost with a loud "ping," the ball caroming off Sproull's pads coming to rest just inches from the cage. Sue Hebert slapped the ball out-of-bounds to relieve the pressure, setting up another Simsbury corner hit.

Off the inbounds pass, Walton again fired another low riser through a crowd, hitting the top of Sproull's pads. The ricochet went to Holly Burk who sent a hard wrist shot that again hit the side post. *"Dammit, Dammit! Keep it up,"* yelled Walton. *"Keep shooting."* On the sideline, Sullivan and her team had edged out onto the field in mass, urging the offense on. Granby's sideline did the same. Fans, too, from both sidelines began creeping onto the playing field. Moving closer to the action with each passing minute.

Walton charged into the circle, her stick in her right hand while she was fending off people including her own teammates with her left arm. There were collisions. No whistles for obstruction. Just lots of people in close quarters. Yelling, pushing and shoving. Simsbury, relentlessly attacking. The game went on.

The timekeeper yelled out, *"One Minute to Play."*

O'Connor broke in behind Sue Jensen, but before she could muster a shot, collided with Lynsie Wickman. No whistle. Lamb sent a low rolling shot that looked like it was going into the goal. It hit the heel of a shoe. No whistle. The ball bouncing wildly back into the middle of the gathering mob in front of the goal. Granby was fighting for its life. The life of its 44 game, four-year unbeaten streak. The respect and adulation of its fans. The pride of the small town of Granby. And, to the now unstoppable, unrelenting tidal wave, that were the Simsbury Trojans.

Almost unheard within the midst of the mayhem, the final horn sounded. The scoreless game was over.

But like two fighters in the ring the two teams did not stop. They kept exchanging blows. Play continued. Sticks banging together. Emotions being hollered. Pushing and shoving. Cries of anguish. Coaches and players from both teams had migrated onto the field along with the large crowd, all screaming and yelling. Forming a canyon-like mob just a few yards away from the on-going action.

Officials kept blowing their whistles. The horn sounded again...and again. Slowly, the emotional play began to ebb. Individual skirmishes ended. The action stopped. The field quieted. For a brief period, players from both teams stood, motionless. When they turned to their respective teams on the sideline, they were shocked to see a most unusual sight. That canyon wall formation. Everyone...just staring at the players. It certainly was a strange sight.

There ensued an uncanny silence. Broken only by the sounds of crying from girls on both teams. Emotions spilling out. Some moved slowly, staring at the sky. A few players from both teams were on one knee, head pitched forward holding onto their stick with both hands. Chests and backs heaving as they sucked in air. They were spent. Their tanks were empty.

Kent Walton stood near the Granby goal. She slammed her stick into the ground...again and again. *"Dammit,"* she hollered out. *"Dammit...Dammit"* her voice trailing off. Walton knew. She and her Simsbury teammates had Granby on the ropes but could not close the deal. Could not overcome the Granby mystique.

For nine minutes, the game never left the Bears' end of the field. The Trojans had been awarded four corners and sent a dozen shots at the goal. They did everything a field hockey team could possibly do against Granby. Except put the ball in the net and beat them on the scoreboard. Walton was down on both knees near mid-field, her chin resting on her stick. She didn't hide her tears.

Yes, Simsbury had now qualified for the tournament. But, at what cost. The answer to that question was less than a week away.

Neither coach wanted to talk after the game. I understood their angst, and I respected their wishes. I'm pretty sure that I knew what each would have said. A few players made quiet comments referring to what had just occurred. Alice Yokabaskas had been right. The game truly turned out to be a dandy. One for the ages. And I too, had been right with my odd, eerie pre-game feeling.

In the end, the results felt like somebody had stepped in and stopped the event that was building to an emotional apex just short of the finish line. Just stepped in and stopped it. No final results achieved. Just tricks and no treats. In some ways the game was over. In so many other ways, it would never be over, because nobody won. They just survived. No *"Thruppence"* to be paid.

After all, it was Halloween.

31

Bubble Week was turning out to be a nasty little adventure with no empathy.

Win and you were considered for a tournament bid. Lose and you were done for the season. Unceremoniously flushed down the drain. It was that sudden and equally cruel. And, for the first time many teams and girls were on a very steep learning curve. They didn't like to be in that predicament, and they certainly didn't like me when I wrote about it. As Jerry Radding had warned me: Don't worry about that crap. Just do the job you're getting paid to do.

Newington bounced back from its loss to Simsbury and played two of their finest games of the regular season when it was needed most. They first surprised visiting Windsor Locks in a scoreless tie, and their record stood at 4-4-2. That set up a season-ending, must win road situation in West Hartford against Conard. Again, the Indians were led by co-captains Mary Bonigsegna and Lisa Meucci, who was known as "Meucci the Masher." She scored the winning goal with three minutes remaining in the game after Nancy Davidson had made a steal at mid-field to set up the final rush. Newington finished the regular season at 5-4-2.

Meucci recalls learning about a post-season tournament at mid-season. Right about the time the team went into a four-game losing skid and on the brink of elimination. *"Our tournament chances were slipping away. So proud of our team. We came together when we had to."*

In Terryville, the Kangaroos rode the inspired play and leadership from co-captains Melanie Kopcha and Patty Reynolds in beating Thomaston to finish at 6-4. North Haven needed a season-ending win over West Haven. They used goals from Sally Erickson and Lisa Cipoloni for a 3-1 victory to become tournament eligible.

For Waterford the tournament was going to be an uphill battle. Coach Vivien Novicki's Lancers had put together a record of 5-2 against schools with losing records. The regular season would end with games against three of the best in the state. Away games vs E.O. Smith and Guilford and home dates with Westbrook and The Williams School. To qualify for the tournament, they needed to win at least one game. That task would take them down to the waning minutes of their final game.

Waterford's fortunes soured. E.O. Smith got a goal from Linda Knapp just before the final horn to beat their shoreline visitors, 1-0. At home against Westbrook Jan Merrill gave the home towners a 1-0 lead they took late into the second half. Westbrook's Rae Hirst tied the game in the last five minutes. The game ended in a 1-1 draw. The unexpected tie keeping their tournament hopes alive. Guilford was the next match and this one was all Grizzlies. Dawn Sprague, Sharon Farquharson and Mary Bunting found the net and goalie Leslie

Gribus could not be dented in a convincing 4-0 win.

Waterford stood at 5-4-1 needing a win or a tie.

It came at home in the season's final game. Novicki used few words in describing the predicament. *"Ladies...you need to win,"* and then walked out of the room leaving her girls to their own thoughts.

Merrill scored in the first. She and Joan Van Ness added second half goals as Waterford got its tournament eligible win, 3-2 over The Williams School of New London. Merrill finished the season with 24 goals and nine assists to lead the state in scoring.

Reaching mid-season, Stamford's Black Nights found themselves at a fork-in-the-road. Ahead, was a daunting schedule for a young team that had made many position changes of players from the previous season. A team that believed they could win the city championship. Now they were coming off losses to Norwalk and Greenwich. Stamford needed wins.

First up was Notre Dame of Bridgeport. Goals from Sue Mihalik and Penny Rickel stood up in a 2-1 win. Mihalik again was the lone goal scorer in a 1-0 win over Brien McMahon of Norwalk. Stamford now had a 5-3 record needing one more win for a possible tournament bid and two wins for the city championship. Both games would be against city rival, Catholic High.

If there was any one game during the year you could point to and say, "This was that one game that made Stamford's year," it was the first game vs Catholic. A huge crowd turned out for the home game. It was, as Coach Pat Pidhirny said, *"The day we came to play."*

Stamford won, 4-0. The game really wasn't that close.

Four different front liners scored, but this day belonged to a smothering defense anchored by fullbacks Brenda Baxter and Toni Rinaldi. They limited Catholic to three shots on goal, all from long range. It was Baxter, one of very few African-

Americans playing field hockey in the early 70's, who kept Catholic far away from the goal. Her booming clearing hits were something to behold. Even her teammates would stop what they were doing and watch her make a clearing hit.

Remembers Rinaldi, *"Brenda could hit the crap out of a hockey ball. It made a noise...like it whistled when it traveled through the air."*

On the next day Stamford's large crowd traveled crosstown as the schools traded fields. The results were the same. Rickel and Mihalik each scored, assisting on each other's score, in a 2-0 win. Rinaldi and Baxter again putting up a wall on defense. Stamford completed the dream and captured the city championship. They were tournament bound with a record of 7-3.

Bubble week was cruel to others. Teams struggling down in the weeds.

Norwalk and Brien McMahon fell into season-ending losing streaks and losing records. Bethel and Andrew Warde each lost key games late and a shot for a tournament bid. Manchester hovered around .500 for the season but could not get a convincing win. North Branford, Wilton and Joel Barlow played well, but not well enough to be in a position for a winning record. Lewis Mills rode the bubble all season unable to get that one, convincing win, late in the season.

Hamden was truly snake bitten with back luck. They were a surprising 4-3 under Coach Helen Bevin. One game rained out and another game lost when the scheduled opponent didn't show up to play at a neutral field. Prior to that game, Hamden was warming up and waiting for their opponent to arrive, two men's teams showed up at the field for a soccer game between neighborhoods. After some conversation and cursing, the men chased the girls off the field and back onto the bus for a hasty getaway.

Bubble week had no impact on those playing in the tall cotton. Those elite teams like Guilford cruised past Old Lyme,

11-0, for its ninth shutout of the season. For the regular season they outscored opponents, 50-3.

Granby ran its four-year unbeaten string to 44 games, shutting out Suffield 3-0 for the conference championship and ended at home with a bitterly fought tie against Simsbury. Maloney had a final game blowout of cross-town rival Platt. Cheshire had an easy win over Lyman Hall and a surprising 1-1 tie with Sheehan to end the regular season at 11-0-1, winning the Housatonic League title.

The standard bearers toiled on. Expected to and already qualified for the tournament, they honed their attacks with final season games. The goal was to avoid injuries in those final games. The teams along preppy corridor honed their skills and looked strong for the tournament.

New Canaan rolled over Norwalk, 4-0 and closed out the regular season with a 7-0-3 record including a well-played 1-0 victory over Greenwich, Betsy Blackwell getting the winning goal. Bea Walko's Cardinals would end their schedule at 9-1-1. Staples rolled on playing Darien and New Canaan to scoreless ties and closing out the season, beating Brien McMahon to finish 7-1-2. Darien won its finale to end regular season play, 7-3.

Old Saybrook ended the regular campaign 9-2 beating Old Lyme and appeared to be a real threat to win the state tournament representing the powerful Shoreline Conference. Joining them were conference foes Westbrook with a record of 10-1-1. A good scoring team led by Rae Hirst, Tammy Husted, hustling Lynn Clements and the play of goalie Rose Weisse. Sandy White's East Lyme squad also figured prominently at 8-2-1.

Coach Pat Small had seen her Roger Ludlowe team fall to 2-3 after consecutive shutout losses to Staples and New Canaan. They needed to win out. They did, running the table with five consecutive wins outscoring opponents 15-1 to finish at 7-3, led by co-captains Sue Morrison and Carol Bonney.

Sheehan, also at 2-3, rode the scoring of Cheryl Eck and Diane Ciccone and play of co-captains Linda Muzyczka, Nancy Dudek and the late Cathy Inglese to go unbeaten in its final seven games finishing 8-3-1 for Coach Judy Samaha. These were huge comebacks as both schools looked dead in the water in early October. Now they were going to post-season play.

Maloney kept up their physical, run 'n shoot game to a season record of 10-1-1 behind the consistent scoring of Shelia Mihalek, Ellen Janiga and defensive leadership of Joyce Allgaier. Nonnewaug finished off its conference winning season playing Litchfield to a tie and beating Thomaston for a record of 8-0-4.

Enrico Fermi rebounded from early season inconsistency. With a scoring flurry the Falcons closed out its regular season blasting Newington and shutting out Bloomfield and South Windsor for an 8-2-2 record. Across town, Enfield, getting big goals from Sue Herter and Kate Mullen, beat Simsbury, tied Conard and shutout East Windsor, finishing 5-4-3, becoming tournament eligible. Suffield, always in Granby's shadow, played well enough for a 6-3-2 mark. Karen Drake's overall play and the scoring of Patty Kelly and Karen Samuelson led the way.

Going almost unnoticed was Windsor Locks, referred to by opponents as the team of *"No Names."* Coached by Cyndy Wilson, they closed out their season shutting out South Windsor and Bloomfield behind the scoring of Nancy Shapiro and play of Lisa Gragnolati to end their season at 8-2-2. After early season losses, the Raiders make player moves, win a couple of big games and find themselves riding a six-game unbeaten string into tournament play.

The real excitement was about to begin.

32

It was late on a Wednesday evening. Patty Mascia sat at her dining room table. Hands over her face. Rubbing her eyes. Peering through her fingers at the board propped up in front of her. The tournament brackets. She was tired and had a pounding headache. You know the kind. We've all had 'em. That stabbing pain behind one eye.

The information had begun being faxed to her on Monday. By 6 PM, Wednesday, 44 schools had faxed in their packages to the CIAC committee for review. Included in that crowd was her own team, Amity Regional. A few members of the tournament committee had met at Mascia's house to sift through the received data and verify who was in and who was out.

Mascia was known for her thoroughness and quality of her committees. She surrounded herself with good people and she always delivered a class product. I once heard a peer refer to her as *"Ms. Committee."* That name hit the target dead center.

The first issues started innocently. During the early edit, one school was found to have a win over a JV program. Wins that did not comply with qualification procedures. A quick audit of all 44 packages ensued. It was found that three programs had such wins listed and each win had pushed them over the required 51% winning percentage. They were eliminated from the list. The qualification pile now stood at 41.

The audit also uncovered two schools with wins over out-of-state opponents, including a win over a private school. Also, not in compliance with set rules. The qualifiers now stood at 39. The final decision was that of Hamden High School. They had a 4-3 record. Just seven games, two under the minimum criteria for qualification. Despite some bizarre and extenuating circumstances, Hamden's bid was rejected. The final count of tournament qualifications would be 38 schools.

Since the tournament had been finalized at such a late date, creating classes for school sizes such as brackets for a Class L and Class M Tournament could not be formalized. For the 1973 tournament, all 38 schools, small, median, and large, who meet qualifying criteria, will play in one division.

Using a simple math formula of quality wins, strength of schedule and conference affiliations, teams were ranked as the scheduling process began. Guilford earned the honor as the top ranked team in the tournament, followed by Granby, Maloney, Cheshire, Weston and Darien as the state's top six ranked teams. It was decided that the top 12 ranked teams would play a first-round home game if it was possible to schedule without disrupting the brackets.

Even with three losses, I felt Darien, player for player, was the best team in the state and Guilford a two seed because of its results in the brutal Shoreline Conference. I believed Greenwich and New Canaan should have been seeded higher. Using my seeding and ranking process, Granby was a fifth or sixth seed. Make no mistake, Granby played a demanding non-conference schedule, but their affiliation in the NCCC, the weakest conference in the state, made the Bears playground bullies in a league of creampuffs.

Teams ranked 13 to 26 qualify for a first-round game. Most will have to travel to play first-round games at a neutral site. The final twelve qualified teams, ranked 27th through $38^{th,}$ are scheduled for a special play-in round to be held on Friday and Monday. The six winners from the 12 teams in the play-in round will move into the six slots available in the first round of 32 teams against one of the top six ranked teams in the state.

Truly a paradox. Their reward for winning became their punishment. First, try to win a play-in game. Then, play against one of the top six ranked teams in the state. A tough road for any team. The belief was that none of the six play-in round winners would make it past the first round. A bit of the sacrificial lamb for the top six ranked teams.

Mascia's committee begins the ardent task of creating and the communicating tournament reporting procedures. This includes confirming game locations and dates. Assigning game officials. The minutia and administrivia of activities that accompany tournament infrastructures. The committee had already begun notifying schools of games that would begin on Friday, November 2nd, just two days out. The championship game is scheduled for Saturday, November 17th to be played at 10 AM on Field B on the Yale University athletic campus. Not much wiggle room to deal with issues, concerns or problem-solving. An issue that will come back to bite them in the ass.

The committee had a mountain of questions to answer. The chain of command. Who will have the final decision-making powers for issues, or protests. What about ties! Overtimes! Games that end in darkness. Injuries and illness. Officials and their backups. Specific rules for specific field locations. What happens if the weather turns bad. If it rains...or snows. Protocols for cancellations and rescheduling! Yikes!

Mascia again buried her head in her hands. Her headache was only getting worse.

33

The stranger innocently introduced himself to me, *"Hi, I'm Warren."* Never told me his last name. Still don't know it to this day. Not even sure if his first name is Warren.

Our meeting would impact both our lives in a way I cannot even begin to dissect. And I would come to understand how Warren would dramatically affect the lives of so many others in the world. Affect them in ways that would go far beyond the perceptions and deep understandings of many, including me.

It was late fall, 1977. I had left the *Farmington Valley Herald* for the glamorous lights of a daily rag, aka a daily newspaper, and was now writing for the new kid on the block, *The Hartford Tribune*. Hired by the late Mort Sharnik, a multi-sports aficionado who lived in West Simsbury. I had done work for Mort during his years as a boxing maven and writer for Sports Illustrated.

I was on assignment traveling with the New England Whalers of the World Hockey Association. Gordie Howe had signed to play with the Whalers that summer and was on the threshold of scoring his 1000th career goal. We were in Houston for a game. He and his hockey playing sons, Mark and Marty, were returning to play their former team, the Aeros at Houston's Summit Arena.

On Wednesday morning, I arose for an early breakfast interview in the hotel restaurant with Whalers' coach, Harry Neale. Following my talk with Harry, I was reading the *Houston Chronicle*. It was mid-week and the NFL's Houston Oilers were preparing for a home game verses the Denver Broncos that Sunday. An 11 AM practice was scheduled at the Astrodome. So, with lots of time to kill, I packed my work bag and headed out to *"The Eighth Wonder of the World"* as the dome was often referred to. Or what the locals referred to as *"The Bump."*

During non-rush hours, the trip from Greenway Plaza to the Dome takes about 20 minutes. I negotiated a rate of $17 with an independent cabbie. The driver matriculated through main street traffic, back alleys, and short cuts. I was left off at one of the Dome's auxiliary entrances as my driver knew the door attendant. This allowed me to enter the facility without the required credentials, though I was given a flimsy one-day paper pass allowing me onto the artificial floor of the dome and the practice field. You know the type. Like you get when you are in a training class and it's pasted to your left breast saying, **"Hello, My Name Is...".** I had been to the Astrodome during my years in the army for baseball and football games, but it was still an awe-inspiring feeling when you entered.

As soon as I entered the Dome things began happening all around me. Oilers head coach, Bum Phillips, appeared in one of the tunnel openings. He was dressed like Gary Cooper in *High Noon*. His signature Ten Gallon hat atop his enormous head. His hair shaved down close in a 1950's buzz-cut style.

Before stepping out into the spotlight, he took a glass from a tray held by a waiter standing next to him. Phillips drained the glass which I later learned was 15-year-old bourbon. He replaced the glass on the silver tray, adjusted his hat and strutted out onto the immense openness that was the Astrodome.

I was told by a writer standing next to me that Bum's entrance signaled the official green light for the 90-minute practice to begin.

To my left, Houston's journeyman quarterback, Dan Pastorini, known to have a volatile temper and short fuse, was being separated and held back by two teammates after a verbal and physical battle with one of his offensive linemen. Pastorini was thrown to the ground and pinned down, ending the skirmish, all the while spewing a barrage of language so vile that even some of the hardened writers in attendance took notice.

The same writer I originally met, now sipping a tall glass of scotch, said it was best Pastorini was pinned, *"Cause that old boy (lineman) woulda ripped his freakin ears off."*

Walking through the fray and never looking at his QB on the ground, Phillips shook his head and growled, *"Goddammed asshole. Gets beat up in practice by his own teammates. And we actually pay him money for this shit to happen."* It was funny and I laughed. I was also thinking maybe Bum wished he had stayed in the tunnel to have another bourbon.

Off to my right an argument was underway between a huge defensive lineman and one of the coaches. The lineman, about the size of my car, stuck a finger in the coach's chest and calmly said, *"Shut up, or I'll knock your ass into next season."* Admittedly, I thought that too, was a funny line. They were quickly pulled apart and the skirmish ended.

On the 40-yard line, kicker Tom Dempsey was practicing field goals as he carried on trash talking with the player who was holding for him. Dempsey was a pudgy, overweight kicker with a stub for a right foot. He was born with no toes on his right foot and no fingers on his right hand. He wore a customized stub-like shoe, if you could call it a shoe. It looked more like a sledgehammer attached to a leg. It had a thick hunk of steel in front, slightly tilted to provide better lift when he kicked the ball. He was the holder of the longest made field goal in NFL history. A 63 yarder against the Detroit Lions in 1971.

Most felt the steel shoe provided at least an additional five to seven yards on each of Dempsey's kicks although tests showed that was not true. Dempsey, usually jovial, was not having a fun day and was yelling and swearing at his holder, a reserve running back. And, like the other previous holders, the running back preferred to be elsewhere and made sure Dempsey understood that fact.

As he readied for his next kick, Dempsey looked over at me, winked and said, *"Watch this. I'm gonna put him on the IR (injured reserve) list."*

Sure enough. He approached the holder and kicked high near the top of the ball and catching the hand and fingers of his holder with that steel stub. The impact was equal in force to having your hand laid out on a work bench, then slammed with a hammer. The man went down in a heap. At first, there were no sounds. Then, like in any injury, the brain's seven billion volts of electricity click, and the sensation begins erupting as pain traverses through the body.

As Dempsey walked past a group of writers, he said loud enough for all to hear, *"Told you so. Hell, he's only a dumb, fucking backup."* I didn't laugh. Just stood there, open-mouthed.

Just two weeks prior, I had been watching high school kids play soccer. Girls battling it out in the state field hockey tournament. Enjoyable. Exciting. Everything I saw as good in sports. Now, here I am at the Astrodome watching grown men playing football. At a practice! With nothing on the line. Acting in ways that left me in a rather confused state. Flummoxed, with a growing litany of doubts if, in my lifetime, I would ever truly find and understand my elusive and, as-yet defined, "Question of Balance."

You see, I could not tell you what I was looking for or specifically define a question of balance. What I could absolutely tell you after seeing five minutes of this Wednesday morning pro-football practice: It ain't this.

I quickly moved away from the action. I walked to a row of concession tables set out and adorned with food and drink for the writers and visitors. Unlike many of the others around me, I wanted no part of late morning and noontime alcohol. I needed coffee. There was a large urn and many smaller pots on hotplates.

A voice said, *"Here, let me pour. Say when. Cream or sugar!"*

The man was smallish in size. Almost childlike as a waif. Perhaps five feet tall. Maybe 100 pounds soaking wet. I thanked him. With a soft, polite voice, he asked if we could sit together and talk. I nodded OK. Together we walked to a bench along the sidelines, away from the practice, beyond one of the endzones.

I was polite. Yet curious. He said he wanted to talk with me. Had admitted that he picked me out of a crowd of almost 200 people. Yeah, I was curious.

He introduced himself as Warren. I said my name was Rob. He said my name was an honorable one. He offered me his hand. So tiny. Smaller than mine. I shook it. We exchanged small talk about the crazy practice and its antics. We talked about the unusual warm weather for Houston and how I came to be in town and here at the Astrodome.

We sat next to each other on the bench. Looked out over the panorama that was the Astrodome. We drank our coffee.

34

Honestly, I thought Warren was a tad strange.

He was not a sportswriter or an invited guest. He said he worked part-time jobs as a writer and editor and decided to come out to practice, searching for a little perspective on an article he was working on. To what subject he never said.

He looked out-of-place. The clothes he wore were too big for his homunculus-type body. His trousers seemed to wear him. Yet each pants leg held an ironed crease as sharp as a razor. You could see the holes that had been punched in his belt so he could pull it tighter around his hips. His cuffs dragging on the ground. His shirtsleeves were partially rolled up exposing wrists so small even my small hands would fit around them. One shoe was untied. The lace was broken. Over his shoulders and tied around his neck he carried a faded and moth-eaten light gray sweater.

His hair was reddish. Wispy and thinning. He was going bald. He had thinning, but evenly cut sideburns. A moustache that kinda looked like a little dead mouse. He was as innocuous as any Wednesday morning person could be.

Warren said he wanted to tell me a story. Yes, he had watched me as I made my way around practice. Said he believed he would be comfortable around me. I was a little surprised, but thought, that was OK. Not too weird. He gently touched my arm and in a soft voice told me he was gay. OK, perhaps now it's a little weird. I nodded saying I would listen. I could have said no...but that's not my style.

I refilled my coffee cup. Sat down next to him. And as the mayhem of a pro-football practice session went on around us, Warren took me on a ride with his story that to this day, I am still pensive and open-eyed when I recall the dramatic details and how this little man and his story would eventually affect so many in the world.

His story began five years earlier in spring 1972. He'd been a student at the University of Texas in Austin. He decided that was not the path he wanted to take, so he left school to begin a career experiencing real life skills and dramas. He wanted to better understand politics, especially Texas politics. He volunteered to do work in the camps of Republican and Democratic parties. Nice way to learn what it's like living on both sides of the street. Well, you know what I mean.

At one of Republican Senator John Tower's satellite offices in Austin, he used his typing skills and ability to edit and re-write. His edits were used by the office in press releases. He was good at wordsmithing the messy and confusing hens scratch that was the handwriting of those authoring the pages. His skills on the keyboards were unmatched. He used an old Olivetti manual typewriter but said he hated that two keys would often stick requiring corrections. He liked the old Royal, though the ink ribbons could be messy.

His preferred tool of production was one of the manual

grays. The Underwood and its smooth applications and what sounded like an almost sing-songy melodic tone of tapping as his small and wiry fingers flew over the keys. He was known to often achieve 60 to 70 words per minute with no mistakes. A secretary I had assigned to me working a project in Canada once referred to that level of production as *"typing that's teetering on hall of fame level."*

I had once typed 71 words per minute in a high school typing class...with 10 errors. I was your typical 35-40 words per minute typist for most of my career.

He would sit at the large table with other typists and work the pile from his *"In Basket."* Quickly, he would level a pile of various documents, usually reviewing his work with the production supervisor. On Wednesday, his day started out as usual. A large pile of documents in need of edits and updates. He was in his own words, *"A whirling dervish of passion and ability."* With that description he stopped his story and smiled. Took a big gulp of his coffee. Perhaps a bit of earned arrogance. I too smiled. I enjoyed the interlude.

He next grabbed a sheet of paper that was folded. He unfolded the document and set it up on his easel. It looked to be about 250 words. Written in a messy handwriting. Like when your doctor writes a prescription and you wonder how the pharmacist can read it. So, away he went, his fingers flying over the keys. Until he typed a line highlighted with the initials JT, which he assumed was John Tower. He consciously became aware of the words...

"...will not pay for the lifestyles of those faggots and lesbos..."

35

Warren stopped typing. Holy Shit! What had he stumbled onto? He didn't know it then, but that inter-office memo, that folded piece of faded yellowish paper, would soon become the uber of smoking guns.

Stunned, he sat frozen in his seat. He re-read the words...over and over. Like letters read by a forlorn soldier in a faraway land who has just received a *"Dear John"* letter from his lover. No matter how many times he reads the words, they do not change. The pain is real. He was disgusted with the words. The words made Warren feel small and insignificant. Like during his years growing up. Pushed and bullied in a world that had made him scared, angry...insignificant.

He ripped the page from his typewriter. Crumpled it up and stuffed it in his pocket. He re-folded the page and put it in his shirt pocket. He looked around the office to see if he was being watched. All were busy with their own wants and needs. Warren whimpered slightly as if ready to cry. He put his hand over his face, swallowed and choked back the sound. He cleared this throat, rose from his seat and headed for the door. Warren felt as if he was going to be sick to his stomach. He needed fresh air.

He walked a few blocks to a small park. A favorite lunchtime place for armies of white collar executives and secretaries working in the area. He sat alone and re-read the paper. The message referred to Senator Tower's supplement to Title IX. It mentioned revenues and expenses for multi-levels of women's athletics.

It was, in Warren's opinion, a loosely written note, ambiguous in structure. What he referred to as, *"A memo with holes, like a piece of swiss cheese."* An inter-office, hand-written note of communication. It included pencil-drawn icons with scribbled words, insertion marks and arrows at points where additional wording could be added. The memo appeared to be more a jumble of loose ideas than a first draft.

He believed it to have been intended as a personal memo between office directors. Perhaps thoughts from JT. Intended for their eyes only. Not to be in a pile of pool documents to be typed. It most likely got stuck to another sheet of paper. Like when new crisp bills in your wallet get stuck together. But, oh boy, this was your massive, *"screw the pooch"* in so many unsettling ways.

Warren's shock turned to anger. He decided to call a friend who worked at the university's, *The Daily Texan*. It took less than five minutes for the friend to call his contact at the city's daily rag, the *Austin American-Statesman*. All were members of an active and emerging gay and lesbian action group. One more call was made, bringing in two independent and trusted lawyers. One was gay, the other a lesbian.

By 6 PM it became obvious that the group had a golden nugget in their grasp. At 8 PM it was decided to confront the

Tower campaign office the following day for a definition of the memo. By 11 PM the group had its action plan and strategy ready to go. They would contact Senator Tower's office at 9 AM requesting a face-to-face meeting to be held at a neutral site.

Remembers Warren, *"It was, as one lawyer shouted, slamming her fist on the table, 'Game On!'"*

The call was made Thursday morning at 9:05 AM. A brief explanation for the call and supplemental actions were communicated to the office manager. The caller asked if the manager clearly understood the gravity of what had been said. Did she understand the next steps being requested. The manager, taking copious notes, said she understood, *"Clearly, concisely and completely."*

It was also inferred by the caller, *"We're not screwing around."*

The office manager walked into the Director's office during the early morning huddle meetings, opening the door without knocking. She was admonished by the Director for interrupting the meeting. She stood in the doorway, ashen faced and waved off the comments. A cigarette between her fingers. She took a deep drag on her filtered Marlboro cigarette, blew the smoke upward in a large cloud. She spoke slowly, in a monotone and cracking voice. Her words echoed like the banging on a kettle drum.

"We've got a big fucking problem!"

36

The Director waved off the call as a prank, saying the caller had nothing. The office manager then referred to the internal communication in question, as the "Fag-Les" memo. She said for all in the room to hear, *"Remember that one, boys!"*

The Director's jaw dropped. The room fell silent.

Over the next few hours, a series of phone calls between the two groups ensued. Tower's office made a list of arrogant requests and demands. All were rejected. Finally, a meeting between the groups was set up for 1 PM in the back room of an Austin city restaurant.

As expected, it was an uncomfortable environment. Tensions ran high, tempers were short. The senator's camp wanted to see, demanded to see, the alleged memo. The group emphatically said, no. The Director demanded a balance of agreements. Political symmetry. The group laughed and reminded him he was not in any position to demand or negotiate anything. Tower's camp pushed harder, trying to make a power play. They wanted, again demanded, a dually agreed-to contact to be in the possession of the Tower group. Threatened legal action. One of the woman lawyers laughed in the Director's face. Then restated her terms. It was to be unconditional surrender to the group's agenda, or they would go public with the memo.

"No goddammed way, bitch" snorted the Director.

The female lawyer had to be held back from going across the table. Pushing and shoving ensued. Cooler heads stepped in and prevailed. Tensions cooled, for a short while, then a new wave of verbal exchanges reached a fever pitch. Another of the group's lawyers pounded her fist on the table. *"Wake up assholes. This is not a game of tavern trivia. This is serious. You will agree to these terms or we go public,"* her voice rising with each word until she was screaming out her final utterances, just inches away from the Director's face as she pounded the table with her fist.

Warren, who was present at the meeting, remembered the heated exchange.

One of the lawyers later referred to that critical point in the meeting as, *"A real crotch grabber."*

It took another two hours. The political group eventually cowered. The Director hung his head. The gravity of their situation was now painfully clear. The Director agreed to and acquiesced to all demands. You could see it in his body language. He was a physically beaten man. Capitulation was his only defense. Otherwise, this situation was going to get way out of hand and go viral.

At 4 PM, and after a flurry of calls to Tower's legal team, the senator's protective posse agreed to all demands. Even the Senator's legal team felt handcuffed. The safest defense for them was not to go on the offense.

At 6 PM a written definition of what the "Fag-les" memo

really meant went through its final edit. The two groups working at another location completed the document, delivering the finished product to the restaurant meeting. The document was heavily wordsmithed, but enough of an admittance by Tower's office to the implications of the ethical and cultural crimes the memo posed.

By 9 PM a directive was sent via twix, an electromechanical device, a pre-cursor to today's email, from Tower's people in Texas, to the Federal offices in Washington saying, in four sentences, the Tower Supplemental Amendment to Title IX was being withdrawn from the proxy. A formal notice would be forthcoming within 72 hours.

All involved parties agreed no newspapers or news outlets would be notified of the private negotiations. That is, unless Tower reneged on the deal and went rogue in a backdoor power play. If that happened, every newspaper in the country with major readership would be issued the story as well as every major TV network. For Tower and his minions, it probably felt like walking around with a hand grenade in their pocket...with the pin pulled. As long as they held on to the handle and didn't release it from the fuse igniter, it wouldn't explode.

What we referred to in Vietnam as *"walking on eggshells."*

On the afternoon of New Year's Eve, 1972, the independent gay/lesbian group again met at the restaurant and toasted their efforts with bottles of imported Chablis and trays of food that were privately donated. Despite not being a drinker, Warren had a glass or two of wine. He said it made him feel silly.

He admitted he had no idea of the impact his efforts had set in motion. The impact to Title IX and the millions of people who, within weeks, and years, would ultimately be affected. To Warren it was a memo whose words made him angry and sad. So, he did something about it. He wanted to right what he knew was a wrong. The impact to his actions would be worldwide and immeasurable.

His story ended, Warren and I sat quietly. Coffee cup empty. Staring out over the now-emptying Astrodome. Practice had ended. I asked if he wished to share any names. He did not. I asked about the memo and the document admitting guilt. He assured me both had been notarized. All parties in attendance to the meeting were required to sign and date an accompanying document. Like a non-disclosure agreement. He said it was put into a standard business envelope, placed inside a safety deposit box in a bank. He did not share its location.

I asked about his signing the NDA yet telling me his story. Warren waved his hand in the air and shook his head saying, *"Rob, I'm way past that."*

I asked how he felt about his contributions to what had occurred. He pondered my question. *"Well...I know I did the right thing."* He added a few rather haunting words,

"I believe, somehow, it will eventually kill me!"

Geez, his answer was like a jab in the stomach. I wanted to say something. How much I admired his will. Before I could get any words out, he thanked me for my patience and for listening to his story. Yes, I was a stranger to him. Why did he pick me to hear his story? Maybe it's just one of those odd, quirky things. He saw something in me, something he trusted. Believed I was a good and honest man with ethics.

I managed to say thanks. Said I thought that I was a good guy, though I could be a real bastard at times. He looked out over the now-empty field. Then, he turned and looked at me, his eyes burned into mine. *"Well, sometimes, Rob, I can be a real bitch."*

For about 10 seconds we stared at each other, then we both just busted into gut-wrenching laughter. He hugged me. I nodded. We turned and walked away in different directions. I never saw him after that day.

With practice over, I walked into the bowels of the Dome.

My mind wildly spinning with thoughts. I spied coach Phillips alone in his office. I knocked. He waved me in. Before I asked any questions, Phillips drained his glass and said, *"That goddamned Pastorini. Can't keep his mouth shut. Can't keep his hog in his pants. Can't play football either. And Dempsey. He's a numbnuts with a steel foot for a brain. And me, I can't keep my mouth shut,"* as he lifted another glass of that aged bourbon and drained it.

I asked about Sunday's game against Denver. Said Phillips refilling his glass. *"We're gonna lose. Cause we ain't ready to play."* I laughed as I left his office. That bottle of bourbon was probably empty before I got outside the Dome and found a cab to the Summit for the hockey game.

That evening at the Summit the Whalers and Aeros skated to a 3-3 OT tie. Howe did not score his 1000th goal. I thought about Warren and his riveting story. Admittedly, I didn't feel sorry for him, or understand his deep anguish and pain. But dealing with my own personal pains, I did believe his agony and frustrations were very real.

During the flight back to Hartford, I shared the story from the Astrodome with Whalers' players, George Lyle and Jim Mayer. Lyle said Warren told me the story because he liked and trusted me. He knew I wouldn't abuse or misuse the information.

Mayer had an interesting observation. He believed that Warren perceived me as a kindred spirit. Like someone he wanted to look like or be. He sensed both of us shared similar beliefs. I was somebody who would do the right thing. Because of those strong beliefs, he wanted me to have that information. To do with it whatever I chose to do. Whenever and wherever I felt it would be a benefit to people to do so.

Those two observations scared me. Not so much for their words. More for the responsibility that accompanied it. The privileged information I was entrusted with.

On Sunday, the Denver Broncos used a late Norris Weese

TD run and did beat the Oilers, 24-14 in front of a half-filled Astrodome. Pastorini played badly. Dempsey wasn't used because during pre-game warm-ups he repeatedly missed field goal attempts from 30 yards out. Another story reported he was hung over. The backup running back was not available to play because of his broken hand and wrist from being kicked by Dempsey in practice. Bum Phillips was right on. The Oilers weren't ready to play.

It was 12 years later I found that kindred spirit, the one Jimmy Mayer said I shared with Warren, when I least expected it.

Ironically, I was back in Houston. I was working a consulting project for Phillips Petroleum in the fall of 1989. Delivering a management training program that I had developed for Phillips' worldwide offices. One of the attendees was a man named Ronnie. Somehow, through a series of innocuous conversations, Ronnie made the connection. During a break near the end of the training he approached me and said, *"You...you're the Rob my friend Warren spoke with at the Astrodome."*

Boy, did that catch me off guard. We were both dumb-struck.

Ronnie shared with me that Warren had died in 1988. Complications from Aids. He had stayed active and worked right up to three days before he died. He worked, passionately, behind the scenes for gay and lesbian rights organizations. He never lost interest in learning Texas politics, and, as Ronnie shared with me, he sometimes would mention me and our brief time together in the Astrodome twelve years earlier.

Warren had been right that day in 1977. He would never see or know the true impact his actions and effects had on Title IX and people worldwide. His anonymous contributions to the world because one day, he found a wrong and tried to make it right.

Perhaps in one of those eerie ways the passions he had for his beliefs really did end up killing him.

Part 4

1973

"The First Tournament"

37

The 1973 CIAC girls' invitational field hockey tournament begins in what can only be described as a state of abstract anonymity.

Like when you're having a beer and say to a friend, *"Hey, the girls' tournament starts today."*

And, the response is, *"Terrific. Ah, what tournament might that be?"*

I was sitting in my apartment working out my schedule for the up-coming week. Where my travels would take me. To soccer tournaments. Cross-country events. Football games. A plan allowing me to see upwards of 30 to 40 events over the next eight days. Including games in the first-ever girls' field hockey tournament.

It was after 11 PM when my phone rang. I knew before I answered the call. It was either: another late-night threat.

Folks who didn't like me or did not share my enthusiasm for covering girls' sports. Or it might be a call from the *Hartford Courant* asking me about field hockey. The *Courant* did not cover girls' games. I had promised the editor, the late Owen Canfield, I would provide information when his folks called. I enjoyed talking with Bo Kolinsky. He appreciated the help, and we always had good conversations. Unlike Woody Anderson, who had the attitude that he was doing me a favor when he called, and I owed it to him. Even with my information, Woody still managed to get it wrong!

If the call was one of the many threats, I found it best to listen to the caller. It was 1973 and for some, change was new, scary and hard to understand and digest. For me the question was more of—hey, it's 1973, way past time for change. If I hung up too soon, they'd just continue calling me back many times.

I got these calls every night. A husky male voice telling me not to cover girls' sports. If I continued to do so it would be hazardous to my health. I would thank the person for calling, and in a dulled voice, wish them good luck, especially on their diet. Perhaps not the best of parting words.

Ironically, I even got calls from girls whose language was downright nasty, explaining to me, in a visceral way, they didn't care for me invading their world and told me what they

Rob Penfield in 1973 Simsbury at Granby Game

would do to me in a rather descriptive and detailed manner. Hey, I was long past worrying about these types of calls and believed those people were more afraid of me than I was of them. Of course, in today's world the FBI would most likely be involved using the technologies of skip-tracing, psychological profiling, cloud access and wiretapping. During those early years, I kept a loaded sawed-off shotgun next to my bed. Like

I said, Vietnam and its memories never go away.

The calls told me in a weird and unusual way my efforts covering sports in the Farmington Valley were having a positive effect. At the *Herald* it was business as usual. The Managing Editor, Rosa Matesky, who was from Canton, told me that since the first week of school, mail-out subscriptions to the *Herald* had increased by 2000. Stores selling the paper off the racks had been selling out and had doubled their weekly orders. I had no idea of the impact my sports coverage was having in the Farmington Valley.

Tournament play begins with teams ranked 27 through 38 required to play in what everybody is trying to avoid referring to as *"Play-in Games."*

That's exactly what they are. Twelve teams—six games. Win and you earn a spot in one of the six remaining openings in the first round of 32 teams. Each of those six play-in winners having now paired against one of the top six seeded teams in the state. It truly was one of those non-refundable, self-fulfilling prophecies. Where your rewards for winning your game become punishment for that very success.

Nothing about any one of the six play-in games would be simple or easy. In fact, these six games would establish a baseline of performance, uniqueness and endurance that would resonate throughout the remainder of the tournament. Literally, one of those classic, *"Who Knew!"*

Due to tight scheduling with little, or in most cases, no wiggle room for rescheduling, the first two tournament games are played Friday. E.O. Smith High School, located on the UConn campus and ranked 29th, travels to Amity Regional in Woodbridge, to take on 36th ranked Enfield High School. Sally Nelson's 6-3-3 Panthers are a slight favorite over the 5-3-3 Eagles of Cookie Bromage.

Smith's Amy Witryol scores a first half goal on an assist from Wendy Chapman. The teams settle into a defensive struggle. Smith wins the opener 1-0, holding off a furious

Enfield rally in the final minutes. The Eagles fire a dozen shots at Smith's goalie. Enfield's sophomore, Sue Herter, has the best shot at tying the game, but her blast from the top of the circle hits the goal post and goes out-of-bounds with 30 seconds remaining. The win earns E.O. Smith a first-round berth against fourth-ranked Cheshire. The first ever, CIAC girls' field hockey tournament game is now in the books.

A small article trumpeting Smith's win appears both in *UConn's Daily Campus* and in the *Willimantic Chronicle*. Nelson assures readers her team will be ready for Cheshire, winners of the Housatonic League crown. No words of attribution for accomplishments and performance of Bromage's Eagles will appear in the *Enfield Press*.

Instead of a season's summation for the Eagles and its field hockey accomplishments, a one column story with two-deck headline, 18-point Badoni Bold typeface, appears. Instead of a game review, the six-inch story, right there, in the middle of the sports page announces an upcoming and free open-house lecture on venereal disease.

Lewis Mills High School in Burlington serves as host for a play-in game between 31st ranked Simsbury and 34th ra

Simsbury's Kent Walton Firing a Shot vs North Haven

nked North Haven. Another of those games that on paper appears to be evenly matched. The 6-4-2 Indians of Betsy Gilmartin are a slight favorite coming off wins over Lyman Hall and East Haven. They feature three all-league performers in Mary Loveless, Lisa Petrillo and one of the best in the state in Jackie Cipollini.

Joan Sullivan's Trojans are 5-4-3. They are improved over their final four games with the insertion of four fiery sophomores into the lineup and still led by Kent Walton and the defense spearheaded by Pat Hoskin. Simsbury, though, is still smarting from its scoreless tie with Granby just two days earlier. And, hungry for revenge. A win over North Haven puts them in a first-round rematch at Granby. The coach and every girl on that Simsbury team knew what was on the line.

Co-captains Walton and Holly Burk give impassioned pre-game pep talks, urging teammates to give everything they had. They want another shot at Granby. Especially Walton, whose emotional words find their mark. She is a whirlwind of action during play, controlling the center of the field, scoring twice in the first half for a 2-0 lead. The spirited defense of Hoskin, Mary Ann DePattie and Sue Marshall, takes over and shuts down the Indians and Cipollini. Goalie Elaine Marcil turns away just three second half shots.

Standing along the sideline watching the game is Mills coach, Linda Hamm. Referring to Simsbury she says for all to hear, *"That's a very dangerous team."* Pressed further Hamm adds, *"I believe the winner of the Simsbury-Granby game will win the state championship."*

When Linda Hamm spoke, you listened. When she made a prediction, you could bet the farm on it. I chuckled thinking that maybe it was Hamm who established Granby's pre-season line on the Las Vegas and Reno betting boards. Honestly, I was too scared to ask for fear she just might say it was her and that she had won a bundle.

Simsbury had re-found that magic and now had another date at Granby. Remembers Granby coach, Dot Johnson, hearing about Simsbury's win. *"We knew what was coming. It was not going to be a friendly contest. This was going to be the toughest game we would play in my five years at Granby."*

Joan Sullivan did not wait around to talk with reporters. Like her players, she hustled onto the big yellow Mack Special school bus owned and operated by Salter's Express on West Street. She began preparing for Granby on their bus ride back to Simsbury. A rematch with their hated rival just nine miles up Routes 10 & 202, along the banks of Salmon Brook.

A third play-in game took place on Friday at Joel Barlow High School in Redding. Waterford High, ranked 32nd, came into the game with a 6-4-1 mark against a 5-3-4 team from Madison, 33rd ranked Daniel Hand High.

Vivian Novicki's Waterford Lancers were a potent offensive threat bringing with them the state's leading scorer, Jan Merrill. She had recorded 24 goals including a nine-goal, one assist game vs Valley Regional. They also had a 10-goal scorer in halfback Joan Van Ness. The team had scored over 40 goals during the regular season. Daniel Hand had scored just 20 goals. They had good front line players in Cheryl Floyd and Kim Punzelt. Their strength was their defense led by Leigh Hudson, co-captains Cindy Horn and Carol Ehrenfreund.

On paper this game should be a blowout by the high-flying Lancers from Waterford, home to the famous 3/8th mile stock car track on Route 85 known as the Speed Bowl. Where the hordes of vacationers from the Rhode Island beaches pack the speedway for Saturday night shows enjoying the exploits of veteran chauffers, Wild Bill Slater, Dick Beauregard, Red Bolduc and Ted Stack.

Waterford was also the hometown of former major league baseball player and manager, Billy Gardner. But, just like the unpredictability of those hot summer nights at the Speed Bowl, or of the ups and downs of a major league career, so too was this play-in game of field hockey. That's why the game is played on a field and not in the newspapers.

Merrill got loose, ten minutes into the opening half scoring an unassisted goal for a 1-0 Waterford lead. Daniel Hand's defense then shut the door, frustrating Merrill's gang of marauders into a defensive game. With Horn and Ehrenfreund repelling Waterford's rushes, goalie Karen Jessey kicked away a dozen shots. But Hand's offense had few shots at Waterford's net. Merrill, assisted by Van Ness, scored her second goal in the game's final minute for a 2-0 win. The

Lancers had now won their way into a first-round game against Guilford, the top ranked team.

Daniel Hand's coach, Wili Roze lamented, *"Geez, we play our best damn game of the year and lose."*

After only three games it was already a memorable tournament. The intensity of the games noticeably ramped up. Emotions running much higher than regular season rival games. This is what the tournament was going to be. One and done for the losing teams. An impact and stress level brand new to so many who thought post-season would be the same as a regular season game. Elimination. It was sudden and it was painful.

Joan Sullivan had commented to me, *"Just the thought of playing one game with a chance of being eliminated scares the hell out of me."* I knew for a fact she was not alone. Even if the others cared not to admit it.

It scared the hell out of lots of coaches.

38

I remember my 82-year-old Aunt Fay saying, *"Do not piss off mother nature. No matter what you do to protect yourself, she always wins."*

We've all heard those wonderful cliches about the New England weather. You know, just wait a minute or blink your eyes and it will change. While serving at Fort Sill I worked for a major who was from Bristol, Connecticut. When the Oklahoma weather got nasty, he'd make some comment like, *"Boy, did she get a tack up her ass on this one."* I never really understood his word association, but, as a Nutmegger, he certainly did get his point across when turning a quirky phrase.

Remember...nothing good ever lasts. Including the weather.

As wonderful as the late fall weather had been, change is

inevitable. During the early morning hours of Sunday, it turned on everyone, like those cold chinook winds that blow down the Canadian Rockies across the Alberta and Saskatchewan plains dropping temperatures 50 degrees in four hours.

The cold front swept down from Canada. Across the upper regions of Wisconsin and Michigan, across northern Pennsylvania and New York. Fully enveloping the areas of western Massachusetts and Connecticut. I grew up hearing the old-timers in Simsbury refer to this weather as, *"The Montreal Express."*

Nobody could have seen this coming. Not the weather forecasters on the local TV stations from New Haven to Springfield. Not the farmers who read the annual Almanac and failed to get the last hay harvest in the barns before the storm. Nor coaches or sports prognosticators. Not even those idiots who fool with Ouija boards thinking that it's just a toy. Not a fingertip-driven vehicle into another dimension. By Monday, skies had that ominous milky white look to them. The omen of rain and snow. The high temperatures for the day hovered around the freezing mark. It was cold and nasty.

Three more play-in games were scheduled. In an unlikely way these three play-in games, in weather unsuitable for war, would stamp a sense of legitimacy on this first-ever tournament. A post-season event that started in anonymity and fighting for its identity, was now at war with Mother Nature. Despite the wicked-bad weather and field conditions, they would become games for the ages.

Bethel High School was the host. The Monday game was between 29th ranked New Milford and Terryville, the 38th and lowest ranked team in the tournament. Coached by Fran Zaloski the 6-3-2 New Milford Green Wave came into the game slightly favored over the Kangaroos of Nancy Neuman at 6-4.

For all accounts this should have been a predictable game.

From the onset, nothing about this game was predictable. It would take on a life of its own. It would not reach a conclusion for almost 27 hours. The game would send a message to all, coaches and teams, that the pressure and intensity of tournament games is a whole different animal than the regular season.

New Milford and Terryville. Each has a core of good players. Both are limited in star-quality players and depth. The offenses like to attack straight into the jaws of their opponent's defense. Both teams like to play the game in the middle of the field using a standard 5-3-2 formation. A basic meat and potatoes style of field hockey.

Terryville struggled defensively in late season games. To compensate for the leaky defense, coach Neumann applies what I refer to as a "Scrunch Defense." She pulls her team's defensive lanes in tighter, bunching her players together near mid-field like a crowded school hallway. This approach leaves the sidelines unprotected. Daring opponents to attack the wings. New Milford is a straight-ahead attack team and will play into the Kangaroos' defensive formation for most of the game.

Early in the opening half, Kim Konapaske and Patty Reynolds combined on a give-and-go score. Terryville takes a 1-0 advantage. In the waning moments of the half penalty, corners give the Green Wave the advantage and LaDonna Bierbower ties the score at 1-1, beating goalie Wendy Watkins who had been bumped out of position by one of her own fullbacks.

The weather continued to worsen. Rain fell harder...the wind howled. The second half became a defensive struggle. Terryville's Melanie Kopcha led a spirited defensive stand. At the other end of the field New Milford's Sue Hess was a defensive roadblock, as was goalie JoAnn Olsen. Regulation time ended in a 1-1 deadlock.

Head official Jeannette Arnold notifies each coach the

game will go on as long as it takes to produce a winner. With the variance in the protocols as to how games would be decided, Arnold and her officiating partner, Carol Robertson, agree. This game will be won on the scoreboard with goals. Not in the scorebooks by penalty corners.

Five sudden death overtimes ensue.

In the end it's Mother Nature who wins the day as darkness prevails. In the 50 minutes of additional hockey the two teams combine for a paltry seven shots on goal. Remembers Laurie Center, senior halfback and motivational leader for New Milford, *"We played the last two overtime periods in darkness. Not dusk. Darkness!"*

She recalled the girls had to call out to each other announcing where they were so as not to collide on the field or hit someone with their stick. Center is tall, strong and fast, and towers over teammates. She also wears a football-like helmet. Protection for a subdural hematoma, a childhood head injury. For Laurie Center, darkness just adds another degree of danger.

The game is called at 6 PM. A decision would be made by the CIAC, with input from the game officials, how to complete the game. At 10 PM, both coaches are notified the game will be replayed beginning at 3 PM the next day in Brookfield. The weather forecast. Wind, rain and snow with temps in the low 30's.

Lee Hough had been New Milford's leading scorer during the regular season. She had been shut out by the Terryville defense and would now have to again go up against that scrunch defense. She remembered thinking of the huge task of having to play another game…just to get into the first round. *"Another full game. A real task. We were not depressed, but it was working on our minds. We were blown away."*

For New Milford's goalie, JoAnn Olsen, it was a simple observation. *"My job is to stop goals. To win the game we need to score goals."* During the ensuing bus rides Coach Zaloski made sure all involved knew and clearly understood the tasks at hand.

Laurie Center took it personally. She felt as if she had let her teammates down. Did not play a good game. It burned inside her as she hungered for the next day's action.

39

Avon and Coginchaug High Schools were scheduled for a play-in game. They have little in common. The schools are located 50 miles apart. Play in different conferences with no overlapping opponents. The 6-3-1 Blue Devils are coached by Deb Haggerty. Bonnie Tyler coaches the Avon Falcons who finish the season at 7-4. A record that raises a few eyebrows when the committee does not award Avon a first-round game.

Avon has a bonified all-state player in Heidi Zacchera and a respected defense.

Coginchaug has a few all-conference nominees. The coaches play different styles, both on offense and defense. About the only thing each team has in common—they both wear the colors blue and white. What they will have in common on this day—both will play in weather that normally would cancel most games.

The Avon-Coginchaug game will take two days to play. They will play 120 minutes of regulation time. Another 60 minutes of sudden-death overtime. Neither team will lose this game on the scoreboard. Both will lose this game in the confusing protocols that are the politics of obstructions. Coginchaug will be declared the winner advancing to the first round.

This contest should have been decided on day-one with Avon the winner. Instead, a simple bookkeeping error, from the Coginchaug scorekeeper would change the outcome. Lead official Karen Schlott notifies the teams she will check scorebooks for compliance and correctness after each period. If there is no winner on the scoreboard after regulation time, three sudden-death overtime periods will ensue. If no goals are scored the winner will be determined by the team having the highest number of short-corner penalty strokes.

Schlott's communication for game protocols are clear to all involved. Both coaches nod their approval. All seems simple enough. So, what could go wrong? Well, about everything that could go wrong, did.

Game action is sloppy. The weather is affecting the quality of play. The Blue Devils from Durham get an early goal from Lynn Johnson and hold a 1-0 lead at halftime. Schlott, as promised, checks each scorebook for the recorded number of corners. Schlott, who keeps her own running total, has a 4-3 advantage for Avon in her small note pad. She confirms that total in the Avon book. The Coginchaug book also has a 4-3 count. But the advantage is for the Durham school. Not Avon.

She declares both books, null and void for penalty strokes. She notifies each coach the game will have to be won on the scoreboard by goals. Just before the start of the second half, both scorekeepers are seen in tears. Schlott bangs her hand on the table and is heard to say, *"Suck it up, Ladies. No time for that shit. Time to play."*

Avon takes immediate control in the second half and Heidi

Zacchera has numerous opportunities to score. In the waning moments of regulation time Karen Poirier muscles through a crowd and beats goalie Linda Stahl on a hard shot for a 1-1 tie.

Five overtimes are played.

Each team has many chances for a winning goal, but every shot is rejected by strong goaltending from Stahl and Avon's Mary Ann Hollfelder. As the fifth OT period comes to an end, the game is called due to darkness.

Remembers Blue Devils goalie, Stahl, *"Coach was walking the sideline. Waving her arms. I could tell she was upset."*

Stahl and her teammates later learned that in the waning seconds Schlott told coach Haggerty the game would most likely have to be replayed tomorrow. When Stahl hears the news, she remembers how she felt. *"Crushed. I had let in the goal. Let my teammates down. It was my fault."*

The Avon scorekeeper continued to mark corner hits knowing it will have no impact on the outcome. Had the books balanced during Schlott's audits, Avon would have won the game on corners with an advantage of 12-8. Instead, the Falcons would now play another full game on Tuesday. Most likely, in the snow.

Both scorekeepers would go on to graduate from college with honors.

40

The sixth and final play-in game was also played on Monday. Stamford beat Newington 1-0 in Woodbridge, advancing into the first round. The game winning goal was scored in the seventh sudden-death overtime period. The game ended in total darkness.

Sue Mahalik scored the winner for the Black Knights in what became known as *"The Goal in the Gloaming!"* Due to the darkness, it's unsure who assisted on the winning score. It's believed left inner, Cindy Sennewald made the pass after stumbling over the ball that was sitting idle in the darkness at the top of the scoring circle. It was just sitting there. All by itself. Nobody could see it, so nobody played it.

Following the winning score, a few of the Newington players engaged in an emotional shouting match with the official saying the pass had been made with the backside of the stick. The official said that she saw the play and the results were final. The exchange was heated, punctuated with words like, *"You Bitch"* and *"You're an Asshole."* The official was challenged by Newington players that she could not have seen the play as she was over 50 feet away from the action that took place in total darkness. She was also accused of being out of the play on the far sideline, smoking a cigarette in the darkness.

Remembers Stamford fullback, Toni Rinaldi, *"It was surreal. Playing in total darkness. I couldn't see my team-mates. Had no idea where the ball was on the field. At times, I didn't know where I was on the field."*

Lisa Meucci of Newington remembers the idiocy of it all. Running head-on into her own players. Meucci also recalled one of those incidents of gallows humor. *"One of our girls thought she was moving up-field with the ball on her stick. Calling out to us. It wasn't the ball...it was a soda bottle."*

Some players used packs of matches, lighting them to let teammates know where they were on the field. Others used Bic lighters being handed out by a man who identified himself as a salesman from the Bic manufacturing facility in Milford. It looked like an army of fireflies had descended on the field. Even fans were flicking their Bics.

As the seventh overtime period began the Newington goalie began screaming for her coach. Coach Karen Erlandson ran the length of field, straining her eyes into the darkness trying to pick up the outline of her goalie silhouetted from parking lot lights almost 500 away. Erlandson yelled, *"What's up!"* The goalie hollered back, *"I can't see the ball. I can't see the damn ball. I'm scared."*

Erlandson cupped her hands around her mouth and hollered back, *"Pick up your fullback. Follow her moves."* A few seconds of silence ensued. Then, a terrified voice shrilly cut through the darkness. *"I can't see the goddammed fullback, either."*

The obstructions of another ilk. Mihalik's goal 45 seconds later, ended the pain, anticipation and the marathon. Just another kind of darkness of the day.

Memories are stark reminders of joy and pain. Often triggered by visuals, physical feelings, sounds or smells. The memory I retain from that day is the pain of the post-battle. The Newington goalie crying. Sobbing loudly. Having to be helped by teammates to stay upright. Helping her walk to the bus in the darkness. Her body laden with the weight of her pads and chest protector. Stumbling in her clownish protective outer shoes. Clutching her field hockey stick with both hands.

As I walked to my car I couldn't see well in the darkness, but I could feel the anguish as it rippled through me. I sat in my car letting the bus traffic out ahead of me. I turned up the volume on my radio. Barry McGuire gutted out the words to "Eve of Destruction." Again, I felt that familiar pain I had come to associate with war. Nobody wins. You just hope to survive a little longer.

41

Two play-in games required a second day of action. New Milford against Terryville. Avon and Coginchaug. When it was over the four teams had played the equivalent of almost four full games.

On day two, New Milford beat Terryville. This time they did it on the scoreboard, 2-0 advancing to the first round.

In the return match with Terryville, it turned out to be the strategy changes by coach Fran Zaloski that turned the tide for the Green Wave. Instead of attacking straight ahead into the Kangaroos' bunched defense, New Milford spread the field, widening the gaps in their 5-3-2 attack. Terryville did not adapt to New Milford's changes.

The ringleader was center halfback, Laurie Center. Still smarting and upset over her play from the day before, she broke out from a group at midfield, hitting co-captain Lee

Lee Hough of New Milford Scoring vs Terryville

Hough with a perfect pass. Hough bull-rushed into the scoring circle and scored for a quick 1-0 lead just five minutes into the game.

Center and Hough combined for another goal late in the first half for a 2-0 lead. Terryville never came close to scoring. Fullback Sue Hess warded off the few attacks that came inside their 25-yard line. Goalie JoAnn Olsen had to make only five saves in the game.

Remembers Center, *"Terryville was a completely different team the second game. Not as aggressive. Not as quick. They seemed to be confused and out-of-sync. We didn't want any part of another overtime game."*

Recalled goalie Olsen, *"It was lonely in the goal. Nobody came near me. Sue (Hess) stopped everybody. It was a great feeling."* It was now off to the first round for the green and white.

Avon and Coginchaug could not settle the deal. Nobody won. Not on the scoreboard. And it's never been accurately determined if they won the game in the scorebook, either. In the end, everybody lost. It would be Coginchaug's Blue Devils who would go onto the first round.

Following their 1-1, five overtimes game the day before, both teams looked sluggish. The weather did not help. Howling winds with rain and snow. The 35-degree temps contributed to the misery.

The girls from Durham got scores from Lynn Johnson and Kathy Fowler, but the defense could not stop Avon's all-state performer, Heidi Zacchera, who scored twice in the second half to knot the game at 2-2. Now, a second day of overtime periods was about to begin.

Officials had notified the teams three sudden-death OT

periods would be used if necessary. If no OT goals were scored the winner would be decided by the total number of penalty corner strokes amassed during regulation and overtime periods. Only, on this day the lead official, Karen Schlott, for a reason never disclosed, chose not to audit scorebooks after each period. Said a fan along the sideline, *"Too many accountants spoil the balance sheet."*

Following the third and final OT stanza with the game tied 2-2, the penalty corner count was made. Coginchaug was declared the winner by out-pointing Avon in penalty corners, 11-10. The Avon scorebook had the count at 10-10. Head official Schlott who was keeping her own tally, also had the count at 10-10. Since Coginchaug was designated as the home team for the second game, their scorebook was the official count. In the end, nobody won. Everybody lost.

Avon's Bonnie Tyler stood speechless. Hands on her hips. Head slumped forward as her team limped to their bus, she sighed, *"Really a lousy way to lose a game."*

Deb Haggerty gently tapped the scoring table and said with a pained face, *"Really a lousy way to win."*

Tension. Stress. Another conspiracy for Avon. Tournament magic. Hell, these were just the play-in games! Skirmishes. The real war was about to get underway.

42

With the wild and unpredictable play-in games finally completed, the 32 team, 16 game first round is finally ready to get underway.

Pat Mascia's headache just kept getting worse. Planned schedules for the next rounds had been dramatically affected. Two-day games, like the ones experienced in the play-in round, cannot be tolerated during the ensuing rounds. Scheduled wiggle room is already used up. Mascia and her committee begin making procedural adjustments on the fly. Lots of late-night phone calls are being made to game officials, timekeepers, on-site support folks and to many of the long-time coaches in the state.

Rules, procedures, and protocols applied by game officials are adjusted into a quasi-standardized approach. Officials are given a wider vista of authorization to call, or not to call violations that are slight, or ticky-tacky. Latitudes are given allowing extra OT periods, only if daylight permits. Or fewer OT periods if so determined by officials. No OTs can begin after 5:45 PM. Rest time between OT periods is dropped from four minutes to two.

Scorebooks will now ultimately determine the winner of a tournament game. Timekeepers will be allowed to keep a clock moving in the case of a minor injury if instructed to do so by officials. If a game starts more than 20 minutes late, only one OT period will be allowed. If it's 30 minutes late, no overtime periods will be played. The bullet-pointed list to expedite games is carried over to a second page.

The Gestalt for all the changes. No game will end without a winner on that day of the game. Even if a contest is to be decided by penalty shots. A last result not favored by most coaches, officials and the CIAC committee. The unofficial instructions to all officials, *"Make sure winners are determined, on the scheduled day of the game."*

Mascia also carries the responsibility to prepare and coach her Amity team in an opening round game against visiting Litchfield the next day.

It seems only appropriate that the top ranked team, Guilford High School, should get the early start on Tuesday hosting Vivian Novicki's Waterford team with a mark of 7-4-1 following its play-in win. The Lancers boast the state's leading scorer in Jan Merrill.

The host Grizzlies, coached by Becky Clomp and the Shoreline Conference Champs, stood at 10-0-1, outscoring opponents 50-3. Their lineup is loaded with all-state and all-conference selections. They are a formidable team.

Guilford's coach, Clomp, remembered, *"Here I am, 22 years old and the coach of an exceptionally good team. Just out of college, I am only a few years older than the girls I am coaching. I had not thought much about the tournament. Suddenly, I had to be an adult."*

217

Waterford gave Guilford all they could handle. The game is a scoreless tie with eight minutes remaining in regulation time. The visiting Lancers hold a 9-7 advantage in penalty corner hits. Lindsay Taylor scored for the home team getting a tap back from Dawn Sprague off a penalty corner. The number one ranked Grizzlies led 1-0.

Still, Leslie Gribus in goal has to make two spectacular saves thwarting a Merrill shot with two minutes remaining and a final save off a rising shot from the top of the circle by Joan Van Ness in the final 30 seconds.

Center forward Mary Bunting remembered Waterford. *"They were better than we expected. That Merrill was a handful. We double-teamed her and she still found ways to get free. We'd guard her close, but we'd turn our head for a few seconds...and she was gone."*

The win moves Guilford into the second round.

Down the road from Guilford about 17 miles east, an old friend from the Shoreline Conference, eighth ranked Westbrook under coach Gail Perzanoski, opened tournament play hosting 25th ranked Watertown. The host Knights had a regular season mark of 10-1-1. Their only loss, a heartbreaking 3-2 thriller to Guilford. The visiting Indians of coach Mary Wollenberg arrived with a 7-3-3 mark led by co-captains Rita Johnson and Sylvia Ledell.

Westbrook, like Guilford, had a skilled lineup and a powerfully strong scoring line. Rae Hirst and Tammy Husted were proven goal scorers. Lynn Clements and Sue Hubbard anchored the wings, and center halfback Chris Rackcliffe's skills were known and respected throughout the conference.

First half goals from Laura Neri and Rae Hirst and a shutdown defense led by fullback Libby Cormier overwhelms the visitors. Lynn Clements added a second half score and goalie Rose Weisse kicked away seven shots en route to a 3-0 win for Westbrook and onto the second round.

Farmington's tournament encounter was a road trip to

Fairfield for a game against Roger Ludlowe, the 21st ranked team. Pat Small's Falcons were stumbling at mid-season with a 2-3 mark and coming off two tough losses to Staples and New Canaan. They regrouped and blitzed through their final five games, outscoring opponents 15-1 behind the scoring of Betsy Thurmond, co-captains Sue Morrison and Carol Bonney and the play of goalie Leigh Coulter. It was Coulter's spirited play between the posts that allowed just one goal during the month of October.

Jean Hunt's 12th ranked Indians of the Northwest Conference completed the regular season at 7-2-3. But the tough end-of-season schedule against tournament-bound teams was costly. Especially in a tie with Granby when three players were injured and two more hurt against Avon.

The Indians came into the game banged up with a variety of injuries to key players. Loretta DiPietro was hobbling on a bad leg and a sore back. Peggy Streich had an injured shoulder. Patty Lavoie was playing on bad knees. Missy Saxton, Farmington's goalie, had so many injuries she did not know which one to complain about.

On a wet and muddy field, Ludlowe dominated the game from the opening bully to the final whistle. Sue Morrison and Betsy Thurmond scored first half goals. Carol Bonney added a second half score. Coulter kicked away just six shots. Ludlowe's Blue and Silver had a 3-0 win and a spot in the second round.

"Worst damn game we played in five years," was the response from Jean Hunt.

If it was not the weather that caused issues, it had to be, and usually was, issues with transportation. The bus or traffic problems.

En route to Joel Barlow High School in Redding, CT for a game against Brookfield, the bus carrying the Nonnewaug girls from Southbury experienced mechanical trouble, arriving 10 minutes after the scheduled start time. Game officials announced that no overtime periods would be played due to the late arrival. A winner would be determined in regulation time, either by outscoring their opponent on the scoreboard or out-pointing them with penalty corners in the scorebook. Maybe...penalty shots if it came to that. That decision was now controlled by the lead official.

Joan Bulmer's 10th ranked Chiefs brought a record of 7-0-4 in the tournament against Cyndie Adamski's 6-3-2 Bobcats. Center Carol Wright scored for Nonnewaug off a penalty corner midway through the opening half for a 1-0 lead. The defense led by Carol Cassidy and play from Liz George and goalie Kathy Deer made it stand as the Berkshire League Champs moved into the second round.

The lead official for the game was the late Charlotte Gallagher. When asked what she would have done had there been a tie both on the scoreboard and scorebook, and no overtime periods would be played, she replied, *"Don't have a clue how we'd resolve the outcome."*

Someone in the crowd commented, *"That's like playing Russian Roulette with a loaded gun."*

Gallagher's response to the quip. She held two fingers against her head and yelled, **"BANG...I'M DEAD!"**

During the return trip to Southbury the bus again had mechanical issues but did make it the 23 miles to the high school to drop the team off at the gym. On the four-mile drive from the school to the municipal lot, the motor died, the driver leaving the vehicle on the front lawn of a neighborhood home. Early the following morning it was towed to the local town garage for repairs.

Shepaug Valley and Windsor Locks meet at Lewis Mills in Burlington in what Shepaug fullback, Liddy Adams, remembers as, *"A very cold, snowy and windy day. We wore our skirts and light jerseys. Most of us had no gloves or sweats. Windsor Locks did wear gloves and sweats."*

The Raiders of coach Cindy Wilson were 13th ranked and

riding a seven-game unbeaten string. At Shepaug, Sandy Bruegger had taken over the reins from Joan Gauthey who was on sabbatical. The Spartans were ranked 20th and stood at 6-3-2 for the season.

Windsor Locks' Senior co-captain Marie Duwell scored twice in the opening half. Early in the second half, Sue MacDonell scored the lone Shepaug goal. Raider's goalie, JoAnne Michalewicz kicked away 10 shots. Windsor Locks held on for a 2-1 win and moved into the next round. Shepaug's Jaye Alex Stuart remembers, *"It was cold. Like the other girls, I just kept moving during the game trying to stay warm."*

Added Adams, *"Even the bus ride back to Washington Depot was cold."*

Cheshire was 4th ranked and opened tournament play at home against 29th ranked E.O. Smith, who had won their play-in game against Enfield. The Rams, champions of the Housatonic League, stood at 11-0-1. Coached by Arlene Salvati, Cheshire had a senior-laden and experienced team. The visiting Panthers' record was 7-3-3.

The home team won the day, 2-0. The game was not that close. Ann Cumpstone and Patty Williams scored for the hosts. Cheshire's attacking front line and halfbacks spent most of the game in the Panthers' end of the field. Smith managed to get off just two shots at Cheshire's goal in the second half.

It took three overtimes and a sudden death goal from Sara Benoit before Enrico Fermi eliminated Suffield, 2-1. On paper this game looked like a mismatch. Fermi played a tough independent schedule. Suffield had an easier time playing in the weak NCCC.

Fermi's coach, Carol Albert, vividly remembered the game. *"Cold, lousy weather. We were the best team and should have easily won the game. The game itself was not that close. The type of game a team with a legacy always wins. We were a new school and as-yet, had not established that legacy."*

Suffield, coached by Bev Thompson, had a record of 6-3-2

and an all-state candidate in Karen Drake. They played the demanding 4-4-2 format, and that seemed to force Fermi out of its comfort zones. Early in the second half, Donna Teske scored for the Falcons. Late in the second half, Patty Kelly tied the game for the Wildcats, setting up the ensuing sudden-death OT periods.

The longer the game went on, the worse the weather got.

Despite both teams being known for their offensive abilities the game turned into a defensive battle. Diane Teske and Gayle Hutchinson playing large for Fermi in front of goalie Debbie Bourque. At the other end it was Drake along with Karen Samuelsen and June Champagney in front of Wildcat goalie, Dawn Burke. A huge defensive battle until Benoit and Sara King combined on a give-and-go for the winning goal, sending the Falcons into the second round.

Suffield's Karen Drake remembered the game. *"Brutally cold. Wind blowing and it was snowing. They were the better team. We got outplayed. But...we had our chances and should have won the game."*

I was beginning to see a common theme emerging with the tournament. Then came the first major, THUD!

43

Weston was a good field hockey team under longtime coach, June Olah. They had all-state and all-conference players. They had won the Western Connecticut Conference title and sported a record of 9-1-1. They had out-scored opponents 31-3. Their ranking of 5th in the state earned them a home game in the opening round of the tournament.

Coginchaug had just completed a foul-weather, two-day battle with Avon in the play-in round and was battling a case of banged-up bodies and tired legs. So, what occurred?

Coginchaug, ranked 37th and coming off a two-day bout with Avon with

Sue Fiolek
Litchfield High
School

injured players and tired legs, upsets 5th ranked Weston 2-1 in sudden death overtime.

The home Wildcats ran into a hot player who was on a roll in Blue Devils goalie, Linda Stahl. She kicked away 15 shots including a breakaway opportunity from Weston's all-state center halfback, B.J. Tomasiewicz with only seconds remaining in regulation. It is believed that Lynn Johnson's stick was the one that poked the ball into the net for Coginchaug six minutes into the sudden-death OT period.

In Woodbridge 14th ranked Amity Regional and tournament director Mascia welcomed 19th ranked Litchfield to town for a first-round game. Amity had a 7-3-3 record and three all-conference players including co-captain Judy Mc-Hugh, goalie Kris Ridinger and all-state candidate, Wendy "Flash" Gordon. A member of the Housatonic Valley League, the Spartans played a demanding conference schedule and an impressive list of independent rivals.

Nancy Lyons of Staples High School Scoring a Game-Winning Goal

Litchfield came visiting from the competitive Berkshire League, earning a spot in the first round after finishing with a 7-3 mark. Their coach, Cindy Ferrarotti, was a Farmington High product and a former player for Jean Hunt. She remembered her Litchfield team. *"We were a little light on overall talent. Did not have much depth and bench strength. What we did have was energy. Those girls didn't run away from a challenge."*

Well, it happened again. Litchfield knocked off the 14th ranked and home team Spartans, 2-1 in the third sudden-death overtime period.

Judy McHugh had given the home towners a 1-0 lead just seven minutes into the game. Litchfield's Sue Fiolek tied the game with four minutes remaining in regulation and she almost popped a winning goal in the final seconds. Only to be rejected by Amity's goaltender, Ridinger.

It was Andrea Lyons who finally ended it 27 minutes into overtime with a nifty flick shot over the shoulder of Ridinger after a nice feed from Fiolek. It was also the play of Litchfield's goalie Ce Query who was able to reject 15 shots, many in the waning minutes of the overtime periods.

Sandy White and her 15th ranked East Lyme team used two second half scores and moved into the next round with a 2-1 over 18th ranked Sheehan. The Titans had rebounded from a sluggish start winning six of their final seven games. The tight, well-played game ended with Titans players Cheryl Eck and Lorie Delguidice firing shots at the East Lyme goal as time expired.

In Westport, Staples' coach Vivian Parker and her 11th ranked Wreckers at 8-0-2 played host to Elizabeth Bouclier's 22nd ranked Nighthawks of Newtown who finished with a mark of 6-2-2. The home team featured a strong defense and had outscored its opponents 28-1 during the regular season.

Despite the wind and rain both teams played a fast-paced game that remained scoreless until Nancy Lyons scored with seven minutes remaining off a crossing pass from Anne Youngling. Initially, Lyons' goal was waved off by one official who called an offsides. Following a discussion with the second official the goal was allowed as it was determined the Newtown fullback had made a lunge for the ball hitting Lyons' stick before she fired the shot on goal.

The exciting and unpredictable tournament games were beginning to draw attention. Fans were beginning to turn out for the action. The press did not.

44

Maloney of Meriden played field hockey at two speeds. Fast, and a little faster. Their up-tempo style of play eventually runs opponents into the ground. They also liked to push their weight around. Get into shoving matches. Toss an elbow or two. They liked to play rough.

The 10-1-1 Spartans are ranked 3rd in the state, and coach Sandy Piantek urges her team not to take their foot off the gas pedal. Stamford's Black Nights are coming to town fresh off their play-in-round victory over Newington in seven overtimes. A game that ended in total darkness.

Stamford coach, Pat Bradbury had heard all about Maloney. She is not concerned about the rough style of play. Her girls, too, are tough, and can handle that type of opponent. She is concerned about the up-tempo game. Stamford cannot get lured into playing Maloney's run and shoot game, or they would get blown off the field.

Maloney's Spartans got off to the races early and center Paula Nessing put the hosts ahead 1-0 just five minutes in. Stamford stayed with its disciplined control game and was finally rewarded when Sue Mihalik knocked in a rebound to tie the score 1-1 at halftime. But that seven-overtime game against Newington the day before is beginning to take its toll on Stamford's tired legs.

Maloney controls the second half from the onset. It is a field-length rush by the Spartans offense culminating in a goal from Cindy Chodkowski that does in the Black Knights. They had thrown everything they had at Maloney but Mihalik and Penny Rickel, running on tired legs, could not shake free for shots, and fullbacks Toni Rinaldi and Brenda Baxter couldn't repel the endless wave of Spartan attacks.

In the waning minutes Ellen Janiga scored the clincher for Maloney after the Spartans' front line relentlessly peppered the Stamford goal. The final was 3-1. It really was not that close of a game.

Stamford's Rinaldi remembered the Maloney game. *"Out of gas. Everyone ran out of gas. That Newington game took a lot out of us. You could see it in our body language. We just ran out of energy. During the bus ride home, a few of the girls fell asleep."*

Seeing the condition and endless energy of the Maloney players did not escape Rinaldi's eyes. She also remembers beginning a new workout regimen that winter to be better conditioned. Many of the girls noticed. You did not have to be the best skilled team, but teams in good condition appeared to have an edge. Especially during tournament time when, in Rinaldi's words, *"Everything about those tournament games seemed to get amped up a few notches."*

45

Bea Walko, coach of Greenwich High School's field hockey team, was nervous and rightfully so.

Playing against rivals like New Canaan, Darien and Staples were tough games but she and her girls knew those schools. Knew what they did and how they liked to attack. She knew the opponents' players and their skills. Knew the coaches.

But this was the tournament. Greenwich was 7th ranked in the state and had drawn a first-round game at home against 26th ranked Hall High of West Hartford. The game was then moved to Amity Regional in Woodbridge. Walko recalled her response. *"Hall High. We know nothing about them. I don't know the coach's name. Or coaches from any of their opponents. Nothing. Not a clue."*

Hall coach Sally Ann Warren had watched her girls finish out the season 5-0-1. Just being in the tournament was a thrill.

"We'll go wherever we're sent and play whoever we're scheduled to play," said the coach in a pre-game phone interview.

The Hall vs Greenwich game turned out to be a marathon in so many ways. It took two days, eight overtimes and lots of injuries just to play the games. It required the two schools to travel a combined 500 miles, spending 10 hours on school buses.

Oh yeah, Bea Walko had every right to be concerned.

Monday's game one was the day of the goalies. Beth Long of the Cardinal and Judy Wince for the Warriors. Both put up a brick wall in the goalmouth. Ironically, both girls kicked away 12 shots. Priscilla McClung and Sarah Sibley had the best shots at Hall's goal. At the other end, Hall's Linda Kendall and Kathy Heubner had scoring opportunities rejected by Long at point-blank range.

Defense ruled. When Hall's attack found its way inside the 25-yard line they were met by Cardinal fullbacks, Joan Holman and Dori Dale. The Cardinal attack that reached the scoring circle was repelled by Warrior captain, Jan Gustafson, fullbacks Linda Sobuta and Marie Bernard.

Eight overtime periods were played.

Just nine shots were attempted during the OT's. Darkness stopped play near 6 PM. The teams bused back to their homes. For Hall it meant a trip of almost two hours in rush hour traffic along the busy I-95 and I-84 corridors. Only to make the return roundtrip 18 hours later.

On day two Greenwich scored what was the deciding goal just six minutes into the opening half. The game was not decided until the last seconds and the final horn. Ann Sneath scored the lone goal on a rebound off the pads of Hall goalie, Judy Wince. The game was far from over.

The next 50 minutes were a defensive struggle and a battle for field position. Hall won the battle and began its barrage on Cardinal goalie Long. It continued to the very last seconds of the game with Long blocking two shots in the final 10 seconds off the sticks of Kendall and Gustafson.

The game had taken its toll. Injuries abounded. Cuts and bruises, fingers dislocated. One person hit in the head with a hard shot. Arms and knees badly swollen.

Walko was once again, nervous. She was not sure her team would recover and be ready for their next game. Maybe they would be OK if the next round was against an old rival. But a team from the tough Shoreline Conference or another upstate team. Someone she just did not know anything about.

Once again, Bea Walko just did not have a clue.

Old Saybrook, 10th ranked at 9-2 and 23rd ranked New Canaan with a mark of 7-1-3 were to meet at Southern Connecticut State College in what looked to be one of those classic games between two established programs.

It was the blue and white Rams of Old Saybrook against the red and black, Red Rams of New Canaan. It was coach Lorainne Splain against coach Sue Schwerdtle. A battle between established programs and well-known and established coaches. Schwerdtle was not happy with her team being ranked 23rd. She believed they were one of the top six in the state. From the eye test, maybe not in the top six, but her concerns did have merit.

The game lived up to its billing.

The two well-skilled and experienced teams battled to a scoreless first-half tie. Goalies Lynn Caley of Old Saybrook and Amy Buckhalter of New Canaan were pitching shutouts, and each was covering the goalmouth like a china wall. Fortunes changed for the Rams in the final 10 minutes of the second half. The winning score came off the stick of Margie Clynes following a penalty corner. Leslie Collier set up a standing screen and Annie Salz back tapped to Clynes who ripped off a shot under Buckhalter's elbow. The Red Rams sideline erupted, yelling at the officials for a third-party obstruction call. There was no whistle. The New Canaan goalie slammed her stick into the cage's post in disgust.

The defense still had to ward off a final wave from the Red Rams. A wild barrage from Jane Stoddard, Laurie Canada and Janet Zucco. Sensational stick blocks were made by Saybrook's Amanda Denny and Barb Brandell. Finally, the horn sounded. Old Saybrook had won a spot in the second round with a sterling 1-0 victory.

The Blue Wave of Darien High School entered the tournament with a chip on their shoulder. Coach Becky Strominger felt her girls should have earned a ranking of second or third because of their demanding schedule and strong finish to the regular season. Said Strominger, *"We are one of the top two or three teams in the state."* I had seen them play during the regular season. I agreed with her assessment.

Even with three losses, they are given a ranking of 6th, meaning they open tournament play with a home game against one of the play-in round winners. In Darien's case, that scrappy band from New Milford. And those kids from New Milford did not give a damn about Darien's feelings or where they were ranked. They had just come off a two-day battle with Terryville and now had to play against one of Connecticut's premier field hockey programs.

Or as New Milford's captain, Lee Hough referred to their venturing into upscale Fairfield County, *"Hey, a trip down to the gold coast, baby."*

Green Wave coach, Fran Zaloski, kept her pre-game talk low key. *"They don't know who we are. We'll give them all they can handle."*

That scrappy bunch from New Milford had made it through the regular season and into the second round without its best player and scorer, senior Elaine Falk. She had broken her leg during a summer softball game. She had collided with the catcher as both went for an infield pop-up. Center halfback, Laurie Center, was the pitcher in that game. *"I can still hear that bone in her leg snapping,"* remembered Center after all these years. Losing Falk was huge. It required others to step up, take responsibility and perform at a higher level.

Darien and New Milford played each other straight up and hard. Good hard-nosed, field hockey and each team had the opportunity to strut its stuff. Darien's Blue Wave was the more skilled team and that was obvious throughout the game. Alison King and Pam Bishop attacked from the right side. Sandy Wilkes and Doreen DeVino from the left. Julie Hendrickson was a go-to scorer at center-forward.

Deb Carella anchored a halfback line with Meg McGoldrick and Leslie Milne, as good as any halfback line in the state and supported with the play of co-captain Jen Barrett at fullback. Janice Prentice and Lorraine Ludwig shared the goaltending responsibilities. The Blue Wave could play.

New Milford played that in-your-face, meat and potatoes style of field hockey. They told you they were coming at you and then did just that. Lee Hough, Jill Southworth and LaDonna Bierbower were the scoring threats. Laurie Center was the glue that held everything together at center-half. Sue Hess was an all-conference fullback and JoAnn Olsen was an active and aggressive goalie. New Milford was a good team, though a notch below Darien.

The game was a classic defensive struggle. To the surprise of the hometown crowd and to the Darien players, regulation time ended in a scoreless tie. The lead official had announced that one 15-minute overtime period would be played. If no goals were scored penalty corners would determine the winner. Heading into the OT stanza, New Milford held a surprising 10-8 margin in corners. Upset was in the air.

Much of the OT play took place at mid-field. Nobody seemed to find a lane to the goal or mount an offensive threat. The timekeeper called out, *"Two minutes to play."*

Darien needed a game-changing play. Deb Carella provided it. She picked up a pass near mid-field and with a nice lead, sent Alison King off and running up the right side.

Doreen DeVino joined the attack that reached the top of the scoring circle.

DeVino unleashed the first shot. Goalie Olsen made the save. King fired a second shot that took a crazy hop, rebounding off Olsen's pads and back onto King's stick. Her second shot was also blocked, but this time the ball went off the side of Olsen's bulbous looking protective shoe covers and out-of-bounds, setting up a penalty corner. There was less than a minute to play.

The in-bounds pass was intended for King. In the last instant, Julie Hendrickson swooped in and lifted a shot into the upper right corner of the net for the winning score. The goal came with just 18 seconds left in the OT. Had Hendrickson not scored New Milford would have won the game with a 10-9 advantage in penalty corners. New Milford fell short by just 18 seconds.

It would have been the monster upset of the tournament.

Darien's co-captain Jen Barrett had played in tough games that season. Demanding games against long-time rivals. She remembered New Milford. *"They were the toughest bunch we faced that season."*

JoAnn Olsen remembered, *"Darien was the most skilled team any of us had seen. We had no idea we were leading in penalty corners. Just 18 seconds away from winning. We didn't embarrass ourselves."*

With each game the tournament seemed to be growing in stature. Along with intensity and the stress and pressure of winning. As I had written in my column, *The Hot Corner,* for the *Farmington Valley Herald,* I had warned a tournament is not like a regular season. It is a whole new season. More intense than the games in September. Every play or mistake magnified. I likened the winning of a state championship as demanding as memorizing the Hartford area phone book.

The deeper a team went into the tournament, the less room there was for error. The short-lived joy of winning. The elevated and immense pain of losing. Eventually, pain for every team, except one. My ever-lasting search for that *"Question of Balance."*

With 15 games in the books, one game remained to be played in the tournament's first round. I remember referring to it as, *"The State Championship Game of the absurd first round."*

Simsbury at Granby.

46

It was a nasty and vicious game. Dirty at times. No other way to describe it.

I do not like comparing sporting events to being at war. I do use similes and metaphors because they are simplistic comparisons. Formations. Strategies. Words, like, fight, attack, and defense. Despite the use of those comparisons, the base premise of sports is competition. Not idealisms or body counts.

During my years covering girls' sports for the *Herald*, this game was as close as it got to a comparison. Two schools who, flat out, did not like each other.

Simsbury's girls, ranked 34th, were fighting for the reputation and credibility of their team. Granby's girls, ranked 2nd, were fighting for the legacy of their small town. It had been just five days ago these two rivals battled to a scoreless tie in the season's finale on this very field. Word spread fast about this game. Field hockey coaches from throughout the state and Western Mass came to watch. Including college coaches looking for recruits.

Nothing about this game was gentle. There were body and elbow checks. Pushing and shoving incidents. High swinging sticks that found their mark on body parts in places I could not mention in the *Herald*. Passes and hard shots drilled at players bodies. On-going vitriolic exchanges were loudly spewed. Even the large crowd of Granby fans, typically regarded as polite and low key, seemed edgy and ornery. You could sense it. Like a tinder box ready to explode.

Nasty or not, it was still a damn good, exciting game to watch.

At halftime the game was again, scoreless. Simsbury held a 5-3 lead in penalty corners. Lead official, Alice Yokabaskas, walked past me, head down while writing a note on the small pad she always carried. Never looking up she said, *"I wish that I was not doing this game."*

Wow, if Alice Yokabaskas would say something like that it had to be worse on the field from what could be heard standing on the sidelines.

The true flavor of the game began happening with 12 minutes remaining in the second half. One of those things that happens in memorable games which you had to be there to see and believe. Granby couldn't believe it was happening to them.

The flow of the game changed. Dramatically. At first, I was not sure what I was hearing. I focused in on the directions being shouted from the Simsbury sideline. The voice become more distinctive. It was Joan Sullivan hollering out to her players when the action carried into Granby's scoring circle. *"Shoot at their feet...Shoot at their feet."*

It quickly became apparent what Sullivan was doing. Creating penalty corners. Simsbury had one of the best defensive units in the state. They had now held Granby scoreless for almost two complete games. Not sure if her team could score against the Bears, Sully chose to try the back door approach. Amass as many penalty corners as possible. That was how she was finally going to beat Dot Johnson and Granby.

Granby's Pam Sproull remembered the ploy. *"Sully wanted her players to create penalty corner opportunities. She was running up and down the sidelines yelling at her players to shoot at our feet. Move us into the (scoring) circle and create a penalty corner. She believed that approach would work."*

Ellen Burbridge saw what was happening. *"They had no interest in scoring. They would shoot at my feet. I would jump into the air. Then, they'd do it again. The Simsbury players would laugh. It was really weird."* Unfortunately for Granby, the tactic was working like a well-practiced magic trick.

Regulation time ended. Simsbury held a margin of 12-6 in penalty corners. They had now shutout Granby for 120 minutes. Sullivan's defense was getting the job done and her backdoor strategy was working like a magic wand. Her team needed to just continue playing their tough defense and they would have that signature win over their hated rival. Stop Granby's five-year unbeaten streak with a monster upset. And earn a spot in the tournament's second round.

Two 10-minute sudden-death overtime periods were planned. If no goals were scored, penalty corners would decide the winner. With Sullivan still urging on her girls yelling, *"Corners...Corners. Shoot at their feet,"* Simsbury dominated the first overtime. Granby repelled every scoring attempt, but the Trojans increased their penalty corners to an insurmountable 14-6 margin as the first OT ended.

The Trojans were now just 10 minutes away from making history. Granby was in big trouble. Every home fan ringing that field could sense the urgency of need.

I had been standing behind the Granby goal watching the *"Corner Conspiracy"* develop, putting the hometown Bears in a very deep hole. Granby needed a goal to survive. To win and move on to the second round. To perpetuate its 45-game unbeaten string. For the honor of tiny Granby High School.

I heard a familiar voice ask, *"So, what are your thoughts!"* It was Tom Weston, a Granby High student. He was a junior. Manager for the soccer, basketball and baseball teams. A member of the National Honor Society. He was a nice kid. Smart with a wonderful sense of humor. I often saw Tom when covering Granby sporting events, and we would always engage in conversation. *"What do you think's gonna happen?"* he added.

Somehow, I had this odd thought, and I knew exactly what to say. I just blurted it out. *"Ellen Burbridge is going to get loose and score the game winner early in the next overtime."* Weston smiled and continued walking along the sideline. I decided to stay at the north goal that would now be defended by Simsbury.

I could hear the bantering from each team's sideline huddles. Simsbury's focus was just keep doing what we are doing. We are going to win. Most of the talk was from the players. Joan Sullivan was eerily low key.

Granby's huddle was, as expected, dealing with the gigantic elephant on the field. Sproull urged her teammates to, *"Forget the penalty corners. We need to score a goal to win."* Dot Johnson then added, *"Just stay in your lanes. Play your game. Create your own opportunities."* She appeared calm. I just knew her insides were churning.

The second sudden-death OT began, and within 60 seconds the Trojans were again banging on the door, inside Granby's scoring circle, only this time they were in full mode attack, firing a flurry of shots at goalie Jo Sproull. Kim Longo's drive hit Sproull's stick at mid-shaft and caromed high into the air. Somehow the ball ended up outside the circle. Sue

Hebert took control, finding a gap between two Simsbury players. She sent a well-placed pass onto Lynsie Wickman's stick. Wickman started right, then, abruptly, sent a blind cross-field pass back to the left. For a strange reason Simsbury's defense kept slowly flowing to the right.

Ellen Burbridge, all alone, scooped up the pass and was off like a sprinter up the left sideline. You could see the dirt clods being churned up behind her by her spikes as she dug in and increased speed while pushing the ball out ahead of her.

Initially, Simsbury's deep defense did not think she would make a one-on-one charge. So, instead of defending they slowly flowed to the right as a group into a zone-type coverage. But Burbridge had shifted into another gear and zipped past the Trojans fullbacks like a sprinter, leaving their competition in the dust.

She was now all alone and closing in on the Simsbury goal.

Elaine Marcil was the Simsbury goalie. The young sophomore nervously watched what was developing in front of her. Knowing her fullbacks would not be able to cut off the Granby attacker. She was on her own. Marcil danced in place to get ready. Slowly, she came away from her goal bending at the knees and waist in readiness.

Burbridge's first shot was a knee-high liner off Marcil's pads. Hard enough that you could hear a thud as the ball hit the pads. The ball caromed right back to Burbridge's stick and she fired again. Marcil was 10 feet out from her net and made a magnificent sliding block. The ball took a funny bounce and with the overspin, climbed up and over the goalie's leg. With Marcil now on the ground the ball continued towards the goal. Slowly rolling over the goal line in slow-motion for the score. Granby had won, 1-0.

It sounded like 10,000 voices had erupted and looked like a tidal wave of bodies charging onto the field from every corner. Sheer mayhem. I was sitting on the ground along the end line and people were jumping over me. Marcil remained laying on the field. She pounded the ground with her fist. Her face looked like she was about to burst into tears.

The field was now a sea of people. Granby players lost amid the crowd. Simsbury players already walking towards their bus. An assistant coach helped Marcil up and off the field. I could not see Joan Sullivan or Dottie Johnson in the throng of people that seemed to be growing. The headline in my head said, *"Nasty Game – Nifty Goal."* Honestly, I was a little numb to the hoopla that was exploding all around me.

I spied Tom Weston to whom I had made my spirited prediction about Burbridge's winning goal. He smiled and pointed at me. Weston would go on to have a forty-plus year career at UConn as a student and in the Sports Information Office.

My thought was to get back to Simsbury with hopes of talking to Joan Sullivan, maybe a few of her players. Due to late day traffic along Routes 10-202, my short trip south through Simsbury's town center took 30 minutes. I drove my car behind the school as I often did. The team bus had already arrived and was unloading.

I saw Joan Sullivan, but I stopped in my tracks. She had her arm around one of her young sophomore starters who was crying, cradling her spikes against her chest. Sully was speaking softly to her. Another girl joined them and the three walked together, arm-in-arm, towards the school. I dared not interrupt.

As I turned back to the bus, I saw one of the Simsbury players crying, sobbing loudly. Her white blouse was untucked, a sleeve torn. Her shoes were untied. Socks had drooped. The uniform skirt was matted and streaked with dirt, grass and blood stains. Her hockey stick had fallen to the ground next to her feet. She was with her mom who had her arms around her daughter as she comforted the teenager, who was distraught and in pain. As I got close enough the mom looked up. She recognized me. And, in a somber and kind voice said, *"And Jesus Wept."*

Not knowing what she meant, I shrugged my shoulders slightly. My face and eyes asking the question, *"What does that mean?"*

In a soft voice she said those words were the shortest verse in the King James Bible. From the gospel of John. Chapter 11. *"When things just don't go the way expected."*

OK, admittedly, I am not a bible reader and knew nothing of that fact. I returned to my car and headed for my apartment. My radio was tuned to WACE in Chicopee, MA. The song playing was "The Israelites" by Desmond Dekker and the Aces. Five years earlier during the third week of November 1968, the song had topped the charts in the UK. My gallows humor was alive as I pondered, *"Jesus wept, huh. I wonder who Jesus was rooting for in this game."*

When I reached my apartment, I sat in the dark. Thoughts of the Simsbury and Granby game were heavy on my mind. As was Vietnam. Maybe it was the other way around. I felt a little overwhelmed. Tired. I titled my head forward. Held my face in both my hands. The pounding ache behind my right eye was debilitating.

Oh, how I wished for some peaceful sleep.

47

The dashboard clock in my 1967 Camaro reads 4:12 AM. It is early morn on the day of November 17, 1973, as I travel south on Interstate 91 to New Haven. I feel like a lone crusader on a pilgrimage. Remembering the catch tune from Dinah Shore singing an advertisement. *"See the USA in your Chevrolet."* Yeah, that was me, all right.

To my right, a November moon was sitting low in the western sky in a waning, gibbous style stage, illuminating the outlines of the high-rise buildings of Hartford's Constitution Plaza. The lone beacon of light atop the Travelers Insurance Company building shone brightly as its beam cut through the darkness. I could see its glistening reflection off the waters of the Connecticut River to my left. My radio played a soft ballad, "Time," by the Pozo Seco Singers.

The Colt Firearms Factory and Armory came into view. Its

cupola dome partially lit. The landmark was an alluring sight. Just south of the armory is Colt's Park and situated close to the highway, Dillon Stadium. Hartford's edifice to big time sports with a seating capacity of 10,000. The lights are on. People working on the field and in the bleachers.

Perhaps cleaning up from a Friday night high school football game or readying the field for a home game for its tenants, the Hartford Knights of the Seaboard Football League. Or, maybe readying the facility for the annual Thanksgiving Day game between Hartford Public and Weaver High Schools. A game played since 1924. My Mom was a graduate from Hartford Public and had gone to Dillon Stadium for the Turkey Day game as a student during the mid-1930's to root for the Owls.

I remember my American Legion, PAL and JC Courant baseball teams playing many games on the fields of Colts Park and in Dillion Stadium when the field and bleachers had been converted for baseball. Wonderful games. Great memories.

Damn, what the hell was that...as thoughts of those memories are erased in a flash of light, a sonic boom and a cloud of smoke.

A car barreled past me on my left as if it had been shot out of a cannon. An old dented and beat-up station wagon that looked like it had served in Korea as an army tank. I figured it had to be traveling in excess of 100 miles per hour. Engine and rattling parts screaming like banshees. Spewing smoke and a light spray of oil onto my windshield, like a WWII fighter plane that has been hit in the oil pan from ack-ack ground fire and was going down.

I had to laugh. My first thought was if I had to follow him the culprit, no problem. Just follow the smoke. He was a moving target for those surprise speed traps that seemed to always pop up on I-91 at the weirdest hours. Especially south of Hartford.

I passed the exit for Brainard Road, home of one of my

favorite places to go as a kid, Brainard Field. My Dad would take me to watch small planes take-off and land. I remember standing on the spots where Amelia Earhart and Charles Lindberg had stood during their well-publicized landings of the early 1930's. I had landed there, myself, in 1969 when I was able to finagle my way onto a Beechcraft 99 flight from New Haven's Tweed Airport.

It was summer, 1969. My military commitment was down to 60 days active duty at Ft Devens in Ayer, Massachusetts. I had been assigned to memorial duty in New Haven. Burial detail. Military people accompanying the bodies of Vietnam vets killed in action. Awful duty. Stressful and demanding. Where you had to walk a fine line in telling grieving families the truth of what happens in Vietnam as opposed to the bullshit stories families receive from the military's PR folks. Those emotional assignments just ate at my insides.

Whenever I could, I'd sneak away earlier than planned. On this day, I got a ride to the New Haven airport and overheard a man talk about flying to Hartford. I asked if I could shag a ride. He welcomed me aboard and brought the beer. The flight took 31 minutes and I downed two bottles of cold Miller High Lifes. *"The Champagne of Bottled Beers,"* I remembered from the days my Dad use to drink Miller High Life.

"God, I hate my memories of Vietnam. They don't go away...never go away!"

Through the early morning darkness, I continue south on I-91. An odd memory finds its way into my thoughts. A field hockey game I had played in during late summer, 1967. My days at Fort Sill. Playing for Colonel Williams. It was against an all-women's team from Fort Sam Houston. They were good. They were rough, too. We won the game, but I recall that I had to pay a pound of flesh for that win. In fact, lots of flesh was bought and paid for during that game.

I learned a lesson from my time in the US Army. No matter who or what, there is always a cost to be paid. And the bill always comes due.

It was one of those games where our opponents were much better than us. Yet, on this afternoon and in the words of teammate, Puss, *"When it came to crunch time, they couldn't even take a piss without making a mess."*

I had made a pass to our center halfback. After the play, their fullback charged at me and we collided. Wildly, she swung her stick at me. Her stick appeared to be honed on the backside of the shoe. Her second swipe cut me on the leg. Her third hit made solid impact on my crotch area. To her surprise the stick made a loud, *"Clang"* on the metal cup I always wore from my baseball playing days.

Everybody on the field saw the hits. Heard the sounds. Watched me go down.

Hey, let's be clear about that third hit. I was wearing protection, but it still hurt enough that I had one of those moments when you open your mouth to breathe...and nothing happens. Fortunately, I was wearing enough protection that it did prevent damage. Like the type of damage that could have provided me with a limp for the next few months.

My attacker was named Wanda. About the only way I can describe her. She was 250 pounds of ugly with a face that could split a rail. Hairy arms with muscles and a torso damn near the size of an outhouse. She had a mustache, too. Not a pencil thin one you had to squint to see. A thick bushy stash that you could hide your lawn furniture in.

She glared at me and with angry emotion said, *"You don't belong here little boy...you little shit."* I held my tongue and did not respond. It took a few seconds to re-focus my thoughts. In a way, she was probably right. An obvious sign of the times. I believe she was about to take another swing at me but broke off her attack.

My coach, Bitchie, came by and tapped me on the ass with her stick. Her words were loud enough for all to hear. *"Hey, get up Rob. You belong here. You're just ahead of your time!"*

As she moved away towards the game action, she again poked me with her stick telling me to get my head back into the game.

With a wry smile and a wink of an eye, she also assured me that Wanda would soon be dealt with. The bill, that payment of sorts, always comes due.

Near game's end I heard a sharp piercing scream and loud commotion at the far end of the field. When I turned, play had stopped. Wanda lay on the ground writhing in pain, both hands holding on to her ass. Like a stuck pig, she was bleeding from her left ass cheek. Her sweatpants already soaked with her blood. My teammates were all around her, except Bootsie who had walked away from the play and was now in our end of the field standing next to our goalie, Killer.

A medic who was watching the game loaded Wanda into his jeep and set off for the ER at the base hospital. The game ended. Bitchie hustled everyone into our vans and we got the hell off the base as quickly as possible. Before the MPs could return and begin asking questions.

It was clear that Bootsie had stuck Wanda with the knife she carried. She had lured her into a scrum with trash talk and then stuck her when they were in close quarters. The knife was passed to Gertie who handed it off to Killer who stuffed it down the leg of her sweatpants, right next to the pistol and knife she carried.

Yes sir, rule number three. There are no rules in war. I really didn't know it at that time but, as Bitchie had said, perhaps I was just a tad ahead of my time. I was now, also, part to a crime of assault and battery. Best defense...get the hell out of there. In the van, I removed my protective cup. It had a half-inch dent, dead center. Yikes!

As I passed the Meriden exit for CT Route 66, flashing lights from three state police cruisers had pulled over the smoking station wagon. The driver was out of the car and was being handcuffed by two large troopers wearing Smokey Bear hats. Again, I had to laugh at the driver as I thought about my Fort Sill teammate, Bootsie, stabbing Wanda in the ass with her knife. I wondered if any of the high school girls I had watched in the tournament carried weapons. I had seen some tough girls out there on the pitch. Some played the game just like Wanda.

Still, debts are a forgone conclusion. All I know is what I am told. No matter how we choose to deal with life's little payments the bill will always come due and is eventually satisfied in one way or another. Wanda's receipt for payment is a roadmap scar for life on the left cheek of her fat ass. Like the guy handcuffed in state police custody in Meriden, I felt no remorse or empathy for Wanda. Rule number three of war.

I picked up speed and continued my journey south. My radio played on. WDRC, 1360 on my AM dial. Jorgen Ingmann, a Danish jazz guitarist strummed a haunting reverberation of his 1960 instrumental hit, "Apache." Steve Lawrence crooned "Pretty Blue Eyes," and I sang along as Patsy Cline belted out her classic, "I Fall to Pieces."

Earl Scheib's voice informed me he would paint any car any color, for $59.99. My Boston Celtics had a big fourth quarter behind Dave Cowens and Don Nelson to beat Milwaukee, 105 to 90 at the Boston Garden. A building that opened on this very day, 45 years ago in 1928. On November 17, 1796, in Russia, Catherine the Great dies.

As I approach New Haven's State Street Exit, I hear Davy Jones of the Monkees solemnly sing the solo, "I Wanna Be Free." I feel a rush in my body. A moment of melancholy that begs to know why I am so fortunate for being a part of what will be today's activities. What did I do to deserve this good fortune. I do not even consider what I do as work. It is absolute enjoyment, and, I'm getting paid to enjoy it. Another day of paid fun. It really is a little creepy.

It is now 5:02 AM and from the horizon over the hood of my car the lights of downtown New Haven buildings are coming into view. From my radio the Beatles harmonize one of their final hits, "Let It Be!" A thought suddenly races through my head. Like a picture, as clear and as sharply focused as a perfect black and white photo. My jaw hangs open. I feel the pulsation behind my right eye. My temple is pounding. From deep inside, words find their way to my quivering lips. I speak them out loud to the only audience listening. Me!

*"Holy Shit. **HOLY SHIT!** Granby is Going to Win the Whole Goddamn Thing!"*

48

Despite my infantile banter and silent disagreeing with the committee, they had gotten the tournament brackets and rankings right. Though I continued to believe the folks in charge were hoping for an all down-state final if it could be arranged.

Looking at the brackets it was rather easy to formulate a final. At the top of the brackets was Guilford. At the bottom, Darien. They jumped out screaming at you in bold, capital letters. Now, just the game scripts remained to be written. What happened, well, other factors got involved and that changed the outcome.

Number one ranked Guilford was strong as they worked through the second and third rounds. On a rain ravaged field at Southern Connecticut State, Sharon Farquharson scored with eight minutes remaining, the Green and White eliminated

Enrico Fermi, 1-0. Leslie Gribus kicked away 14 shots including spectacular sliding saves against Falcon's front liners, Sara King and Sharon Benoit, during the last minute.

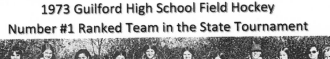

**1973 Guilford High School Field Hockey
Number #1 Ranked Team in the State Tournament**

**Front Row L-R: Mary O'Grady, Beth Mermann, Lorainne Delabry, Leslie Gribus, Lindsay Taylor, Deb Crosby, Amy Cunningham, Dawn Sprague.
Row 2: Sharon Farquharson, Nancy Nettlton Mary Bishop, Nancy Evans, Shelley Palmieri, Wendy Monroe, Tammy Edwards, J Edwards, Debbie Laine, Amy Schulz, Lis Neydorf, Nancy Capezzone. Row 3: Coach Linda Gavin, Mary Bunting, Meghan Devaney, D Edgehill, Cathy Corning, Lisa Sikes, Lori Schulz, Cathy Benton, Julie Loveday, Nancy Cantey, Lorraine Rogers and Head Coach, Becky Riggio**

Two days later at Coginchaug's field, an old friend from the Shoreline Conference was waiting to do battle. Westbrook had put the only blemish on the Grizzlies season with a mid-season tie. The Westbrook Knights had the talent to match-up against Guilford.

Dawn Sprague scored twice in the first half on assists from Lindsay Taylor and Deb Crosby for a 2-0 Guilford advantage. Rae Hirst cut the lead in half for Westbrook with 10 minutes to play off a pass from Lynn Clements. The Knights will get one more good shot at tying the game, but Chris Rackcliffe's drive is kicked away by Gribus as time expires. Guilford hangs on for a 2-1 win and a spot in the semi-finals.

The players from both teams put all they had into their play. Every player left it all out on the field. As the game ends, many from both teams are on hands and knees, heads bent forward. Totally spent. Another typical encounter between Westbrook and Guilford.

As Westbrook headed for the buses an assistant coach from another school who happened to be at the game noticed something that made her uncomfortable. Post-game reactions in some of the Westbrook girls' behaviors. Some were short of breath and struggling to breathe. Some sweating, others noticeably not sweating. Still, others are sobbing and retching, their bodies doubled over in pain. Many appear to be experiencing a general lethargy in actions and responses.

The woman has a nursing background and is uncomfortable at what she is seeing. She has one of the Westbrook team coaches call ahead to the downtown clinic in Westbrook, describing symptoms and alerting the medical folks the bus will be stopping at the clinic. Please be ready.

The 22-mile trip is made in a quick 33 minutes. On-duty physicians, nurses and nurses-aids attend to the girls. Many are treated on the bus as a first-step triage. Some are brought inside the clinic. Most are treated for exhaustion, exacerbated by dehydration. A few have general hyperextension of limbs. Some are cut and bruised and have other minor injuries. Physically, the girls' energy tanks are empty. Mentally, most are exhausted. What is called the real pain of defeat. In a cliché of sports, *"They left it all out on the field."*

Lyn Clements remembers the day. *"Field hockey was not our lives, but during the season it meant so much to every one of us. Playing together and what we accomplished as a team. Each girl giving everything she had in every game. That game...we just could not get into a rhythm. We hated to lose. That loss to Guilford really hurt."*

They did not know how much it affected them until checked by the medical folks. Had it not been for that coach whose nursing background allowed her to see what was happening, some of the Westbrook girls could have gone into minor shock.

That evening, after the team bus has been towed back to the municipal lot after breaking down at the high school, someone spray paints the letters DOA on the side of bus for *"Dead on Arrival."* Two years later an experienced Westbrook team will win the Class M Title beating a mature Canton team, 2-1 in sudden-death overtime.

Guilford's captain, Lindsay Taylor recalled, *"Westbrook... every game. Every time we play them the outcome comes down to the last seconds. It's always a tough game."*

Number two ranked Granby took an equally exciting path into the semi-final round. The day after beating Simsbury in sudden death OT the Bears followed the same game script against a suborn and defense-minded East Lyme. Regulation ended in a scoreless tie. Just one overtime was scheduled to be played, and Granby, as they did against Simsbury, entered the OT trailing the Vikings in penalty corners, 8-6. Overtime waned into the final two minutes. As she had done against Simsbury, Ellen Burbridge broke free down the sideline, cut across the goal mouth and from 15 feet out fired in the winning goal sending the Bears into the next round.

The second game in two days where the Bears, trailing in penalty corners, had to score a goal or be eliminated. And Burbridge scored the key goal in both games.

Granby, playing their third game in four days, was the host against a dangerous Old Saybrook team. The game was played at the Ethel Walker School in West Simsbury. One of the best playing surfaces in the state. Despite the weather being cold and windy, one official, Lucy Goodridge, would call it one of the finest, most well-played field hockey games she had the pleasure to be a part of, either as a player or an official.

Lynsie Wickman scored the game's only goal seven minutes in, a bouncing shot that caromed off the stick of Rams fullback, Amanda Denny. The ball then goes airborne, bouncing off the arm of goalie Lynn Caley. One of those odd goals that on any other day would have been blocked. The remaining 50 plus minutes is a contest of stick-handling skills, defensive sets, crisp passes, slick moves and very few whistles.

The two teams combined for only ten penalty corners.

Caley had to bat away 11 shots by Granby. Jo Sproull rejected 10 including two in the final three minutes. One from Margie Clynes and a point-blank shot from Leslie Collier just 10 feet out. It truly was one of those games where every player in both lineups touched the ball and had an opportunity to make a critical play.

"Actually, the best game we played all year," remembered Old Saybrook coach Lorainne Splain.

Staring out over the pitch Granby coach Dot Johnson said, *"Wonderful game."*

Windsor Locks finds its way into the semi-finals vs Guilford by first stopping fourth ranked Cheshire, 3-2 at Southern Connecticut State on a cold and rainy day. Nancy Shapiro scores two first half goals for the Raiders. Ann Cumpstone and Patty Williams score for Cheshire and the half ends at 2-2.

Marie Duwell scores the winner for the Locksters with five minutes remaining on a crossing pass from Liz Gragnolati. Defensively, Sue O'Brien and Kathy McCarthy set up a wall in front of goaltender, JoAnne Michalewicz, holding the Rams to just three good shots on goal in the final 20 minutes.

What Cheshire coach Arlene Salvati remembers about that day, *"The long, cold and wet walk up that steep hill to the buses. We were the better team and should have won that game...we should have won that damn game."*

Windsor Locks then stops Roger Ludlowe's run in the tournament shutting out the Falcons, 3-0 on a rainy, snowy day at Joel Barlow. Ludlowe had reached the quarter finals beating Coginchaug in a blowout, 5-1. Coginchaug, after winning two games in the tournament, will drop field hockey in favor of soccer in 1995.

For Windsor Locks, once again it was Shapiro and Duwell doing the scoring. Goalie Michalewicz blocked 10 shots for the shutout.

"They dominated us," remembers Roger Ludlowe goalie Leigh Coulter. *"We were, absolutely, the better team. On that day, we could not generate any offense. I mean, nothing. And they kept firing shots at me the whole game."*

Darien reached the semi-final round, beating rival Staples 3-2 and then surviving a rough, physical game against Maloney, 2-1. A game that was more like a roller derby match than a game of field hockey.

Against Staples, Julie Hendrickson got the Green Wave on the board at the ten-minute mark of the opening half. At mid-point in the second half, Nancy Lyons tied the game for the Wreckers. Alison King was the benefactor of a perfect pass from a penalty corner. Her goal gave the lead back to Darien, 2-1.

Staples then went the length of the field in three minutes. Anne Youngling hit Janet Lane with a pass resulting in a goal, tying the game at 2-2. Once again, it was Alison King who stickhandled her way into position for an angle shot that caromed off the goalie's pads for Darien's winning score with 1:57 remaining.

What made King's goal more impacting was the pre-game decision by the lead official that no overtimes would be played. It was a rather odd and head-scratching decision for many. Especially with the number of sudden-death, overtime games already in the books. Unknown to the Darien players was the simple fact that when King scored her game winner, Staples held a 10-8 advantage penalty corners.

Friday's game in Fairfield, Darien against Maloney, was played in freezing temperatures, pelting rain and 20 mile per hour winds. When a team had to play east to west on the field, the wind made it hard just to go in that direction, having to run into the relentless and blustery headwinds. Some wind blasts reaching 30 mph.

Darien brought its skills to the game. Maloney brought its up-tempo and patented rumble-in-the-alley style of game.

They battled for 45 minutes until Debbie Grant got her stick on a rebound and scored, giving Darien the lead. But in the final minute of regulation Maloney's tri-captain, Joyce Allgaier, muscled up, knocked two players off the ball and took aim at the Blue Wave's goal. Her first shot hit goalie Ludwig mid-body and bounced back onto her stick. Allgaier's second shot was a vicious liner that hit Ludwig's arm bouncing off and onto Patty Zamoik's stick who jammed the ball through the pads and into the goal to tie the score with 30 seconds left on the clock.

On this day, officials did have plans for three overtimes if needed.

The first sudden-death stanza was quiet. Neither team coming close to getting off a clean shot on goal. Maloney looked as if it had won the game late in the second overtime. Ellen Janiga had an open corner of the net and her shot looked like it was going in. It was sweeper back, Leslie Milne, diving and while airborne made a valiant stab at the rising shot, redirecting the ball into the ground. While lying on the ground, Milne swiped at the ball that sat just six inches from the goal, the ball exploding off her stick traveling outside the scoring circle. Half the Maloney team stood watching the play, their jaws hanging open in awe. Milne had made the play of the game. Perhaps the play of the year for Darien.

Less than a minute later Deb Carella and Meg McGoldrick made passes that set up Alison King for her game winning goal in the waning seconds of the OT. Darien was now 10-3 and on their way to a semi-final game against Granby.

Thirty-four tournament games had been played. The committee had engineered the brackets and results had played out to expectations. Three schools, Guilford, Darien and Granby had been the favorites to reach the semi-finals. Windsor Locks had caught everyone off guard. The committee did not want to admit it, but it was no secret what they were hoping for. A downstate championship final between Guilford and Darien.

Then, there was Granby. That little school from...well, somewhere upstate near the Massachusetts boarder, biding its time.

Just waiting for Darien.

49

The tournament semi-finals and its games are becoming an enigma. A list of contradictions to be sure.

Both games are to be played at Southern Connecticut State College in New Haven. On Tuesday, Guilford and Windsor Locks will play. Darien and Granby will then go at each other on Wednesday. Tuesday's game begins at 2:30 PM. Wednesday's game at 3:15 PM. Tuesday's game is scheduled for Field One. Wednesday's game to be played on Field Two. Both fields are in terrible condition, ravaged by the week-long foul weather. It is reported some maintenance has been done to Field One. Nobody was sure if any maintenance had been done to Field Two.

Except if you ask the SCSC Facilities Manager who assured all that many hours of maintenance had been dedicated to each field. I come across an SCSC maintenance worker in a battered blue and white pickup. When asked what he had done to prepare the fields he laughs saying, *"We ain't done shit to them fields...especially not in this weather."*

Contradictions, all right. Like when you flip a coin and call out, **HEADS** or **TAILS**. Only this time the coin lands precariously on its thin edge. What the hell are the protocols for that situation? Well, we were about to find out.

In Tuesday's Guilford-Windsor Locks game, one overtime period would be played if necessary. In the Darien-Granby game, three OTs were scheduled if needed.

In game one the CIAC supplied a timekeeper to run the clock. For game two, officials found a volunteer from the SCSC field hockey team to run a hand-held clock.

For game one, scorebooks kept by each team's scorer, would be official for penalty corner counts. In game two, even though each school would keep a scorebook, the second official's count would be the deciding component.

About the only common thread folks could agree on for these two games was the weather. It stunk. Temperatures in the low 30's. Rain, snow, and wind. And the fields. Each one looked like it had recently hosted a demolition derby. Mud pits. Like the seas of mud and huge crowds I remembered from my time at the New York Woodstock Music Festival in 1969. Now, in the 1973 field hockey semi-finals, again we had the mud, but unlike Woodstock...there were no fans.

Selected people in the know were asked for predictions and outcomes for the semi-final games. The consensus appeared to be, *"Guilford will run Windsor Locks off the field. Darien will outclass and beat Granby."*

Well, they forget to ask the underdogs how they felt about their chances. Yeah, contradictions. About as unpredictable as the predictable untruths.

In Tuesday's first semi-final, Guilford did beat Windsor Locks, 1-0 on a muddy, sloppy field. This one could have gone either way. Just ask any of those girls from Guilford who felt more like survivors than winners. Sharon Farquharson scored the lone goal late in the first half, set up on a nice pass from Mary O'Grady. The Green and White of coach Becky Clomp earned a spot in Saturday's state championship game to be played on the campus of Yale University.

Guilford was clearly the better team. Well-skilled and experienced players at every position. Windsor Locks had skilled players in Nancy Shapiro and Marie Duwell.

The Cinderella run ended with the shutdown play by the Grizzlies' halfback line led by Lindsay Taylor and the deep defense of Amy Cunningham and Lorraine Delabry. The Raiders did manage to outshoot the Grizzlies, 14-10. Including a pair of tough saves for Leslie Gribus in the final three minutes.

"I was so scared I was going to slip and fall in the mud," said Gribus, remembering her saves late in the game.

Remembers Taylor, *"The weather and the field actually made it easier to cover their players except their center (Shapiro) who's a terrific player."* Most of the Guilford players agreed, Windsor Locks was much better a team than pre-game information given to them in a loosely produced scouting report.

Half of the committee's wishes had come true. Guilford was now in Saturday's final.

Darien coach, Becky Strominger, remembered seeing the condition of the SCSC field and thinking, *"Not good for our style of game. This is going to be messy."*

Granby's Dottie Johnson took one look and said, *"Hey, both teams have to play on it."*

On Wednesday, rain fell during pre-game warmups. A tape player atop the scorers' table blared out the words to Helen Reddy's, "I Am Women." Her 1972 international signature song. I was close enough to the Darien team to catch some of the pre-game banter. One amusing interaction caught my ear. One girl said she did not know there was a Granby in the state. Another asked where it was located. There were a few retorts that put the town, *"Upstate somewhere. The other side of Hartford. Near Springfield (MA)."*

Obviously, for one of Connecticut's highest rated academic high schools, state geography was not part of the college-bound curriculum.

The game itself was a titanic defensive struggle affected by weather and field conditions. The goalies, Darien's Lorainne Ludwig and Jo Sproull for Granby, made few saves. Field conditions became the most pressing opponent. Most saves resulted from penalty corners. Pam Sproull and Val McCord each got off shots that were knocked down by the deep defense led by Leslie Milne. Sue Hebert was the spirited leader at the Bears' end of the field.

After 60 minutes of regulation time on a messy field, the game ended in a scoreless draw. You could hear it in that fearful tone as a few Granby players came off the field. *"Overtime. Here we go again."*

For the third time in a week, it was overtime for the Granby Bears. There were three sudden-death periods. Forty-five additional minutes of scoreless overtime play ensued. The Bears did manage to create three penalty corner opportunities. The final OT period ended with Granby leading in corners, 9-6. The girls from, *"Somewhere upstate"* were declared the winners. They had played their way into the state championship game.

The enigma had become the answer. On Saturday at Yale, the first-ever state of Connecticut field hockey championship game would pit Number One against Number Two. An odd feeling. Like this was destined to be. Almost as if this script had been written many years before.

There were no post-game celebrations. No jumping up and down. High-fives. Loud bantering, singing of songs or indirect taunts towards opponents. The game and its conditions had used up almost every ounce of energy in both teams. The teams quietly acknowledged each other and began the long trek back up the steep hill to the buses.

Granby's girls walked slowly. Sticks dragging on the ground behind them. Bending forward into the pelting wind. Unlike the Granby team I had come to know. This tournament was draining. And these girls still had one more very steep hill to climb. The wind was relentless and the wet rain had turned to snow.

Jill Barrett, one of Darien's co-captains, shared an amusing story about the night before the Granby game. *"We were feeling pretty confident. We got together at one of the girls' houses. Made spaghetti and meatballs. A little celebration. Next day in the mud, we played sluggish. Like we were still trying to digest that meal. Perhaps a celebration that was premature."*

Barrett also remembered, *"It was a long, quiet ride back to Darien."*

Remembers Granby's Sue Jensen, *"We were happy and thrilled about going to the championship game. We were also cold and tired. More tired than usual. Some of the girls fell asleep on the long ride home."*

I reached my car and watched the Darien girls board their bus. I laughed as I recalled their pre-game jocularity about Granby and its location. Hell, I had grown up in Simsbury when it was still a farm town. Downstate folks didn't know where we were located. Well, Darien now had a lot of free time on their hands to locate Granby on a state map.

I had a half-pint of Hiram-Walker peppermint schnapps in my army shoulder bag. I spun the cap off and took a large gulp. I could feel the warmth and its bite as it rushed down my throat and began spreading out in my innards. I swallowed hard. Licked my tongue. Blinked my eyes and tears rolled down my cheeks. Immediately, I had a renewed focus as my body and mind snapped back to life. Like being poked with a hat pin.

My clothes were soaked, clammy and uncomfortable. I was cold and hungry and once again, a long, snowy ride from home. One of my wipers was worn and left a streak across my windshield's center of vision. Yup, another typical day at the *Herald*. I started my car, turned on my Motorola dashboard radio and began my trip back to Simsbury.

"Bottle of Wine," an early '60's hit by Jimmy Gilmer and the Fireballs played on the radio.

50

Friday, November 16, 1973, was the eve for three Farmington Valley schools and their date with destiny in a state championship game.

Farmington and Canton would be playing in the boy's Class M and S soccer tournaments, respectively. Both games to be played at Hall High School in West Hartford. Granby's girls were in the inaugural girls' field hockey championship game in New Haven. I would be busy on this Friday trying to visit with the three coaches, looking for a few pre-game thoughts. Perhaps even running into a few of the players.

Larry Dubac was Canton's soccer coach. He was a longtime athlete and coach. A member of the 1948 National Championship soccer team at UConn. A multi-sport coach, he had started the Canton soccer program in 1964, and the Warriors, a respected member of the Northwest Conference, were now in the title game against Old Lyme. He had returned my call to the *Herald* saying he would be available after 11 AM. Farmington coach, Jack Casper, said to stop by sometime after 1 PM during a light practice. His undefeated Indians, also a member of the Northwest Conference, were scheduled to play Guilford's Grizzlies. Farmington had given up just two goals to opponents all season. Both scored by Canton in a 2-2 tie.

My first stop would be just 3.4 miles up the road from my apartment. It would be an unannounced cold call. I was hoping to spend a few minutes with Granby Coach, Dottie Johnson. I ran into AD Kenny King in the hallway. He said I might find Dot in the gym. He said she was a little under the weather. And, from a personal perception, King said, *"She's exhausted. She might not want to talk."* I spoke with one of the janitors who said he had seen the coach behind the upper level of the bleachers.

I found her. Sitting on the floor. Propped up against the backside of the bleachers. Hiding from as many intrusions as possible. Her legs straight out, slightly elevated on a pile of towels, covered by a maroon-colored school jacket. Arms crossed on her lap. Her eyes were closed, mouth slightly open. Asleep. I took one look and slowly backed away.

"Rob," I heard her say, *"it's OK. Always have time for you."*

Like her coaching moves, it was uncanny how she knew I was there. I felt humbled and apologized for waking her. She smiled, weakly. She covered her mouth and coughed. Tapped the floor with her left hand, wanting me to sit next to her. She looked awful...and I told her so. She nodded and laughed. Said she had one more gym class to lead. Most likely to be led by a student teacher. Then, she was heading home. I asked if they were ready for Guilford. *"Yes...there's nothing more we can do. We're ready."*

I got up to leave. Wished her good luck. Chuckled at my own words. I really did not believe in luck. To me, luck is when lots of preparedness and a tad of karma and a little good fortune from the cosmos comes together. As I turned to leave, Dottie said *"Hey Rob…thanks, for everything."*

Choked up a little, the only words I could utter were, *"Dottie, it was my pleasure."*

I set out for Canton High School riding the backroads through West Simsbury. On my radio, Chicopee's WACE plays "No Good to Cry." The 1966 and first chart hit by The Wildweeds from Windsor and their leader, Big Al Anderson. In 2000, Al Anderson will be honored as Broadcast Music, Inc. (BMI's) songwriter of the year. An extremely prestigious award from the USA's premier music performing rights and licensing fees organization. Al Anderson, the talented song-writer, had come a long way from the 21-mile strip of Route 159 between Hartford and Springfield and the cramped bars and American Legion halls where it all started.

51

It was a little after 5 AM on November 17, 1973. I exited Interstate 91 at North State Street. Drove south towards the center of the Elm City.

I passed Grove Street. The old New Haven Arena. The memories of so many events I had seen in that building. High school basketball between local powers, Hillhouse and Wilbur Cross. The New Haven Blades of the American Hockey League. Yale University hockey. When former major league pitcher for the 1962 New York Mets, Canadian Ken MacKenzie, had skated for the Elis. Mets manager, Casey Stengel referred to MacKenzie as a smart pitcher...who was now working as the lowest paid member of the 1956 Yale graduation class.

Downtown New Haven was eerily dark and desolate. Remnants of another ravaged inner city. The results of 1960's turmoil and migration of folks to the suburbs. On Chapel

Street was the four-sided clock next to the old Edward Malley Department Store where my Mom had taken me shopping with her many times during the 1950's. Just down the block from Liggett's Drug Store where we would eat lunch. Next to Gilbert's Bakery which sold day-old doughnuts for two cents each. I drove slowly through the main streets. Wondering... remembering. Turned on Chapel Street and began the mile and a half trip to 81 Central Avenue. The Yale Bowl.

I reached Central Avenue driving along the practice fields where the championship game would be played. I parked in an empty lot near Derby Avenue directly across from Yale's Field B. It was 5:25 AM and I was alone in the darkness. In an ironic and haunting way, the song on the radio was "Everyone's Gone to the Moon." A ballad from the mid-1960's British Invasion by Jonathan King, a music writer and promoter who would later be convicted and imprisoned in the UK for child pornography and molestation.

It was dark and cold, so I bundled up in my field jacket, scarf, and gloves. I walked to the middle of what would be that day's field of battle. It was a little unsettling. The moon, low in the western sky, offered an eerie blue-black light. The temperature was 28 degrees. I tightened my shoulders and shivered. The ground was hard and frozen. I could sense and smell the coldness all around me. Like when you walk alone in a cemetery. Surrounded by that thundering quiet. The biting loneliness that creeps up your spine when you walk among the spirits. That strange aroma that is the home for the dead. Sounds and smells I remembered from Vietnam. TET, 1968.

Suddenly the dark was interrupted by the bouncing beams of the on-coming headlights that sliced through the darkness. Jesus, my head was throbbing at a fever pitch. Once again it was my gallows humor. One of those welcoming lights at the end of the tunnel. For me it usually turned out to be an on-coming train. I stood frozen in the dual beams of light. Just waiting for the blast.

The driver of the small university maintenance vehicle rolled to a stop next to me. Used his flashlight to check me out. Said his name was Juan. Probably because of the look on my face he asked if I was OK. He seemed sincerely concerned. It took a few seconds to get enough air in my throat, and I assured him I was OK and all was well. Just a bit startled. He nodded and drove to the sideline and began to unload a few tables and chairs for the game's sideline officials. I walked over and helped him unload. He smiled, nodded in appreciation and said, *"Gracias."*

He asked if I would like some coffee. He had a large urn inside the cab of his truck. Unfortunately, no cups. I went to my car and checked my truck. I had an old, dented WWII-era army helmet. That would be my coffee cup. Juan roared with laughter. It really did look funny watching me sip my coffee from an army helmet. The coffee was black and hot. Man, it hit the spot. I could sense the on-coming dawn. Though its subtle first light had not yet appeared I focused my attention on the eastern horizon.

I held my coffee cup...the army helmet in front of my face. The steel pot was warm. I patiently waited. First light always meant new beginnings.

I could sense the memory almost before it began invading my thoughts. I tried to shake it...but it would not go away.

On this very day, November 17, 1968, Viet Cong rebels overrunning the helicopter pad at Dong Tam. Deep in the Mekong Delta, it was the base camp to the US Army's 9th Infantry Division. It was a hot night, so I went to sleep on the topside of a bunker. You could always catch a nice breeze once the sun went down. Like sleeping out on the back deck. Around 2AM all hell broke loose. Incoming mortars and rockets. Small arms fire from three sides. People screaming as they were hit with shrapnel and AK-47 fire. Explosions so loud and hot it felt like being in Hell. The two-hour attack would kill and wound more than 100 US, South Vietnamese, South

Korean, Filipino and Australian soldiers. Another 30 civilians and Vietnamese locals would die.

As I search for cover trying to outrun the on-rushing waves of attackers, I will fire more than 200 rounds from my WWII-era carbine rifle. The barrel will get so hot I will burn my hand when I grab it while running to a bunker. I will not know if my defensive fire hits anything until the dawn.

At first light there is a smokey fog. New beginnings. The aroma of burnt flesh and the smell of death hangs heavily in the air. Fires are burning all around us. The ground littered with bodies, alive and dead. We begin counting bodies. A few are still alive. Medics arrive. Airlifts to hospitals begin. The attack is never reported in the US news services.

In the heartbeat of a thought, I'm back in the middle of that dark and cold field-like cemetery at Yale and overcome with a wave of nausea. I hold both hands over my mouth to choke back and swallow the puke in my throat. My face is flushed, breathing accelerated and my heart is pounding in my chest. My thoughts plead with my very being. *"Please...It's not fair. Go away. Get outta my head. I don't wanna remember."*

Juan joins me in one of the chairs we had set-up along the field. He reads my face...gives a cautious smile. Asks if I'm OK. I nod. He offers me half a doughnut. I think of old Gilbert's bakery in downtown New Haven...two cent doughnuts. Juan asks me why I am here so early. I didn't know what to say. I tell Juan it's a little confusing. Something inside urging me to be here. I tell him that I don't have an explanation. I just chose to follow my gut feeling.

Juan nods. Sips his coffee and takes a long drag on a filtered Marlboro. After a silence he says, *"I don't know what...but I think you make the right choice, amigo."*

Softly, under my breath, I say, *"I hope so."*

52

Dawn arrived as the sun peaked above the horizon and began to rise into the eastern sky. The quiet of the Yale Bowl area began to awaken.

By 8 AM people began arriving, trickling in from every direction. By 9 AM it had become a steady stream of cars, bicycles, trucks and people on foot. Team buses arrived at 9:15 AM. Granby's team bus was followed by a caravan of yellow school buses and cars making the 60-mile trip. Students, parents, shopkeepers, town officials. It's been reported that an estimated 50% of the school's student body has come to cheer for their team.

Students and fans are wearing their high school colors and jackets. They have blankets and banners. Megaphones and airhorns, which by CIAC rules, are not permitted to be used at tournament games. Small groups, combos, have musical instruments, also not permitted by CIAC doctrine.

I chuckle thinking, *"Hey, it's about time to face the horns and music."*

I walked the field checking on its condition. I gave it a mark of C minus, at best. It's hard as rock. There are many ruts made from the tires of bicycles and small vehicles. It had been a muddy field when driven across, yesterday, and now those tracks are frozen. With the row of elm trees, buildings and the time of the year, the sun's low mid-day position in the southeastern sky, the sun's rays will not soften the field on this day.

This playing field is going to be extremely fast and very bumpy. Certainly not the best or desired playing surface for a state championship game.

As I come off the field, I notice the lead official for the championship game has been watching me. Adorned in her snappy white blazer and gloves, Angela "Chickie" Poisson smiles and says, *"I've heard about you from coaches. What's your opinion of field conditions?"* I answer, *"Fast and bumpy."* She nods and says, *"I think so too."*

Angelia Poisson has heard about me! Wow. I am humbled.

Poisson, who I often refer to as the Babe Ruth of field hockey due to her reputation and legacy, will be the lead official on this day. I can think of no other person in the state to be the lead official for this game.

Her running mate will be Lauren Anderson. She is young, a former high school field hockey coach and has credibility and respect for her officiating skills throughout the state. She is an excellent choice as a second. Charlotte Gallagher will be the alternate on site if needed. She has replaced Alice Yokabaskas from Simsbury who was originally chosen. Alice had to decline the assignment when a summer house on Cape Cod was damaged by a storm, and she is with her family clearing away debris.

I study each team as they go through warm-up drills. Try

and read body language and the faces of the players. Co-captains Pam Sproull and Sue Hebert perform their co-captain roles overseeing pre-game drills. Lynsie Wickman runs through her paces and hollers out, *"Fast field, ladies. Very fast field."*

Val McCord is talking trash. To everyone within earshot. Sharon Schneider practices her patented stop and go's. Sue Jensen smiles, but you could tell she is shivering. She does not like to play in cold weather. Ellen Burbridge appears sedate, unlike her usual outgoing and bubbling self. Mary Byrnes practices stickhandling. She says nothing.

Jody Wickman works on short passing. Linda Dewey goes through her warm-ups in her usual perfunctory manner. Nancy Hutchins stands tall. Her stick is upright, both her hands overlapped on the top of her taped handle. She watches the Guilford girls go through their drills. Jo Sproull kicks away soft shots and does leg exercises to loosen up. Dottie Johnson studies a few notes on a small pad. She takes in the sights and sounds that are now all around her. Dottie coughs, still a tad under the weather with a cold. She waves to the Guilford coach. The coach waves back.

I turn and do a second take. Closely stare at the Guilford coach who waves back. I looked at the crumpled-up paperwork and documentation I had put together for my pre-game prep activities. I look at an early season team photo. The person who waved back is not the person I have in a photo of her and the Guilford field hockey team.

I scan the sidelines. I do not see the Guilford coach from the picture.

53

The first-ever, CIAC field hockey state championship game starts at 10:07 AM. Temperature at game time is 34 degrees. The sun is still hidden behind a row of elm trees and buildings. The game will evolve into the event that the founding folks had hoped it would be. Perhaps the most important girls' high school sporting event to date, ever to take place in the state of Connecticut.

The game is a marketing agent's gift from heaven. Number one ranked Guilford High School (14-0-1) from downstate against second ranked Granby High School (13-0-3) from upstate. Just the way the tournament committee drew it up on the blackboard. Well, almost.

The game begins with emotions at a fever pitch. Once the initial adrenaline eases, the simple complexities of the game, strategies and player's skills, take over. Early action moves, stickhandling, passing, shooting and triangular executions elicit screams and cheers from the huge crowd. Granby's 4-4-2 format entices Guilford into attempts at taking advantage of the large visual splits in the Bears' disciplined positioning. Luring them into the web before the gap quickly closes creating turnovers.

On the other side of the ball, Guilford, their five-girl attacking front line, uses short passes and angle cuts that seem to defy calls of obstruction because of the angle of the cuts and distances maintained to avoid the inference of a penalty.

Early on it's obvious to all. These are two really good teams, evidenced by the level of play that is breathtaking. In a cliché of sports, they came to play and play they did.

The game is played at a good pace. It's only time before one of these teams will carve out an edge. Granby is the first to find that path. It starts with a nice give-and-go pass from Jody Wickman, sending Pam Sproull inside Guilford's 25-yard line. Sproull carries the ball into the scoring circle. She back-taps the ball into an open area 25 feet directly in front of Guilford's net.

Linda Dewey's long-legged strides catch up to the pass. Dewey tees off with a blistering shot about 18 inches off the ground into the Guilford net. Standing close to the sideline, I hear the ball make a *"Whooshing Sound"* as it cuts through the cold morning air. Goalie Leslie Gribus never moves. She stands straight up, shrugs her shoulders and slowly shakes her head. She never sees the ball.

The first half ends with Granby leading, 1-0.

Just 30 minutes of field hockey remain. Or maybe more. I scribble thoughts from the first half into my weathered notebook. For Granby, I note they played well, disciplined. Maybe even too hesitant. Deep defense had not been tested. Some of the girls looked tired. One big concern: Ellen Burbridge had played as if uninspired and sedate.

For Guilford, I wrote they were a ticking time bomb ready to explode.

The coach for Guilford is Becky Clomp, and I notice she is not here today. As the halftime meetings are taking place, I learn from folks in the Guilford crowd Becky is walking down the aisle at her wedding, becoming Becky Riggio. The on-field coach for this day is her assistant, Linda Gavin, a physical education teacher at the high school.

Lindsay Taylor, Co-Captain
Led the Guilford Attack

The Granby halftime huddle is upbeat, though low key. Coach Johnson reminds all not to overplay. Maintain areas of responsibility. Create opportunities. Pam Sproull adds one inspiration, *"Don't give up. If you need help, you'll have it."*

Guilford's halftime huddle is different. Center halfback, Lindsay Taylor appears to be the center of control. She is on one knee communicating instructions. She urges front line players, *"Be more aggressive with your attacks."* To her halfback line mates she says, *"Make quicker passes."* To the fullbacks she reminds them, *"When you clear a ball, let it fly."* And, to her goaltender, her best friend, she points to her and gives a thumbs-up. After all, Leslie Gribus is one of the best in the state between the pipes.

What is noticeably absent. Acting coach Linda Gavin is not involved in any of the discussions. She stands outside the group. Ostracized. Head down. Hands in her pockets.

The first half play had been 30 minutes of beautifully played field hockey. The second half will make that first half look like a junior varsity practice game.

And tension. It will be so thick it's palpable.

54

As the teams took the field to begin the second half, I notice Ellen Burbridge is not in Granby's line-up. She had not had a good first half. Her play was sluggish. She seemed slow afoot. Always a step behind the play, and that was unlike her. It happens to anyone who has ever played sports. Some days, for so many reasons, the parts just don't work quite as well.

She is replaced on the halfback line by Mary Byrnes, a junior, who is quick afoot with a solid stick and a good sense for the game. Byrnes would be a regular starter on any team in the state. Except the 1973 edition at Granby.

The Guilford girls came out for the second half with a bounce in their step and a look of stern determination in their eyes. Mary Bunting hollers for all to hear, *"I'm scoring the next goal."*

Nine minutes into the second half, she does just that. Her

field-length dash and goal can only be described as athletic and spectacular.

Amy Cunningham starts the play with a short pass to Bunting who has swooped back into her end of the field. Bunting pushes a short pass to Deb Crosby who deflects the ball to Nancy Nettleton. Granby defenders go after Nettleton who rolls a slick pass to Bunting who is in full stride. With a burst of speed, Bunting kicks in the afterburners and explodes up the middle of the field, leaving defenders flat-footed in her dust.

She leaps into the air and smashes between two defenders. Dekes a fullback and sprints headlong at Granby's goal. Jo Sproull sees her coming. She leaves her goalmouth and heads out to meet her attacker, trying to cut down the shooting angle. Bunting beats her to the spot and rolls a hard shot past her into the net to tie the game, 1-1. Bunting, unable to slow her momentum, follows the ball into the Granby net while trying to put on the brakes. She is mobbed by teammates.

Before the ensuing bully, Sproull's sister, Pam, jogs the 50 yards to her sister. Her message delivered with a stern and pained look on her face, *"That one's on us. They won't get another one in this game."*

Guilford's potent offense, though, is now unleashed. Dawn Sprague and Sharon Farquharson are next to attack Granby's deep defense. Sue Hebert blocks one shot. The other hits the goalpost. It takes a clearing pass from Lynsie Wickman and a head-on collision with Val McCord to relieve pressure. Granby's defense re-gathers. Guilford re-groups at mid-field.

Eight minutes remain to be played in regulation time.

Beth Mermann and Bunting lead the next onslaught into the scoring circle. Two more hard drives are fired at goalie Sproull. Both are rejected. Lindsay Taylor picks up one of the rebounds. Her shot clangs off the cross rod and the top of the net and out of bounds. Sue Hebert is shouting to teammates, *"Could use a little help here."*

Wave after wave of Grizzlies' attackers push the Bears deeper into the defensive zone until their backs are against their own goalposts. Mary O'Grady gets off a hard shot that tips off Sprague's stick, only to be repelled by Sproull in a last-second kick save. The ball had not left the Bears' end of the field in almost five minutes.

Jensen sets up about 20 feet in front of goal. She claws at the ground with her spikes as she digs in. Points at the Grizzlies' attacking line with her stick. *"C'mom-C'mom...come try me,"* she yells aiming her stick at Lindsay Taylor. *"You're not getting past me."* There is a look of astonishment on Taylor's face. She knows Jensen means business.

I walk past the scorers' table. Less than five minutes remain in regulation.

Taylor again initiates the next charge with line mates, Crosby and O'Grady. Again, it's Bunting, bouncing off people like a pinball, finding herself face-to-face with Granby's goaltender. With a flick, she lifts a shot for the right corner that first hits Sproull's stick at mid-shaft before ricocheting off her shoulder and out over the top of the net. One of those once-in-a-lifetime saves.

The timekeeper hollers out, ***"ONE MINUTE TO PLAY."***

Bunting and Taylor combine for one more rush. Bunting gets off a hard rolling shot stopped by Jensen who hollers out a few choice words at her opponents as she tees off on a clearing hit. A vicious drive that had Guilford attackers diving to the ground to get out of the way of the screaming high riser.

Regulation time ends with Granby ragging the ball near midfield, killing time. When the horn sounds Lynsie Wickman can be heard saying, *"Damn, that was a long minute."*

The first 15-minute sudden death overtime period beckons.

I spied tournament committee Director, Pat Mascia standing behind the scorers' table. She looked gaunt and tired. Yet, she stood proudly watching a game take place that once had only been a dream. Her committee had the right to do a little chest pounding and howling at the moon. They had earned the accolades. As we used to say as kids in the neighborhood, *"They dun good."*

Team huddles went on during the break. Scorebooks were checked to validate penalty corner hits. The count was knotted at 8-8. The official game timeclock was set for 15 minutes. A Bulova wristwatch was being used as a back-up. When I saw the watch, I had to laugh remembering watching TV as a kid, a 1950's NBC News Anchor, John Cameron Swayze, whose nightly news show was highlighted by his quote, *"That's the story folks—glad we could get together."* His show is sponsored by Bulova Watches, *"They take a licking and keep on ticking."* Like the players in this game.

I hear a voice yell to me. *"Hey Rob. What's gonna happen in overtime?"*

I mull over the question for a few seconds. Look at each team's huddle and holler back, *"Nothing. Nothing at all."*

That's pretty much what happens in the first OT. Nothing.

The overtime is a tug-of-war at mid-field. A battle of attrition about as exciting as watching vanilla ice cream melt on a hot August day. Linda Dewey got off the only serious shot for Granby. Gribus easily turned it away. At the other end of the field, Lindsay Taylor had Guilford's lone shot on goal. Sproull kicked it back at her so hard that if the ball had hit Taylor it would have knocked her senseless.

As the period ended the usually stoic Pam Sproull came off the field in a huff. Something had stuffed a burr in her ass and she was letting teammates know she was a little pissed off. I edged over and got as close to the Granby huddle as I dared. Pam's message was clear and emotional.

"Look! We're going to win this game. We have to! They're a good team. We're a better team. All right. Just do your job," was the message as she pounded her stick on the ground. I remembered Pam once telling me a team is like a mosaic. Lots of little pieces that make up one picture. It was time for all

those little pieces to become one.

That same, inquiring voice rang out from the crowd. *"Rob, what's gonna happen?"*

My response was terse, if not a tad arrogant. *"Granby's going to win."* The crowd near me went silent. My words were a little ballsy. But that's what I believed. It was 11:54 AM. The sun finally peeked through the row of elm trees on the Yale Bowl side of the field.

"Ah, post tenebras lux," I murmured, recalling a Latin phrase I had learned from years past. Its meaning, *"After darkness, light."* For Granby, it was now the moment of their dawn and time to wake up. Time to finish the mosaic.

As I walked the sideline , I passed Chickie Poisson. I asked how many OTs. She was a little iffy, but said, "Two. Maybe three." We both knew there would be three sudden-death OTs if needed. I mumbled some words that it needed to end, soon. Chickie nodded and

Granby Goalie Jo "Baby" Sproull Makes a Save Against Guilford

admitted that she thought Guilford was going to end it in regulation. She said the Granby team had a lot of guts.

Guts, yeah. They had lots of that. What they needed was just one goal.

55

The second sudden-death over-time was a battle. As brutal and demanding as any part of any game either team had played during the 1973 season.

First it was Guilford mounting the attacks. All five girls on the scoring line crashing in on Granby's goal. Hebert, Jensen and the Wickman sisters fighting them off. Heart throbbing action where, even as a fan, you found yourself gasping for breath. Granby counter-attacked, going the length of the field for a pair of corners and a barrage of shots on goalie Gribus off the sticks of Sproull, Mary Byrnes and a laser drive from Linda Dewey that nicked the post. The penalty corners gave Granby the advantage, 11-9, in case the outcome came down to penalty corners.

Dawn Sprague had the best opportunity to win it for Guilford. Sprague stickhandled deep into the scoring circle to the right of Granby's goalie, Jo Sproull. Sprague was hugging the end line so the angle of a shot to the goal was awfully wicked. Still, she got off a hard shot aiming at Sproull's feet and her protective shoe covering. What goalies refer to as their clown shoes. Perhaps a ricochet off the goalie's shoe would find its way into the net.

**Mary Bunting & Dawn Sprague
On the Attack for Guilford**

En route, her shot hit one of those frozen ruts that had a lip about five inches high. The ball, heading directly for the goalie's shoe, took a sharp left turn and went out-of-bounds about a foot short of the net. The kind of shot one couldn't repeat if they tried for ten years. Sprague slowly shook her head and just stared in astonishment at the raised frozen turf.

What happened next is one of those moments in sports, and in life, that transcends the game itself. Its memory and the stark realism to its empathy and respect has stayed with me for 50 years. Still chokes me up a bit. One of those occurrences that helps us to better see the path ahead in our lifetime search for an understanding to *"A Question of Balance."* It tells us who we are in stark and realistic terms. And it happened right before my very eyes.

With six minutes remaining, Pam Sproull took control of the ball just inside midfield. She started her attack near midfield and stopped. She just...stopped. Perhaps, to catch her breath or to see where people were on the field. Instead, she let the heel of her stick fall to the ground. Stood straight and upright. Proud. Legs slightly parted. Head held high. Chin out. Her kilt rippling slightly from the morning breeze. Behind her, teammates also stopped and emulated her stance.

Across the mid-field line was Guilford's Lindsay Taylor. She stood directly in Sproull's path about 15 feet away. She, too, came to a stop as did teammates behind her. Like her counterpart, she let the heel of her stick drop to the ground. She too, stood tall and proud, head slightly raised.

The two young girls, teenagers, stared at each other.

Each was her team's co-captain. Team leaders. Battling for recognition and perhaps, lifetime memories. For a legacy. Their chests heaving in and out as they breathed in the still, chilly November air. Sweat dripping from noses and chins. Uniforms streaked with dirt.

The playing field was eerily silent. The crowd noise slightly muffled.

Sproull pursed her lips and nodded in recognition at her worthy opponent. Taylor nodded back, swallowing hard as if to choke back a sound. They were saluting each other in a way only the girls on that field would ever be able to understand. No words or hand gestures. Just body language, facial expressions...an approving head nod. Young ladies in a battle against each other. But this. Whoa...this was something that went way beyond the 17 years of their lives.

Jeez, at that moment, I thought somebody had reached down inside of me, grabbed my guts and yanked on them. Maybe there were gentler rules of war. You can and should respect your enemy. Sproull gave a slight smile, nodded one more time. Picked up her stick, took in a deep breath and once again began her journey up field.

The moment and its subtle nuance had passed in a heartbeat. Few along the sideline ever really saw the salute. Just an epistle in a pause that now exists on the fringes of time's conscience. Hidden away in the hearts of friends, enemies and two teenage girls playing field hockey.

Two young ladies. Standing at the threshold to the rest of their natural lives, took time to honor the moment and their opponent's efforts.

56

The critical play of the overtime, and the game itself, began in a harmless way.

Two minutes remained in the second overtime. Sue Jensen made a clearing hit to the right side of the field. Sproull picked up the ball that was bouncing wildly over frozen ruts. She pointed for Jody Wickman to head up the sideline ahead of her. Sproull was boxed in by Crosby and Beth Mermann. She scooped the ball over Crosby's shoulder to Wickman. You could hear lead official Poisson call out her verification, *"Good hit, good hit."* Jody stickhandled up the sideline until she too was boxed in along the sideline, just outside Guilford's 25-yard line.

That's when things just started going badly for Guilford.

The ball was back passed to Sproull, which in the general scheme of things was a rather gutsy play by Wickman. It drew the Guilford defenders to Sproull, who was now being triple-teamed. The senior co-captain waited until the last possible second before she scooped and lifted another soft floater toward the Grizzlies' end of the field where it was picked up by Lynsie Wickman who continued the journey stickhandling through a double-team before being stopped near the right edge of the scoring circle.

A mass of six to seven girls from both teams surrounded the ball in what can only be described as a group scrum. All the while the group kept shuffling their feet drifting closer towards Guilford's scoring circle. In retrospect, it was a rather amazing sequence with no penalty whistles. No one person was able to make a breakout play.

From her goal, Leslie Gribus yelled, *"Get the ball out of here. Clear it."* She repeated her call more emphatically, ***"GET...IT...OUT...OF...HERE!"***

The scrum's whirling dervish of activity kept migrating closer. A whistle sounded for an obstruction, giving the ball to Granby. Sproull's free hit deflected off Taylor's stick. Another group scrum ensued on the fringe of the circle. Wickman yelled out, *"Don't let em clear it. Play tight,"* meaning don't let any of the Guilford players extend their arms for a clearing hit.

"ONE MINUTE" was the cry from the timekeeper, now on her feet running along the sideline. She had to go about 10 feet out onto the field, screaming out the time above the roar of the now raucous crowd. Many of whom had drifted onto the corner of the playing field.

Gribus had ventured a few feet farther away from her goal. In case of a shot, she wanted to be ready. Able to cut down the angle of her attacker.

Fullback Amy Cunningham had joined the scrum. Lorainne Delabry stationed herself about 15 feet behind Cunningham as a safety valve in the event the ball might be hit out of bounds, giving Granby a corner hit. Gribus was now left alone near her goal. Deb Crosby was positioned about 20 feet to her right.

Gribus remembered, *"You could feel it. Something was going to happen!"*

Lynsie Wickman decided it was time for her to make one of her patented hell-bent-for-leather plays. Throw a few elbows and bounce off a few people...see what happens. She made a loud sound, *"Arrrrrgh Yeouza"* and went crashing into the mass of bodies.

Suddenly, the ball squirted out from the scrum's mass of legs and sticks. It shot between Cunningham's legs and past Delabry before she could react. It was headed for the center point of the scoring circle. Gribus saw the play developing and reacted in the blink of an eye. As she looked at Crosby to her right, she came eye-to-eye with Granby's Mary Byrnes who had quietly migrated into the scoring circle.

Byrnes, who was the halftime replacement for Ellen Burbridge, was on-sides, about 20 feet away, standing directly in front of Gribus. That elusive loose ball was now hugging the shoe-end of Byrnes' stick. Their eyes locked on to each other. Byrnes then did what she worked on every day in practice. She stepped into the ball and fired her shot.

Fifty years have passed. Gribus still vividly recalls the shot. *"She (Byrnes) looked at me, then looked down at the ball on her stick. Bending at her waist and knees, she shot the ball at me with a full follow-through as she went down on one knee. Stick ending up shoulder high. I saw the ball coming at me."*

"The ball was moving fast" said Gribus. *"It bumped over a couple of ruts. It had a funny spin and was slicing away from me. I had made up my mind I was going to make a kick save. Kick it back between the shooter and the group scrum to my left."*

Gribus continued with her memory of that moment. *"It was quiet. Like I was the only one on the field. I was focused and had the shot all the way. Just as I was about to plant my left foot for my right foot to make a kick save, a stick appeared reaching across in front of me. It was Deb Crosby. She made a poke at the ball. It ticked off the tip of her stick, changing directions slightly, deflecting about a foot to the left."*

Gribus had already planted her left foot and was paralyzed as the ball shifted farther away. She pushed off with her left foot, trying to fall backwards while reaching out with her left arm. The shot was already past her. She rolled to her left and while on her knees, turned to see the ball cross the goal line and disappear into the corner of the net. She looked back at Byrnes.

Recalled Leslie Gribus, *"Her (Byrnes) face. She had this odd look. A blank stare. Then, her eyes got large like someone in awe. Her mouth hung open. Then I started to hear the screaming all around me. Sticks were being thrown into the air. I knew it was over."*

Granby had scored and won the game, 2-1. There were 28 seconds remaining in the second sudden death overtime. For the fourth time in less than two weeks, Granby had won a field hockey game in the waning seconds of sudden-death overtime.

Sticks continued to fly into the air. Granby's players were screaming and jumping up and down. Fans rushed the field like a tidal wave coming onshore. Pandemonium ensued. Players from both teams disappeared into the wave of humanity. More people than I had ever seen at a field hockey game. Dottie Johnson stood on the sideline. Mouth open, that half smile that would find its way to the corner of her lips. She stood, stoically, and watched her team in jubilation. She then ran onto the field and picked up Sue Jensen in a bear hug.

I admired her. The person and the preparation. I quietly mouthed the words as I had done earlier that morning, *"Wow—Granby won the whole goddammed thing."*

Chickie Poisson checked the net and found the ball tucked behind the backline pipe. She went to the scorer's table. Confirmed the shot was a goal. Declared the game over and

Granby the winner. Ensured the appropriate documentation was made in scorebooks including signatures. She shook hands with her partner, Lauren Anderson.

There's an old saying in sports. If you can't remember much about the officials and calls during the game, they did their job the way it was supposed to be done. In all my years covering field hockey, it was the best officiated game I can recall. And I remembered her words about wearing a white blazer and gloves. She declared proudly, *"They are part of the official uniform for the officials of field hockey."* Angelia "Chickie" Poisson was one classy lady who brought dignity to the game of field hockey.

I sat down on the playing field. Just plopped down in the middle of all the mayhem and watched what was happening all around me. Why not! From a tape player the voice of Eddie Hodges shouted out his biggest hit "I'm Gonna Knock on Your Door." A song he recorded when he was just 14, at the urging of The Everly Brothers. Hell, why not sit there? What was going on all around me was the best damn show in town.

57

Eventually, I regained control of my euphoria, found my way into the large crowd and began mingling, my trusty pad and Paper Mate Pen at the ready. Snapping a few pictures with my newest motor-driven TopCon and Yashica Mat-12 cameras.

When asked how she felt, Coach Dottie was breathless and said only, *"I don't know. Good, I guess. It hasn't set in yet."* Her eyes twinkled, ready to emit tears.

Pam Sproull, excited but reserved, reminded folks, *"This was our game and we were going to win it."* She had never lost a field hockey game in her four years at Granby and the unbeaten streak now stood at 50 games. She said, admittedly, *"It felt like we were fighting for our lives out there."*

Sproull later shared with me that during second overtime she thought about the unbeaten streak. It had to continue. For that to happen, Granby was going to have to win this game. I asked if that scared her. She said it didn't. Though, the thought of losing was like a hard slap in the face. Kind of a wake-up call.

Sue Hebert, in a stunned wonderment, held her hands out in front of her, palms up. Speechless, just slowly shaking her head and wearing a beautiful smile. When asked about the winning goal, Mary Byrnes just smiled and shrugged, not knowing what to say. She had replaced Ellen Burbridge in the second half. Burbridge rejoiced with her teammates. She knew she was having a bad game and needed to be replaced. It was my belief that, despite having a tough game on this day, Granby would not be here without her. Ellen Burbridge was a consummate teammate.

Lynsie Wickman flit from person to person yelling, *"We did it...We did it."* Val McCord hollered shouts of her team's accomplishments to and at everyone within earshot. Linda Dewey, her red hair tied into a ponytail, carried the team's teddy bear in her arms. Sue Jensen cried. Still shivering and cold. She came from a tough home life. Cradling her hockey stick in both arms. The one she bought with money she earned from babysitting. Other Granby players were in various degrees of celebrations with friends and family.

Guilford's Leslie Gribus and Lindsay Taylor stood together watching the winning team's celebrations. Taylor had her arm on Gribus' shoulder. They were teammates. Good friends. Yeah, they had lost the game and most likely weren't thinking that, even with losing, they had been a part of something special. Perhaps it would take a lifetime of friendship to realize they, too, had played in a game that will become an important piece of history. A piece of the legacy and their part in time that had yet to be written.

At that moment, Mrs. Rebecca Riggo and guests were settling into the post-wedding reception. She had coached the Guilford girls to their number one ranking, but today, her wedding day, she would be there only in spirit. Linda Gavin would assume coaching responsibilities. To many on the team, she was an outsider.

I caught up with Gavin along the sidelines asking for a few thoughts. She turned. Looked me over with a laser stare that would penetrate steel. She began nodding her head, pointing one finger at me. She fired off a fusillade of wide-ranging verbiage spoken so quickly I couldn't write it down fast enough to keep pace. Her words were hard and biting. No warm and fuzzies here. Perhaps it was her way of reacting to her team's disappointing loss. Or deep-rooted feelings of rejection by the team, girls she knew from years of gym classes, that saw Clomp-Riggio as the coach. Not Linda Gavin.

When my editor Lou Ball saw what I had written capturing Gavin's tirade, he said in that all-too familiar and curmudgeonly manner, *"Nope...Can't Print That!"*

Mary Bunting chased down local folks asking if anyone had heard how the Guilford boys' soccer team had done. They were playing that morning in the Class M state championship game against Farmington. They won the title, 1-0 on a goal by Lee Ramosco in the second sudden-death OT. The boys winning in the second sudden death overtime. The girls losing in the second sudden death overtime. One of those legendary symmetries in and of sports.

Amy Cunningham and Deb Crosby stood together with family, talking. Dawn Sprague, hockey stick held proudly between her knees, sat quietly in one of the folding chairs. Sharon Farquharson, her shoulders sagging and a blank look on her face, stood looking out over the playing field. Mary O'Grady cried. Comforted by friends and family. She will wake up on Sunday morning and again start crying when she hears on her radio the Four Seasons singing, "Big Girls Don't Cry."

I spied Juan, the Yale University maintenance worker who shared coffee and doughnuts with me standing near his truck. He smiled and pointed at me. He hollers to me words barely audible. *"You made the right choice, Amigo."* I waved back. I mouth the word, *"Gracias."* For a strange reason I also say, *"C'am o'n."* It's a slang expression and a way to say thanks, in Vietnamese.

Granby players are mobbed by a crowd. Kids asking for autographs. The girls sign every request. As the Granby team makes its rounds a little girl follows behind them dragging a field hockey stick that is taller than she is. On the edge of the field two young boys, perhaps seven or eight years old, pass a soccer ball back-n-forth using field hockey sticks. Amid the crowd a small combo plays a lively high school fight song. There are air horns blaring. When I closed my eyes and listened, it all sounded normal. Like a deck of cards being shuffled, multiple sounds meshing, all in perfect harmony like a Sunday morning chorus. Maybe there really were field hockey gods.

I realize *The Farmington Valley Herald*, me, is the only

Granby High School
1973 Connecticut Field Hockey Champions

Front Row: Sue Hebert, co-captain, Pam Sproull, co-captain and Ellen Burbridge. **Second Row:** Nancy Hutchins, Linda Dewey, Lynsie Wickman, Jo Sproull, Jody Wickman, Mary Byrnes, Val McCord, Sharon Schneider, Sue Jensen, Coach Dottie Johnson

newspaper covering this game. I squat down on my haunches along the sideline. I let my eyes perceive and my mind wander. So much is going on all around me. I need to assess what I am seeing. What's going on in my head. My heart. Hell, I don't know where to start.

Just 100 feet from me, Dot Johnson, surrounded by her team and fans, accepts the trophy for winning the title from Tournament Director, Pat Mascia. I have one frame left on my Yashica Mat camera. I am fortunate to get all the girls who played in the game together for one shot at a team picture. I struggle with focusing and I am not sure if I got a good shot. I will not know what I have until the next morning when I get into the darkroom and develop the film. My good fortune is that I do get a decent and focused picture.

Another 500 feet away from the hockey field I see the berm-like hill that is the top of the historic Yale Bowl and its entrance portals. Unlike the above-ground stadiums for most of college football, the bowl is a mounded reminder of a military-like redoubt of earlier centuries. Where one enters, then walks down into its bowels. A place where I had watched football games before there was an official Ivy League beginning in 1956.

I vividly remember. Me, a ten-year old, listening on my Zenith transistor radio to the voice of Sid Jaffe on WNHC as he extolls the virtues of Eli quarterback Dean Loucks and the crazy legs running of Dennis McGill. Just six days earlier I had been here to watch former Yale All-American, Calvin Hill, return to the Bowl with the Dallas Cowboys and run for 100 yards in a win over the New York Giants who had moved to the Bowl as the original Yankee Stadium began its refurbishing.

Hey, what if this field hockey final had been a prelim to a home game for Yale. It would have drawn thousands of spectators. Just imagine, Yale's Boola Boola tune harmonizing with Granby's fight song.

Twelve miles away on I-95 crews are finishing up repairs to the Stratford toll booths damaged when a Consolidated Freightways semi-trailer crashes into them earlier in the week. An omen of sorts. Two more fatal accidents with trucks and toll booths will hasten their removal from the nearby interstate in the 1990's. Yale will no longer receive a stipend from the state for toll booth revenues from the once-owned Yale land, ceded to the State of Connecticut in the 1930's.

In Meriden, 27 miles up Interstate 91, Hector Goncalves, which is an alias, is brought before a weekend magistrate for his moving violation earlier that morning when captured in a speed trap driving his battered and smoking station wagon that looked like a Korean War tank. He pleads not guilty. Bail is denied when it's learned he has many aliases and is wanted on a number of outstanding warrants in Massachusetts and Rhode Island, including one for child sex charges and one for attempted murder.

Like I said, the bill and payment, demanding satisfaction, always comes due.

To the north, 59 miles away, folks in Granby have already learned their girls' field hockey team has won the state title. Word spreads quickly throughout the small community. On the bus ride home, Granby girls will stop at a McDonald's in Cromwell. They will take over the building. Sing songs and eat Big-Macs. The bill comes to $94. A huge crowd will welcome them back when they arrive at the high school. Celebrations will follow that evening and throughout the ensuing weeks.

Also, 87 miles north, my girlfriend waits on this day for a phone call from me that will never come.

To the south, 132 miles from where I am sitting, the tenants of the Yale Bowl, the university's football team is taking the field at Palmer Stadium in Princeton, New Jersey. The Elis of coach Carmen Cozza will upset Old Nassau 30-13, behind QB Tom Doyle and the running of Rudy "Bam Bam" Green and Tyrell "Hurricane" Hennings. The next week's win over Harvard will give them a share of the Ivy League Title.

Granby field hockey and Yale football. Appropriate both should share championships in the lengthening afternoon shadows of the Bowl.

On this day in Atlanta, 951 miles south, a young man named Wil, sitting at his kitchen table, will answer his phone. The call is from his VA appointed psychiatrist. Wil is the recipient of the Bronze Star for heroism and a Purple Heart in Vietnam. The doctor hasn't heard from Wil in two weeks and is worried. So, he phones.

The doctor will spend an hour on the phone talking Wil out of committing suicide. Wil, staring at a photo of his family and with his hands shaking, will remove the bullets from the Smith & Wesson .38 special, placing the gun on the kitchen table. My friend from the 9th Infantry Division will live on, becoming an advocate to prevent veterans' suicides.

Wil dies in 1982 from complications of and exposure to the killer defoliant, Agent Orange, that has ravaged his body. One of his daughters will spend her lifetime on crutches because of AO passed on to her genes. Another will struggle with heart problems. The VA will never pay Wil or his family members any reparations for his wounds, disabilities, medical costs or service to his country. It just didn't matter to the VA, who lies to the family when they say his records were destroyed in a 1973 fire at the VA records warehouse. A lawyer, hired by the family, will find his records in 2001 buried in a VA storage archive in Georgia. A decision on a family claim from 2015 is still pending.

On this day in 1863 Abraham Lincoln will pen the first draft for his speech that will become the Gettysburg Address. Words of empathy. "For the people."

On this day in 1956, Russian Premier, Nikita Khrushchev will arrogantly vow to the world press, *"We will bury you,"* referring to his being present for the demise of the US and western democracy.

Also, on this very day in a Miami hotel suite, 1357 miles away, Ray Price and Aram Bakshian are word-smithing the finishing touches for that evening's nationally televised speech by President Richard Nixon to the Associated Press Editors Convention.

In the TV speech, Nixon will utter his infamous line to the world, *"I am not a crook."* More of his self-evident lies. "For the people."

As I leave New Haven, my radio plays The Chambers Brothers. Wailing out their classic, "Time Has Come Today." The Dave Clark Five sing out their percussion-driving hit, "Do You Love Me." Eric Burdon and the Animals belt out, "We Gotta Get Outta this Place." A theme song of sorts for every Vietnam vet.

My ride home to Simsbury is long and I am pensive. I make three stops. The first is to watch the second half of a state championship soccer game at West Hartford's Hall High School, won by Canton, 3-1 over Old Lyme on a key goal from John Incillo. The very same field the Guilford boys had won their title earlier that morning. For my second stop I cross the Connecticut River to speak with a long-time Connecticut stock car racer who races on many of the local tracks for a story I am planning to do in early 1974. My final stop is at Antonio's Restaurant in the Weatogue section of Simsbury. I eat spaghetti and meatballs and have a couple of glasses of chianti.

It's 10 PM when I arrive at my apartment. I am tired and have a killer headache. I sit on my daybed. Take a handful of aspirin. Wash 'em down with a glass of wine. Smoke a Winston. I think of the Granby girls. Their wonderful state championship. Dottie Johnson, how proud she is of her team. Sue Jensen, crying tears of happiness. Sue Hebert's wonderful smile. I chuckle to myself, *"My '63 team at Simsbury's Henry James, my senior year. They would have beaten Granby, today."* I take a deep drag on the cigarette. I drain my glass of merlot. On my radio, Dicky Lee sings out his 1962 gut-wrenching song, "Patches," about forbidden teenage love within social classes.

For what it's worth, sleep does not come to me on this night.

58

Lives change. Like I said, nothing good ever lasts. The relationship with my girlfriend will end just four days later during the early morning hours of Thursday, Thanksgiving Day. The roll-away couch bed in the living room has been made up for me. A large turkey day family dinner is planned for 2 PM. But I cannot sleep. It's 2:30 AM and too many unbridled thoughts are running wild in my head. And I cannot stop them.

As Colonel Williams at Fort Sill had taught me, it's time to pick a lane. Despite the oddity of the situation, it's time for me to go.

Quietly, I dress. Gather my things and tiptoe out the front door. Get in my car and begin the 90-minute drive to Simsbury. I am embarrassed and feel shame at what I am doing. After 20 minutes, I am cruising south on Interstate 91, the lights from the city of Springfield, Massachusetts on my left. The Bee Gees sing "Massachusetts" on WHYN, 560 on my AM dial. The station is located just three miles west of downtown. In an odd and strange way, I begin to feel a calmness in my body. My hands no longer are choking the steering wheel. The throbbing behind my right eye has stopped and the dull ache in the back of my head has eased. My breathing has slowed. In a move that seems to use every part of my body, I loudly breath out a sigh.

As painful and embarrassing, perhaps as wrong as it is, I am doing what needs to be done. What one of us should do. No justifications. No point-counterpoint discussions that drone on at a kitchen table. No do-overs. I have made my decision. Colonel Williams always urged, *"Pick a lane. Stay in it. Defend it. Then live with the results of that decision because you now own it."*

Like the Granby girls. They picked a lane. Defended it to the end. And now own the right to be called Legends. I wonder...what the hell will people call me.

As I cross the state line from Southwick, Massachusetts into Granby, Connecticut, I light a cigarette. WHYN still on my radio. Rick Nelson's "Poor Little Fool" and Don Gibson's "Oh Lonesome Me." Neal Young sings, "Heart of Gold." And Johnny Horton belts out the words to his 1959 classic, "Sink the Bismarck." Horton, another legend, will die less than a year later in a head-on crash traveling from Austin, Texas to Shreveport, Louisiana.

Surprisingly, the words just started coming to me in a gentle flow from a place I know not where. Those final words to that poem I had tried to write to my girlfriend. My rather lame and feeble attempt at an apology. Because I had not yet found the courage to pick a lane. I took a drag off my Winston, exhaled and as the words came into my head, I spoke them slowly out loud as I drove through the center of Granby.

Tonight, I found a path to walk
    and for the first time,
    it's not a yesterday path.
It's my sanctuary of forgetfulness,
    a way for me to just drift away.

So, now all my issues both alive and dead
    can somehow, now, be put to bed.
Understanding the pain and regret
    in those many places where I should have been
    and with those caring words that I should have said.

At last, I can now see and deal with my adult shame,
    because I am no longer afraid
    to wear the cloak of blame.

I have picked my lane.
My decision is out there for all to see.
Now, I am truly a solo, and singing slightly off-key.

The Five Satins and the voice of Fred Paris sing, "In the Still of the Night." My journey continues. I pass by the original Granby High School building atop the hill. The back-to-back signals in the center of town. Past South Congregational Church and Powers Chevrolet. The new Malibu and Nova highlighted in the showroom by small floor lamps. And the town recreational fields that once served as the Granby Public Golf Course. Over Salmon Brook and the last few miles before reaching the Simsbury town line and my apartment. From my radio Martha and the Vandellas sing "Nowhere To Run".

It's 4:11AM when I reach my apartment. Directly across from the town line sign that proudly announces, *"Simsbury Incorporated 1670."* I stop at my apartment to change. Knowing the phone calls would soon be coming, I decide to clear out of my apartment and head for the *Farmington Valley*

Herald. I'll be safe there. Away from having to answer painful questions on the phone. I turn on the radio and loose myself in the music listening to Chicopee's daylight-only station, WACE. The Teddy Bears harmonize, "To Know Him is to Love Him." Tommy Roe rocks out with his classic, "Sheila." Booker T & the M.G.'s spins its soulful jazz with "Green Onions." I spend the day cleaning up a pile of paperwork. I prep for the on-coming seasons. Basketball and ice hockey. I develop film in the darkroom. Print a few photos that I will sell for pocket cash.

The phone rings six or seven times. I don't answer it. I turn up the radio. The Ventures meld together guitars and the driving beat of the snare drum to "Walk Don't Run." Johnny Tillotson finishes off the set with his nasally version of "Poetry in Motion."

On a lark and looking to kill time, I decide to make holiday phone calls to folks I don't know. I call a 319 area code number in Cedar Rapids, Iowa. Nobody answers. The folks in 419 Lima, Ohio are not pleased with my interrupting their Thanksgiving Day dinner. I dial a number in the 603 area-code. The couple in Melvin Village, New Hampshire are nice, but are heading out the door for a family dinner in Wolfboro. My conversation with a family in Hull, Quebec Canada ends when it dawns on me, Canadian Thanksgiving was in October.

I call my Mom and Dad in Largo, Florida. It's a nice conversation. My Dad, Canadian born in southern Quebec, reminds me that as kids, most of the families in their farming community celebrated both Canadian and US Thanksgivings.

Later that evening, I return to my apartment. I disconnect the phone and settle in for my Thanksgiving Day meal. I eat hotdogs with mustard and relish. A dish of mac and cheese along with a few glasses of Luigi Cavalli Lambrusco. I sit in the darkness thinking about the decisions I have made on this day. I have picked my lane. Now, I must defend it. Because I own it. I think about the state championship game. Guilford and

Granby. I wonder. Do the girls have to pick a lane and defend it?

My cat crawls onto my lap. She gives a quiet, open-mouth meow.

In the darkness of the small apartment, my memories carry me back to Thanksgiving Day, 1968. I am part of an army convoy returning through the confluence of landlocked Laos and the Cambodian Triangle. Very dangerous territory. We're on our way back to South Vietnam's northern border following a supply drop. Near dusk, we're ambushed by a combined force of VC and a group known as, "The White Mice." Vigilantes who will fight for whoever is paying the best price that day. Twentieth century Hessians.

We dig in and make a Mayday call for help. To our incredibly good fortune, two AH-1 Huey Cobras are nearby and are on the scene before our Captain finishes his message. Helicopter gunships that can bring lots of firepower and kick ass. They decimate the dense foliage on each side of us with mini-rockets and withering blasts of strafing fire. Machine gun fire from mini guns that hits just five feet from where I am laying on my back. The noise and vibrations of their attack enough to make you piss your pants. Infantrymen embedded in our convoy will find over 30 mangled and bullet-ridden enemy bodies. Many attackers are killed just a few feet away from our position. Our embedded Vietnamese rangers scour the landscape taking prisoners of the attackers still alive. Prisoners are dragged off into the jungle. After brief interrogations, we hear screaming and automatic small arms fire in the jungle. The prisoners are being assassinated.

Had the Cobras not been close by, perhaps I might not be sitting here recalling the incident in my apartment's quiet darkness and the late hours with my cat. You might sometimes hear a veteran say, "Guess it just wasn't my day to die."

Yeah, Thanksgiving Day. Once, it meant family, a yummy

turkey and lots of stuffing. Watching the Detroit Lions. Or Macy's parade. The first Macy's Thanksgiving Day Parade held on this day in 1924. I had been to a half dozen parades in my lifetime.

Now It means something a little different to me. I chose this day to pick a lane and defend it because it was time for me to do so. Now I own that decision and will live with it. As I live everyday with my memories. My legs stretched out on the ottoman, I lean back in my chair letting my head rest on a large, soft pillow, listening to my cat purr in my lap. On the radio, Rosie and the Originals sing, "Angel Baby" and The Danleers croon, "One Summer Night." There is a strange restful silence all around me.

For what it's worth, that evening, I will fall soundly asleep for more than six hours. The first night I have done so in over five years.

Part 5

"Through the Years"

59

Being a good athlete is one of those wonderful gifts we get from God. But you don't have to be a good athlete to play sports. Having the choice to participate because you want to, is a good thing. Sports does not determine who or what we are. Or what we will become during our life's journey.

Choosing to play sports becomes one of those station stops along the road of life. You pick a lane and defend it. You choose how to manage the perception of your lifetime choices. Or, as I have come to know in my lifetime, playing competitive sports is another in those lines of learning that is a part of our lives. And some of those lessons we come to learn are life changing.

I left sports writing in 1978 looking for a new challenge in my life. Searching for a new perception. Because I began struggling with the idea of sports and the game itself. I had to learn how to understand one of my life's monsters. That, when the game is over...the game is really over. I liked the games. I hated the final whistles that ended them. Leaving me with too much time to think about too many unpleasant things. Alone with my thoughts and with no short or long-term plan how to deal with those monsters that were the everyday thoughts in my head.

I entered the field of management consulting. A decision prompting me to move from Simsbury to Baltimore. My specialty became the development and implementation of business training programs in multiple industries worldwide. I will always believe that a base education, steady learning environment, my days playing sports, my years at the *Farmington Valley Herald,* even my military years, were the ascending stairsteps of preparation that eventually jettisoned me into the tall cotton of the consulting world.

I will spend the next 38 years implementing my business training programs in every US state and Canadian province. Throughout Europe and Asia. Central and South America, India, Pakistan and a list of islands and countries dotting the globe. I liked what I did and I was good at generating results and satisfying client's needs. It was financially rewarding and it was one hell-of-a-ride. Along the way, I learned how to deal with that game-ending final whistle. Learned how to manage and live with those awful thoughts and some of those monsters that never die. Fortunate to have my best friend and loving wife, Bonnie, in my life to help me along the way. I will retire in 2015, because of wounds and nagging injuries from Vietnam.

Shortly after retiring, I will begin writing books because of my 50-year battle with the Veterans Administration for disability, medical and medal benefits never awarded from my injuries in Vietnam. The VA constantly reminding me that I did not have the appropriate documentation for those claims. They will deny my claims saying I am losing my memory and cannot recall key events and critical information to support my claims. When I do produce viable documentation, it will be waylaid, damaged or fall through the processing cracks slowing the process and requiring me to reapply.

Well, they're right with one point. I don't have all the required documentation because the 9th Infantry Division destroyed over 80% of its hard-copy paperwork, beginning in January 1969 and continuing to August 1970. The very people denying me my claims...delaying the process and the ones saying I was suffering mentally with my memories, are the ones who destroyed the evidence. The frustrating protocols harken back to the days in late 1969-70 when suspicious fires begin destroying hardcopy veterans' records in the St Louis archives.

I am not losing my memory. So, I start writing about all those wonderful years being a kid and young adult in Simsbury. Writing stories to get them down on paper before I really do begin to forget them. My published books allow me to highlight to the VA...to all who care to read my words, the fact that my memory of years gone by is just fine.

And because of that fact, I cannot...I must not let the story of my time at the *Farmington Valley Herald*, my involvement with field hockey and that 1973 season go untold. Tell the story so I will never have to suffer the indignation and embarrassment of one day having to say that I could have or should have done it.

60

The story about the 1973 high school field hockey season comes back to life in summer 2019. I wanted to begin searching for players from the fall of 1973 because it was these folks, not the CIAC that owned that tournament. Once the young girls of history. Now the adults of the world and the keepers of those memories.

Wow, did I ever find a cache of buried information just waiting to be discovered. A virtual population of people who represented the ways and means of the living americana. It was a double-edged sword of discovery. I will find many, at home, only because of their being locked in due to the killer pandemic. Like me, suffering the mental and physical stresses resulting from those continuing strange times.

These girls from history are living in all 50 US states and Canada. In Europe and Southeast Asia. Many, like me, working their professions in every corner of the world and have stories to tell. Memories to recall. I find a girl, a mom and her family, living in New England and hear James Taylor sing, "Sweet Baby James." To the music of Billy Joel's "Living Here in Allentown," I find the co-captain from the state's top-ranked team in 1973 living in central Pennsylvania.

To the poignant and haunting words from Iris DeMent's song, "Our Town," I find moms, single moms and family partners living in Oklahoma, Texas, Utah and Minnesota. Trini Lopez sings, "If I Had a Hammer" as I find ex-pats living in the U.K., Canada and Laos. I discover moms, wives, business owners, living in or near my Simsbury, Connecticut hometown as I listen to the sad echoes of the edgy, Queens-based girls' group, The Shangri Las, sing through their 1965 hit, "I Can Never Go Home Anymore."

These folks have lived their lives, becoming teachers of English, math, chemistry, history and physical education. Working their skills and trades at public and private schools and within general business organizations. They are school principals and presidents of universities. Many will coach at multi-levels of sports and general activities. Others work in the public or private sectors managing multi-type park and recreation operations.

They've become doctors practicing general and specialized medicines. They are surgeons. Veterinarians and in multi-levels of dentistry. Psychologists and psychiatrists. Medical forensic examiners. Emergency room nurses, nurses' aides and volunteers. Audiologists and opticians. Many still active and prominent on the frontlines during the all-encompassing pandemic.

Some are private investigators. From common people searches to stakeouts, assisting law enforcement in making arrests. There are lawyers, paralegals and legal aides. Administrators to litigators. Their involvements running the legal gamut from common torts to grand juries. Simple obstruction of justice cases to the epitome of white-collar crimes. Armed robbery to murder.

Many have found a niche within corporate management or government agencies. Operational leaders in finance, transportation, human resources and in the ever-evolving world of change management. They are the owners of small businesses and boutique shops. Dealers in imports, exports and antiquities. They sell insurance and real estate. Futures and financial plans. Automobiles, new and used. Others have found their way into support services for town halls, county, state and federal offices.

I found writers and editors. Artists, painters, and graphic designers in the fields of advertising, general publishing for specialty and children's books. Businesses providing special services within federal government guidelines in European and Asian countries. Supporting projects in the fields of engineering, construction, transportation, communications, supply chain applications, looms and weaving, technology transfer and cyber security.

We learned about elected officials, mayors, selectwomen and local representatives. People in the civil services. Pilots licensed in multi-style aircraft. Folks working in the broadband services for commercial airlines, private air industry and military support, specialized air support groups and the long-respected Civil Air Patrol.

Military service becomes a chosen path for many. Career commitments for some. Reserves and National Guard duty for others. In places such as Iraq, Afghanistan, Abu Ghraib and others in the long list of Gulf War locations. In Mogadishu and along Korea's 38th parallel. Fighting the world-wide war against external terrorism. And now battling the threats of home-grown terrorism from the emerging internal groups on the streets and in communities across the United States.

Athletic accomplishments are many with those who ascended to the top of their peer groups representing the USA in the Summer Olympics. Those who made the final cuts on teams only to be denied by the USA's boycott of the 1980 games in Russia. Many will go on in their careers to play on teams at gold medal levels in multiple sports in numerous worldwide sponsored games. A few still playing today in senior Olympics including the USA Seniors Field Hockey Team, gold medal winners in 2019.

For years, many have been greeting you from a teller's cage at the local bank. Comforting and welcoming customers into salons, drugstores, department stores and at checkout counters in local supermarkets. Serving you coffee at the diner on main street. Cleaning a home or walking your pets. Repairing your car or truck. Living just down the street from you and providing so many of those everyday common professions we never think about until we have a need for their services.

We found stay-at-home moms. Single moms, grandmas, and widows. Battered and beaten women. Members of law enforcement and those who had run afoul of the law. We found many in good health. Sadly, there were others who battled a lifetime of obstructions. Illness and injuries whose mobility was hindered. Lives of multiple addictions and those with stories of death. We continued searching for the ones we couldn't find. We identified and cried for those who had died.

The people we found were white, black and brown. English, Italian, Latino, African, Jewish, Irish and Dutch. They were tall and lean. Others were short and zaftig. A few still skilled, quick afoot and agile. Most, though, now slow as molasses. Many living with the general aches and pains of life. And others who struggled with body aches and pains and with life itself.

There were those who were in national honor societies. And those who were not. Folks who graduated from a wide range of colleges...Ivy League schools, junior colleges and online universities. Those with high school diplomas, GED's and folks with trade school certificates. And there were those who left high school before graduating, choices made as a result of the many decisions we are faced with in our lives.

I found many who had wonderful and detailed memories to share. And those who could not remember much, other than they had once played in high school. They played for the enjoyment, because they were competitive or due to peer pressure and a sense of wanting to...or a need to belong. Some were thrilled I reached out to them. Others requested that I please not bother them. And a few who, despite name changes and guarded communication paths, were upset with me that I was able to locate them. As if I had somehow breached the sacred walls of the witness protection program.

They were hard to find. Those who married and changed their names. Re-married and changed again. Then, went back to using their maiden names. Others legally changed names. Some took their partner's name, or the name of their pet. Still, others had hyphenated names, using either name depending on the situation. There were folks who wanted to be known only by a one-word name.

There were many people who had not given up on life. Unfortunately, there were a few who had.

I kept looking over the list of folks I had found in my searches. Their lives and their times. Some thrilled with the ride back in time. Others numbed by the passage of time. There were those pained by their recollections and frustrations of a life filled with unmet expectations. As I pondered their input, Alexa continued playing one of our home playlists. The Highwaymen sang, "Michael Row the Boat Ashore."

I wondered if the people I had located will continue performing in classrooms or in emergency rooms. Pouring cups of coffee for folks along the counter or cutting somebody's hair. I marveled at legacies they had chosen or found their way into. Another one of those station stops we all occupy as we roll along on the tracks of life. A mixed cacophony of hopes and dreams from those people, who were the faces of that first tournament in 1973 and, like now, became the persona of the times. I was blessed with the kindness most showed in letting me be invasive into their lives. They allowed me to bang loudly on the pipes in hopes of waking up a few dormant memories from a long time ago. Some memories were enjoyable. Others rekindled old pains.

And, just as I was awed by these young women in the fall of 1973, I am still in awe of these people and their contributions to history. Perhaps one day, even in the White House. Maybe the answer to my endless search for *"A Question of Balance."*

61

In the fall of 1974, Granby repeats as state champions. Adding to their legend winning the first-ever Class M Title over valley rival Lewis Mills. Beating schools two and three times the size of their enrollment. The Bears run their undefeated streak to 67 games over six years. Granby will then make it a clean sweep when, in 1978, they will also win the first-ever Class S title game beating Litchfield, 1-0.

Once again in 1974, it's Simsbury who had the best shot at ending the Bears' streak. In an early season home game, the Trojans held a 1-0 lead on the Bears who got a goal from Val McCord with 30 seconds remaining for a 1-1 tie. Sue Jensen had the most emotional line. *"They (Simsbury) think they're going to shove the winning streak up our asses. Never happen, baby. They don't know how to beat us."*

Many of the girls from the '73 team led the way in 1974.

Linda Dewey, Val McCord and the Wickman sisters, Lynsie and Jody. Sue Jensen and Jo Sproull. Mary Byrnes and Nancy Hutchins. A new wave of sophomores and juniors breaking into the lineup. And, led by their unflappable coach, Dottie Johnson. She will continue as coach until 2003 turning over the reins to a former player, Sandy Wickman Mason. She will be assisted by her older sister, Jody Wickman Bascetta who had teamed with her sister Lynsie on that '73 title team. Both will retire in 2021. Since 1969 Granby had just two head coaches in field hockey. They won or shared 14 state titles, played in 23 state title games and reached the Elite Eight round in 30 seasons.

A footnote to their 1974 Class M Title. It comes against Lewis Mills of Burlington. It had been just a year before when Mills' coach, Linda Hamm's lamented need for one more quality player for her team to go deep into the tournament. She found that key player. Then stepped down as coach, handing over the reins to the late Karen Schlott. With Hamm's players and strategies now in place and Schlott's leadership, the Spartans blazed their way into the title game.

During the fall of 1974, Simsbury finally unburdened themselves and got out from under Granby's shadows, beating a good Wreckers team from Staples High School, 1-0 for the Class L Championship. A cadre of experienced seniors anchored the team. They were supported by that core group of sophomores from the previous year who now took control of the team as juniors. The speed and quickness of Denise Lamb and Pinky O'Connor. The smooth and silky play from Kim Longo and fiery play of Elaine Marcil.

Late in that title game, and with the Trojans holding onto their slim lead and being urged on by their fans, a voice in the crowd was heard yelling, *"C'mom, Hold On! Hell, it's Not Granby this time!"* Even coach Joan Sullivan turned her head towards the voice shouting those haunting words and smiled. As did Staples' coach, Virginia Parker. Both chuckled.

317

The powerhouse Trojans will repeat as champions in 1975, not only beating back but dominating a good New Canaan team, 3-0. The win cementing Sullivan's legacy as a successful coach in the annuls of Connecticut high school sports. Her 1975 team will be considered as one of the most powerful teams during the years of tournament play. Perhaps, one of the best, ever, along with Sullivan's undefeated 1963 team.

Gail Juday will arrive at Canton in the fall of 1974 and field hockey fortunes will skyrocket. The Warriors will make their first tournament with an 8-5 record. The following year they will produce a 13-4-1 mark and reach the Class M title game. Losing to Westbrook in sudden death overtime on a controversial goal. She stays on the scene for only three years. Wins more than 30 games and her legacy of disciplines and strategies will become a part of Canton's winning approach in field hockey for the next 40 years.

She is paid $300 by the town of Canton for her yearly services as coach.

One of Juday's starting fullbacks on the '75 team, Nancy Grace, will return to her alma mater as the field hockey head coach. In her long tenure as head coach, Grace will win and share in eight state titles and play in the championship game 14 times. Her teams will reach the Sweet 16 and Elite 8 rounds in 21 seasons.

Over the next 50 years, enrollment at Granby High School will double. The school will be ranked in the top 10% in combined groups of overall test scores. Their academics place them in the top 20% in coveted Advanced Placement Coursework. Almost 60% above their peers being measured in math proficiency. Over 60% above state baselines in reading and the arts.

A local politico is overheard boasting, *"Not bad for a little ole farming community in northern Connecticut that plays a good game of field hockey."*

Over the same period, Simsbury's population increases

almost 50% with high school enrollment peaking at 1600 students. Avon High School's enrollment doubles and the town population increases by a whopping 130%. Farmington becomes the most-populous town in the valley. Lewis Mills and East Granby High Schools and town populations double in size in less than 30 years. Growth becomes an epidemic.

Since the inaugural 1973 field hockey tournament and over the ensuing 47 years, Farmington Valley teams will appear in 64 state field hockey championship games in three designated classes. Collectively, they will win 29 state championships, co-share in 8 titles and lose in 27 state finals.

Field hockey will continue that eternal fight for an identity and survival.

Rivals will include the omnipresent tidal wave that has become girls' soccer. There are changing lifestyles and attitudes in young people and their parents. Prohibitive costs. Legal lines that make up today's borders of what coaches are allowed to say and do within the boundaries and scope of their responsibilities. The never-ending struggles that have become the world of litigious sports where lawyers, and their cell phone numbers, usually on speed dial, have become more important than the uniform numbers worn by the players.

Boys' sports will remain as the dominant expense drain and revenue makers at most schools. Title IX affecting women's sports, will live on, ambiguously administered, loosely interpreted, and typically misunderstood. Same as it was 50 years ago.

Republican Senator John Tower, his daughter, and 20 others will die on April 5, 1991, in a plane crash just outside Brunswick, Georgia. Atlantic Southeast Airlines flight, 2311, will go down resulting from a catastrophic failure in the propeller control units. After Tower's 1972 supplemental amendment to Title IX is withdrawn, it will never again appear as a roadblock to finances and revenues targeting women's educational opportunities and sports.

From the end of WWII to Connecticut's first field hockey post-season tournament in 1973, women's sports expand at what can only be described as a snail's pace. Since the 1990's and into the new millennium, expansion has been, in an overall collective approach, meteoric.

Headlong into the 21st century women's sports are now world-wide. Professional and amateur leagues in multiple sports that occupy a calendar's 12 months. Girls will compete with boys playing in midget football, baseball, and softball leagues. Co-ed basketball and soccer leagues will begin for kids as young as five years old as well as volleyball and ice hockey teams throughout the country.

In its 50 years, Title IX will run full circle, eaten away by the pesky rodents of time. As a result of class-action suits, boys will begin playing high school field hockey on girls' teams in a dozen states. Their physical size and strength once again rekindling the search for that ever elusive "Question of Balance." Of gender designations and boundaries, legal rights, and ownership to pathways. And, for the sarcastic pre-Title IX warnings which flowed from those arrogant souls of yesteryears. Those long ago and self-anointed protectors of the systemic and institutionalized obstructions who kept crying wolf with their threats, *"Be careful what you wish for."*

Lou Ball will tell me that that my presence did have an impact on sports in the valley. For both girls and boys. That I did play a part in the change process. I don't believe that I had anything to do with the actual life changes that took place. I do believe my efforts and presence did, like a tiny cog on a big wheel, earn a degree of acceptance and respect from within the Farmington Valley. From some of the players, girls and boys. From coaches and folks who, because of the coverage, began reading *The Farmington Valley Herald*. Even from those folks still mired in the systemic and institutionalized protocols of the world.

During my five years at the *Herald*, paid circulations for

our weekly publication will increase from about 4000 to almost 12,000. Estimated weekly over-the-counter sales will increase almost 300% to 4000 with point-of-sale locations jumping from about 75 to 350. I am told advertising revenues triple in volume and a backlog for advertisers wanting space in the *Herald* is created. Many requesting their ads be placed on the sports pages. I will never earn more than $152 in any week during my time at the paper. Still, those are the types of growing pains I can live with.

My heroes of the day were a menu of "Who's Who." Ted Williams of my beloved Boston Red Sox. Willie Mays, the greatest player in my lifetime. Bob Cousy of the Celtics and Don McKenney of the Bruins. Glenn "Fireball" Roberts on the budding NASCAR circuit. Red and Leo LeBel from West Hartford, Connecticut in the annual barrel jumping championships at Grossinger's in the Catskills. I always rooted for professional golf's underdogs. Doctor Carey Middlecoff, Art Wall, Charlie Sifford and Ted Kroll.

So, my years at the *Herald* were a connection period for me...to go back in time and remember those few women athletes I knew as a kid from the 1950's and 1960's and followed in the newspapers and sports magazines. Occasionally getting to see them perform during national TV appearances. My dad was a scratch golfer. We'd watch the LPGA exploits of Patty Berg, Mickey Wright, Kathy Whitworth and my favorite, tall and lean, Carol Mann.

We'd watch bowling. Marion Ladewig and LaVerne Carter. And Cathy Dyak from Connecticut who would bowl on Hartford's WHCT, TV Channel 18 duckpin show before the station converted to Pay TV...the first Pay TV channel chartered in the US.

There was Billie Jean (Moffitt) King, Maureen Connolly, Althea Gibson and Margaret (Court) Smith in tennis. Carol Heiss and Peggy Fleming in figure skating. Louise Smith, Ethel Flock and Sara Christian in the early days of oval track stock car racing. Janet Guthrie, the first woman in the Indianapolis 500. Shirley Muldowney will emerge to become one of the NHRA's Top Fuel dragracers.

Babe Didrikson (Zaharias) will star in any sport she chooses. I will watch the exploits of home-grown star from Waterbury Connecticut, Joan Joyce and her accomplishments in softball, basketball, and golf. Wilma Rudolph's three gold medals in the 1960 Rome Olympics. Penny Pitou's medal-winning skiing exploits in the 1960 Winter Olympics at Squaw Valley.

In wrestling, Mary Ellison is "The Fabulous Moolah," ranked number one in the World for 28 years. She performs in the WWWA created by Mildred Burke, the world's top wrestler from the 1930's to the 1950's, Joanie Weston, known as the "Blonde Amazon," will become one of the highest paid female athletes during the 1960-70's as captain for the San Francisco Bay-Area Bombers of the International Roller Derby League.

Right up to Jan Merrill's long distance running performances in the 1976 Montreal Olympics. The same Jan Merrill who, during her senior year, will lead the Connecticut high schools in field hockey scoring during that fall of 1973. Her Waterford High team will come within a heartbeat of upsetting the number one team in the tournament, Guilford, in a thrilling first round game.

I was humbled to witness changes in real time. Surprised and pleased that after all these years, I could still remember the sights, sounds, even the smells that became memories of my life. That I still remembered the benefits and concerns of crossing that line drawn in the sand drawn by Colonel Travis at the Alamo. Or Lou Ball, my editor after reading my game thoughts, drawing endless lines through my notes saying, *"Nope...Can't Print That."*

What I vividly remember are the words and stories Lou Ball did let me print.

His words of support and encouragement. The latitudes he gave me with his blessings. The wiggle room he allowed when I saw a wrong and tried to do the right thing. Sometimes, I wrote words that climbed mountains. Other times, I created dumpster fires. Just a bastardization of participles and infinitives and abuse of sentence-beginning words such as "But, Just, Because, And"...as I still do today. His confidence in the power of the press provided a wonderful message. Change was happening. I was fortunate I had the freedom to pick a lane. Defend it. And be part of that change.

I was thrilled to remember the names of so many wonderful individuals from the schools in the Farmington Valley and from throughout the state. The fond recollections I have for all those folks I met, especially the girls from Granby High School, who treated me with courtesy and respect throughout that fall of 1973, while making their mark in the world in such a simple way. I recorded their accomplishments as best I could during those times. Though the true depth and complexities to their accomplishments, may never be fully acknowledged or appreciated.

Yeah, Lou Ball may have been right. Perhaps my days at the *Farmington Valley Herald* did have an impact in a small way.

Hey, I was just a young guy who found his way into the right place and at the right time. Fortunate to have the opportunity to be a part of an exciting period of change. To enjoy myself with five of the happiest, most wonderful years of my life. It wasn't work. It was pure fun. Waking up every morning knowing I was going to enjoy my day. Being a part of the family that was *"The Farmington Valley Herald."* A passionate love affair in my life, that I am not ashamed to say I still cherish to this day.

For me, it was truly a thrill to just tag along for the ride. For all those wonderful rides. To be there, everyday, but especially to be in New Haven on that Saturday in November of 1973, when the world really did change. And a legacy was born. Right there, in front of the eyes of the world.

EPILOGUE

Many years have passed by since that special day, November 17, 1973. The day when the girls from Granby and Guilford High Schools played each other in a game of field hockey in Connecticut's first-ever, post-season tournament championship game.

The date has become a kindred spirit of sorts, with November 17, 1797. The day Eli Perry of Plymouth, Connecticut was issued the first-ever clock-making patent in the country. Clocks to tell time. That ever-churning, eternal pendulum that continues ticking. Linking eras and events together. Living on inside all of us. Measuring the existence of lives and legends. Reminding us, without empathy, and in a not-so-gentle manner, that time, like a memory, is a precious thing worth saving and really is of the essence.

Those 38 high schools...over 800 young ladies, coaches, officials and support services folks from that first tournament all played a living part within a special event in time. They lived the cliché, *"You don't get a second chance to make a first impression."* They are now, and forever will be, a sorority of souls who have become another of life's living monuments to a real life happening that a half-century later has slowly, quietly, become a fading memory.

And time, that eternal pendulum recording history, just keeps on ticking.

Time has recorded history from those who existed before us. To leave their mark, they built monuments to honor and perpetuate the self-engrossing guile for accomplishments of the human spirit. Structures for the living and for the dead. Tokens of the good we all hope for. Or the bad that exists within the survival for all living things.

There are moss-covered and faded obelisks dotting the Gettysburg battlefield representing the struggles of man. North and south. Black and white. Misguided idealism verses hope. A world truly in battle between hatred and lifestyles. The eternal quest for finding acceptance and peace through war. Perhaps to what we often refer to as the battle between heaven and hell. Right verses wrong. Women against men! The unsure and the unknown. Those unwritten rules of war. The ever-continuing search in humanity for a definition and answers to *"My Question of Balance."*

The Pyramids of Giza, machines of math, built for the Kings, so it's said, to assist the departed with their journey into the afterlife. Stone monoliths in Central and South America, to cultures and believed-in gods, who whence from the skies. Intelligence-like structures rumored to be on Mars and the backside of the Moon. To those living legends and entities not yet believed in or identified. And, to the arrogance of their existence.

Or perhaps, just one monument of granite. A lonely tombstone in a cemetery. A memory to a loved one no longer here as a part of our lives. To their accomplishments and to the life they lived. To the precious memories and to the legend they have become.

The metaphysical understanding, of course, are those energies and memories that dwell within those structures, have no boundaries in time. They are forever. Or, legends for as long as we wish to believe in them. A continual lifetime battle of overcoming those eternal systemic and institutionalized obstructions.

On a Saturday in November 1973, a band of girls from tiny Granby High School, standing at the threshold of their adult lives, won a field hockey game. History has recorded this accomplishment as fact.

This, too, is a fact. Unknown is the impact this event will eventually have on history. On the lives of those who lived it. Granby's girls walked onto a field of battle and played a game. They scored more than their opponent and to the acknowledgment of how we have come to gauge sports competitions, won the game....and a place in history.

As a testament to their accomplishment, that time-honored monument for rewarding achievement, a gift was given by the good citizens of Granby. A brand, new dictionary was presented to each girl on that team. A quirky gold medal to be sure. An edifice of information. The book of words. From *"aardvark"* to *"zyzzyva."*

Granby's girls were then and remain today, a cultural and product mix of people and human traits. A few belonged to the National Honor Society. Others struggled to get C's. They came from middle class families of closeness and from families that were poor and lived hard lives. Some went to college. Others began their life of work. Some went on to live lives of enjoyment and success. Others carried the burdens of life's human failures. Addictions, injuries, illness, and death.

Granby's girls lived in colonial homes and little cape cod houses. Split-level ranchers on dead-end streets. On farms with acreage of rich loam. They walked to school. Rode the buses or rode their bikes. As a team, they wore the same uniform and came together with multiple personalities and a wide range of athletic abilities. And despite the living menagerie of road maps that have taken the Granby girls in so many different directions, there remains a unique bond within this group. A bond that words cannot even begin to describe.

A bond that is worn by every girl who was a part of that 1973 tournament.

Granby's girls walk their own paths in history where each perceives her own accomplishments as either a self-fulfilling or a self-loathing prophecy. Her monument to an accomplishment. To a lifetime of accomplishments. Or, for a few, maybe a path to that chilly November day in 1973 and to one important moment in time.

Perhaps the memories to those paths in life are as near to them as their bookshelves. They need only open that dictionary, their monument to words and definitions, given to them so many years ago by those good folks from the town of Granby.

Look up the word, *"**Legends!**"* The traditional definition will focus on that of, *"A popular story regarded as truly historical but needing authentication."* You see, monuments, like memories, good or bad, can sometimes get lost in time. Or misplaced on a bookshelf. It's OK if you struggle with emotions. Having passion is just another of life's gifts allowing us to better understand why certain things happen, when one signs up for life's journeys.

Granby's girls...whether they wear that title as an honor, or struggle to carry it as a burden, it's one of those quirky oddities that is not their choice to make. Long ago it became a lifetime responsibility to its weighty ownership. To the decision each girl must deal with. Either to proudly wear or painfully endure the weight of the cloak that goes along with the word, *"Legends!"*

Show me a legend, and I will show you someone who

wears humility. Legends, such as the Granby Coach, Dot Johnson. Whose care and love for her players and responsibilities is immeasurable. Legends such as Co-captains Sue Hebert and Pam Sproull. Their on and off-field leadership qualities. The way their lived their lives.

To every girl on that Granby team whose dedication and toil made them a living part to that legend. To their school and its support services. To the teachers and students, then and now. The town of Granby. The local grocery store. Places of worship. To the library and the news from The Drummer. To the volunteer fire department. The pub, flower shop, the local pizza joint and other boutiques. To the calmness of the paths in the woods, to listening to the gently flowing waters of Salmon Brook.

To all the multiple personalities that are the symmetrical happenstance that makes up the soul and heartbeat of any hometown. To the legacy and its humility. Wherever the eternal responsibility for managing and protecting that honor exists. For Granby...and for those girls from every school in that first tournament who are now a living part to that humility. For all those who kept reaching for the prize that always seemed too high for them to touch...or too far away to ever reach. Well, they kept trying because that is one of our human frailties most folks are proud to display. We see the critical importance of achieving a goal and in knowing, there's always hope if we just keep trying.

You see, it's never about winning a game. It's more about the understanding of losing. Because in most competitions, every team but one will end its season with a loss. The winning, be it a sporting event or in life's demands and challenges, is in how the masses manage the perceptions of what is learned along the way. Then, collectively, take the next steps. March up to the next level...take the new high ground. Pick a lane, dig in, defend it and begin the next fight...and the beat goes on! The rules of war.

Time will then dictate its own standards of historical importance to the events of the day.

Like November 17, 1913, the first ship will pass through the Panama Canal. During the early morning hours of November 17, 1939, wolf packs of German U-Boats sink the first passenger ships in the North Atlantic. A continuing prelude to WWII and the deaths of over 75 million people, worldwide. The movie, *Casablanca* will have its Hollywood debut on this day in 1942. In 1953 the St Louis Browns franchise will move, becoming the Baltimore Orioles. The first franchise shift in major league baseball in 51 years.

During the early morning hours of November 17, 1973, on Practice Field B at Yale University in New Haven, girls' teams from Granby and Guilford High schools played a game of field hockey. One of those distant memories that, in life's human frailties, tends to fade with time. But is no less important than any of history's actions of that date in the annals of time.

Dare we have the self-audacious nerve to believe events from that day...that one championship game played by girls' teams, worthy enough as a memorable occurrence in the ever-lengthening milieu of our world's comparative history and in the endless journey of time? God, yes! A foregone conclusion to all of history's memory of that day, living and dead. Remembered or forgotten. Time, though, will not forget.

Like Eli Perry's ticking clock. Time continues its emotionless, never-ending journey. Time will deny us our needs of arrogance. Empathy, degradation, hubris and ego satisfaction to our very existence. It will, however, relentlessly pass by, always providing us new sets of opportunities. A chance to search for balance and symmetry in the road ahead using the triumvirates of simplicity, pathos, and the repetitions of our very being. It will consume our hates. Outlive our loves. Eventually, taking us into eternity. Along the journey, offering us only the learning opportunities to better understand the rationale of, *"Why things happen to us and why our lives are affected in so many indescribable ways."* Often, without us even knowing, or understanding, that a transformation in our lives has occurred.

All, traceable back to one event in time. Our lifetime.

At times, I am overwhelmed by my memories and emotions. Trying to comprehend...or simply understand, the impact from all those subtle and dramatic events that this memorable November date in history has had on me and my life. And, perhaps, one day, my death.

Yeah, it was just a simple game of girls' field hockey played on a cold Saturday morning, November 17, 1973. The day legends were born. For both teams who were not even aware it was happening. To the history being made and future paths of expectations created. Lost and forgotten minutiae of a simple day so long ago.

Time, its endless journey and sterile personality, will not let us forget. For on that memorable day, Granby's girls earned the right to call themselves champions. For the first-time. And to call themselves legends. For all-time.

Because, what occurred on that chilly morning of November 17, 1973, really did change the world for so many people, including me, in ways far too innumerable to easily explain or ever fully comprehend.

Truly, it was dramatic and legendary change. For a day...for a lifetime.

Forever!

Acknowledgments

I owe a special thanks to Nancy Grace, long associated with the field hockey program at Canton High School as a player and a coach and renowned throughout the state of Connecticut. I've had the honor to call her my friend for 50 years. Without her help this book might not have been written. Her wisdom, experience and knowledge of the game and her efforts in searching for and finding lost information led the way for me, filling lots of gray areas of information for many people from so many years ago... all while she battled a painful cancer diagnosis.

Nancy Grace

To all those wonderful folks who shared memories with me. Former players Leslie Gribus, Lindsay Taylor, and Mary Bunting, Jan Merrill, Loretta DiPietro, Kim Longo, and Heidi Zacchera. Pam Sproull, Sue Hebert, Lynsie Wickman, Ellen Burbridge, Jo Sproull and Sue Jensen. To Lynn Clements, Leslie Collier, Carol Cassidy, Andrea Lyons, Candy Thierry, Melanie Gibson, Laurie Center and Lee Hough. To Jill Barrett and Deb Carella, Liddy Addams, Joyce Allgaier, Lisa Meucci, Toni Rinaldi, Karen Drake, Sue Michaud, Debbie Teske and Lee Coulter. And so many others who were kind to me with their time and memories.

To all the coaches who took that extra time to share stories and guide me to resources: Lorainne Splain, Arlene Salvatti,

Sally Nelson, Sue Swerdetle, Bea Walko, Becky Strominger, Pat Mascia, Cookie Bromage, Gail Juday, Carol Albert and Linda Wooster. A special thanks for support and information to Angelia "Chickie" Poisson who I have always referred to as *"The Babe Ruth of Field Hockey."*

For all the athletic directors from yesterday and today: current coaches, the media specialists at both local and high school libraries who listened to my pleas for help. I thank you for your support and valued information.

Thanks go to Judy Sylvester and the folks at the CIAC office who said, yes, every time I asked for help, guidance or information.

To my loving wife, Bonnie, without whose help, support and understanding, I would not have even attempted to take on this three-year project. She again listened to all my stories...to the phone calls from former players. She read my words, made suggestions and gave me that kick-in-the-ass when it was needed. And I love her.

Somewhere in the universe, I want to send thanks to Lou Ball, my Editor and my friend at the *Farmington Valley Herald*. He gave me the green light and the freedom to roam, write what I saw and what I felt. Lou would often say my time at the *Herald* would change my life, forever. He was right.

ABOUT

THE AUTHOR

Rob Penfield is a Simsbury, Ct native with a passion for writing stories about his hometown. He attended Northampton Commercial College where he captained the basketball team and is a graduate of American International College in Springfield, MA. He is a twice wounded and decorated Vietnam veteran who served with the 9th Infantry Division during the TET offensive.

Author Rob Penfield
Phoenix, Maryland

Rob was the Farmington Valley Herald's Sports Editor during the 1970's, the lone sportswriter covering women's high school sports on a fulltime basis, including 1973's first-ever field hockey tournament. He covered the World Series, The Super Bowl, NCAA tournaments, professional golf, tennis tournaments, NASCAR and local stock car racing and the Montreal Olympics for nationally known sports publications.

He worked as a professional consultant developing business training programs in every US state and for more than 200 clients in over 30 countries worldwide.

He ran his own boutique consulting company for 27 years.

He's a lifelong athlete including his playing field hockey at Fort Sill, OK. An opportunity which provided him with a special insight and understanding to tell the story of Connecticut's first-ever high school field hockey tournament. To tell that story before those memories were lost forever.

As a published writer, Rob has previously authored the riveting books, *"The Monsters That Never Die"* and *"The Last Echoes From Down "N The Hole."*

Rob and his wife, Bonnie, originally from Shamokin, PA, live a comfortable retired lifestyle in Phoenix, MD with their cats and rebuilt Model A Fords. Find out more at www.robpenfield.com.

ABOUT ATMOSPHERE PRESS

Atmosphere Press is an independent, full-service publisher for excellent books in all genres and for all audiences. Learn more about what we do at atmospherepress.com.

We encourage you to check out some of Atmosphere's latest releases, which are available at Amazon.com and via order from your local bookstore:

Twisted Silver Spoons, a novel by Karen M. Wicks
Queen of Crows, a novel by S.L. Wilton
The Summer Festival is Murder, a novel by Jill M. Lyon
The Past We Step Into, stories by Richard Scharine
The Museum of an Extinct Race, a novel by Jonathan Hale Rosen
Swimming with the Angels, a novel by Colin Kersey
Island of Dead Gods, a novel by Verena Mahlow
Cloakers, a novel by Alexandra Lapointe
Twins Daze, a novel by Jerry Petersen
Embargo on Hope, a novel by Justin Doyle
Abaddon Illusion, a novel by Lindsey Bakken
Blackland: A Utopian Novel, by Richard A. Jones
The Jesus Nut, a novel by John Prather
The Embers of Tradition, a novel by Chukwudum Okeke
Saints and Martyrs: A Novel, by Aaron Roe
When I Am Ashes, a novel by Amber Rose

Made in the USA
Middletown, DE
17 December 2021